THE SPORTS MANAGEMENT TOOLKIT

The Sports Management Toolkit is a practical guide to the important management tools and techniques available to those working in the sport and leisure industries. Designed to bridge the gap between the classroom and the workplace, it includes ten free-standing chapters, each of which provides a detailed introduction to best practice in one of the core sports management disciplines.

Written in a clear and straightforward style, and free of management jargon, the book covers all the most important elements of contemporary sports management, including:

- marketing
- performance management
- risk management
- human resource management
- project management
- finance.

Each chapter includes a detailed, step-by-step description of the key tools and techniques and their application, a 'real world' case study to demonstrate the technique in action, and self-test questions. The final chapter offers an extended, integrated case study, demonstrating how all the key management techniques are combined within the everyday operation of a successful sport or leisure organization. Online materials include an extensive guide to further resources and guideline answers to the self-test questions for each chapter.

This book is essential reading for all students of sport and leisure management, and for all managers looking to improve their professional practice.

Online resources are available at www.routledge.com/9780415491594.

Paul Emery is a Lecturer in Sport Management at La Trobe University, Australia.

D1340033

THE SPORTS MANAGEMENT TOOLKIT

PAUL EMERY

Routledge
Taylor & Francis Group

LONDON AND NEW YORK

First published 2011
by Routledge
2 Park Square, Milton Park, Abingdon, Oxon, OX14 4RN

Simultaneously published in the USA and Canada
by Routledge
711 Third Avenue, New York, NY 10017

Routledge is an imprint of the Taylor & Francis Group, an informa business

British Library Cataloguing in Publication Data
A catalogue record for this book is available from the British Library

Library of Congress Cataloging in Publication Data
The sports management toolkit / by Paul Emery.
    p. cm.
  Includes bibliographical references and index.
  1. Sports–Management–Handbooks, manuals, etc.
  2. Sports administration–Handbooks, manuals, etc.
  I. Emery, Paul.
  GV713.S6779 2011
  796.06′9–dc22   2010043569

ISBN: 978–0–415–49158–7 (hbk)
ISBN: 978–0–415–49159–4 (pbk)
ISBN: 978–0–203–88027–2 (ebk)

Typeset in Univers and Melior
by Swales & Willis Ltd, Exeter, Devon

Printed and bound in Great Britain by
CPI Antony Rowe, Chippenham, Wiltshire

Dedicated to my extraordinary parents, my loving wife Coral, and my treasured children Sabrina, Sean and Jamie. Thank you for teaching me to laugh, love and live life to the full.

CONTENTS

IEC	International Electrotechnical Commission
IPL	Indian Premier League
IRM	The Institute of Risk Management
IRR	internal rate of return
ISO	International Organization for Standardization
KPI	key performance indicator
MIRR	modified internal rate of return
MoS	margin of safety
NPV	net present value
PAQ	position analysis questionnaire
PB	payback
PERT	programme or project evaluation and review technique
PIMS	profit impact of marketing strategies
PLC	product life cycle
POWER	Personal experience Order Weighting Emphasize detail Rank and prioritize
QSPM	quantitative strategic planning matrix
SBU	strategic business unit
SMART	Specific Measurable Achievable Realistic Time-based
SPACE	strategic position and action evaluation
SS	start to start (logic relationship)
SV	sales value
SWOT	Strengths Weaknesses Opportunities Threats
TC	total cost
TOWS	Threats Opportunities Weaknesses Strengths
UK	United Kingdom
USA	United States of America
USP	unit selling price
VC	variable cost
WBS	work breakdown structure
WPS	work profiling system

CHAPTER 1

INTRODUCTION

CONTEXT

To meet the complex demands and challenges of the emerging sports industry, future managers will need to be everything to everyone. In an unprecedented world of technological connectedness and social diversity, sport managers will need to know how to maximize income, be resource smart and time precious, and simultaneously minimize their footprint. Evaluated against new output metrics, this dynamic global industry will require knowledgeable and innovative problem solvers who are competent in a broad range of management tools.

Historically, such education and training have largely been the responsibility of tertiary institutions. However, as Mallinger (2009) suggests, 'Several recent business journals suggest a growing gap between those who teach in graduate business programs and those who practice business in corporations and agencies.' Elaborating further, he argues that, while academics encourage theoretical input and thoughtful reasoning, practitioners face real-life deadlines and bottom-line pressures and require urgent practical solutions. The outcome is an emergent theory and practice divide, limited dialogue between the two entities, and significant barriers to the development of mutually beneficial partnerships.

The purpose of this textbook is to help bridge this gap between class-room teaching and workplace needs. It is intended to be a sport and leisure management student *and* practitioner text that applies conceptual, procedural and professional knowledge to real-world case studies. As an introductory textbook, this process-oriented practical management toolkit covers the broad remit of management disciplines. Through selection of fundamental analytical and planning techniques to the key resources of people, products, money and time, the long-term aim is that this book will

1

become one of those rare essential sources that every manager keeps and uses in the workplace.

ORGANIZATION

Given that this is not a standard textbook, it is not intended to follow the norm of developmental and sequentially read chapters. Instead it adopts an active learner approach that encourages independent chapter reading. Each free-standing chapter presents a management tool or set of tools that is suited to a particular purpose. In the same way that a tradesman would not use a hammer to cut a piece of wood or, to use a sports analogy, a golfer would not use a driver to sink a final putt, a manager should use a tool that is fit for purpose and solves a problem. Possessing its own unique assumptions, processes, limitations and applications, each chapter – and tool – provides a framework for practical use and where possible will adhere to the following structured format:

■ technique description – defines the nature and key concepts of the management tool(s);
■ purpose – elaborates on the benefits of using the tool;
■ theoretical overview – clarifies broader concepts, key principles, historical development and theoretical underpinning;
■ practical application – provides examples of tool use;
■ assumptions and limitations – establishes the application and interpretation boundaries of the management tool;
■ process – illustrates step-by-step procedures;
■ common mistakes – identifies frequently encountered errors;
■ interpretation and management decision – explains what the data mean and possible decisions derived from them;
■ summary – paraphrases and draws together the key points of the chapter;
■ self-test question – provides one or more tasks to help assess understanding of the tool application.

Guides to further resources, useful web links and guideline answers to all the self-test questions featured in this book are available on a companion website at www.routledge.com/9780415491594.

Each chapter will additionally include either an applied sport management example or a case study. In some cases this is essential and covered within the process section; otherwise the procedures would be difficult to engage

2

with. In other instances, separate case studies are provided to view real-world outputs of the technique.

Text is often kept to a minimum in order to put over management tool principles in a concise way for time-precious practitioners. To additionally ensure personal and meaningful engagement, case studies are drawn from both work and non-work sources, as organizations in the future must meet personal aspirations as well as task-oriented goals.

Furthermore, to reflect the broad remit of the global sport industry, diverse examples are selected from contexts that cover private, public and non-profit sector organizations and from destinations as far spread as America, Australia, China, Europe and India. Popular sports will be alluded to and reference made to services and goods that are produced and delivered by small local enterprises through to multinational conglomerates. Similarly the self-test tasks reflect contrasting demands, ranging across short-answer, essay, mathematical and even theoretical critique questions.

CHAPTER CONTENT

Integrating these personal and organization perspectives, chapters are logically organized as a 'developmental journey through life'. For example, Chapter 2 introduces the SWOT analysis tool as the first stage of this journey, as if addressing the question 'Where are you now?' If you do not know where you are, how do you know the route to your desired destination? This analytical technique is used to develop a situational audit establishing where you are as well as identifying the most influential factors currently affecting you. This is achieved through applying the SWOT tool principles and process to the instantly recognizable brand of Nike Inc., as well as to you as an individual commodity.

Once you know where you are, you can determine where you wish to go. Setting a measurable course or direction is the purpose of Chapter 3. This entails establishing clear targets or ends by constructively aligning aims, objectives and performance indicators. This process of detailing realistic outcomes is initially demonstrated through a personal non-work scenario of New Year resolution setting, before applying it to the Tennis Victoria (Australia) case study.

Having decided where you want to go, you need to be aware of what could go wrong along the journey. This is covered by Chapter 4, where risk management tools are examined. Being a legal requirement, a risk management framework is presented whereby the processes of risk assessment, treatment and control are explored. Practical industry examples given relate to the risks encountered in sports clubs or centres, a marathon, Formula 1 and even the 2012 London Olympics and Paralympics.

In sport management, nothing happens without people making it happen. In other words how do you find the right people to help you reach your destination? To this end, Chapter 5 focuses on three vital yet interconnected tools of the recruitment process, namely job analysis and the writing of effective job description and person specification documents. Acting as communication tools to inform the recruitment and selection process, real-life case studies are provided from contemporary public sector and national governing body positions from New Zealand and Australia.

Who helps you and how are important factors to consider along your journey. But you also need to continuously look back at your collective outputs, as well as forward, to determine whether you are still heading in the right direction. Times change, and you need to appraise where you focus your energies now so as to create new directions and opportunities for the future. Chapter 6 focuses on strategic business units and the competitive market-place. It incorporates some of the most popular diagnostic tools of marketing, namely product life cycle analysis and portfolio matrices, with application of the latter being demonstrated through the hugely successful Twenty20 Indian Premier League.

However, time is always of the essence. Common questions on any journey include 'Are we nearly there yet?' and 'What is the quickest route from here?' Chapter 7 provides a condensed view of project management schedul-ing tools that are applied to a non-profit local ice hockey club in Canada. Introducing manual and computer processes of constructing and calculating the critical path, this chapter explores the planning, monitoring and trade-off decisions that ensue from the important project drivers of quality, resource and time.

Can we afford to undertake this journey? Resource issues underpin every management decision we make. In practice, it is rare that a sport organization can survive any length of time without money, which makes financial accounting tools vital to current and future success. Chapters 8 and 9 respec-tively address these important short- and long-term business planning deci-sions. Using a small video analysis start-up project as well as a local football synthetic pitch example, Chapter 8 illustrates the relationship between income and expenditure or more specifically sales volume, costs and profits. Constructing and interpreting the graphs and calculations of break-even and

4

sensitivity analysis tools help in appraising an organization's financial viability. Chapter 9, on the other hand, extends the financial principle of contribution and profitability, by looking at capital budgeting or long-term investment decisions. By means of the most frequently used appraisal tools of payback and average rate of return and the discounted cash flow methods of net present value and internal rate of return, the economic viability of the decision-making process is applied to a sport venue development project of the Beijing Olympic Games.

The final chapter offers an example of a sports organization as well as an event that has already made such a journey and continues to do so. The Great North Run, the largest half-marathon in the world, and Nova International Limited, the UK's leading event and sport marketing management group, demonstrate the power of sport. Through extensive partnerships, this integrated case study demonstrates how all of the key management tools introduced in this text could combine within the everyday operation of a very successful sport organization that achieves social, health and economic objectives simultaneously.

However, to conclude, it must be remembered that management tools and techniques should not be considered a failsafe panacea for diagnosis and decision. Whilst they offer useful insights, they rarely offer definitive answers on their own. They should not be a substitute for management judgement but be used as an aid to inform a creative yet systematic decision-making process to real-world problems.

CHAPTER 2

UNDERSTANDING THE CURRENT ENVIRONMENT: THE SWOT ANALYSIS

TECHNIQUE DESCRIPTION

Before sport managers can manage anything they first need to understand the context in which they work. At the least, this involves carrying out a SWOT (strengths, weaknesses, opportunities and threats) analysis. This is a marketing tool that determines where an organization is relative to its internal and external environment. As a situational audit it examines the most influential factors that affect the sport organization at a moment in time and becomes the fundamental building block as to where you will be in the future. In essence the SWOT analysis is the auditing cornerstone of all strategic, tactical and operational business decisions of an organization.

So that you can better understand what a SWOT analysis is, this chapter first provides you with an overview of the audit outcome, explaining how components are linked to one another, as well as to other concepts and theories, before introducing a case study demonstrating its practical application.

PURPOSE

The nature and purpose of the SWOT analysis can be diagrammatically represented by the matrix shown in Figure 2.1.

The internal environment recognizes current organizational attributes that can be considered positive (strengths) or negative (weaknesses). Respectively these determine the internal value-creating or value-destroying factors of an organization. Once these have been identified, the organization needs to build upon its strengths or capabilities and eradicate its weaknesses or deficiencies.

The audit additionally focuses on the macro- and micro-environments that contain the external value factors from the environment. Whereas the

6

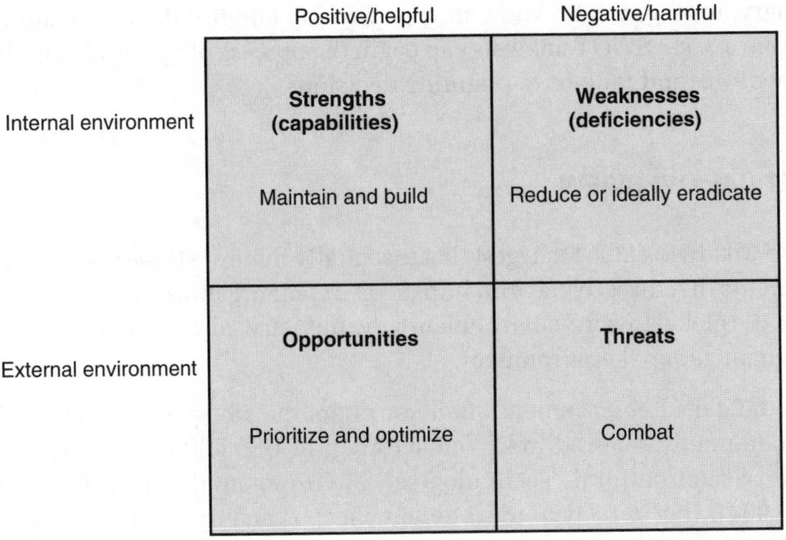

	Positive/helpful	Negative/harmful
Internal environment	**Strengths (capabilities)** Maintain and build	**Weaknesses (deficiencies)** Reduce or ideally eradicate
External environment	**Opportunities** Prioritize and optimize	**Threats** Combat

Figure 2.1 SWOT matrix

internal variables are assumed to be under organizational control, the external factors are typically considered to be outside the control of the organization. For example, the global financial crisis is directly outside an organization's control yet will directly affect consumer spend and hence an organization's activities.

The two environmental analyses, internal and external, are further differentiated by their specific focus on the time dimension. Namely the internal analysis appraises and determines where you are now, whereas the external analysis assesses what might happen in the future. Opportunities are therefore potential strengths of the future, and the threats are potential weaknesses. The implication is that any tactical or strategic decisions derived from the SWOT should prioritize the opportunities whilst combating the threats.

The purpose of a SWOT is to strategically align the two environments, creating forward-planning opportunities that are based upon the most relevant internal and external information available. This permits sport managers to:

■ capitalize on strengths, reduce the effect of weaknesses and maximize opportunities, whilst minimizing threats;
■ identify the most realistic and viable strategic, tactical and operational decisions in determining business, market, financial, and human resource planning activities.

In summary, managers who know how to develop and use the information gained from a basic SWOT analysis can begin the process of optimizing their short-, medium- and long-term planning decisions.

THEORETICAL OVERVIEW

Beech and Chadwick (2004) suggest that essentially there are three interactive environments that directly have an impact on a sport organization's success. These are the global (macro-environment), the industry (micro-environment) and the organizational environment.

Whereas the global environment often considers the key generic drivers of change, commonly referred to by the acronym of DESTEP (Demographic, Economic, Social/cultural, Technological, Environmental, Political/legal) (Kotler, 1994), the industry environment more typically refers to closer organizational variables that directly affect industry competition. For example the nature of the competitors and the reliance on an organization's supply chain(s), as well as the power of its customers. Analytical models and theory focusing on this micro-industry environment commonly derive from Porter's (1979) five force competitor model and value chain analysis (Porter, 2004).

The internal or organization environment however must not be forgotten or underestimated. Blythe (2001) for example suggests that this internal environment is a microcosm of the external environment, with its corporate culture typically possessing its own language, symbols and traditions. Political agendas will interact with organizational rules and expectations, and employee attitudes of loyalty, commitment and morale will directly affect and be affected by external environment attitudes (Lashley and Lee-Ross, 2003). In this sense the organizational environment should be considered an equally important and influential component of the SWOT analytical process.

Based upon Johnson and Scholes's (2002) marketing premise that an effective organization strategy is derived from an appropriate fit between an organization's internal resources and capabilities (strengths and weaknesses) and its external competitive environment (opportunities and threats), the SWOT analysis involves inside-out (resource-driven strategies) and outside-in (market-driven) data collection and analytical processes.

Understanding the complexities of these rapidly changing yet interconnecting environments must be continuously monitored so that a sports organization can be proactive in its management activities. It is from the results of the SWOT analysis that the organization can plan its sustainable competitive

8

advantage (for further information see Porter, 2004) and develop strategically aligned options such as those of market penetration, market development, product development and diversification strategies (Ansoff, 1957).

PRACTICAL APPLICATION

The SWOT analysis can be used in a variety of scenarios, for example at the organization or business, unit and/or individual levels. Used in a business context, it provides the basis of organizational planning and is commonly used either before a business commences (as a component of the business plan) or annually during its life cycle. Furthermore it can be used as a simple ice-breaker activity to commence strategy formulation or as a more rigorous tool to appraise competitor offerings.

An example of use at the unit level could be the human resource department of a national retail chain, a community development unit of a sport governing body, or even a subject area or school in a university setting. Similarly, at the individual level, a personal SWOT analysis could be used for career development purposes and/or in the preparation of applying for a particular position. For example, what would be your strengths and weaknesses relative to those of your competitors, and how might these be used to exploit the opportunities and thwart the threats related to the position applied for?

ASSUMPTIONS AND LIMITATIONS

The flexibility of the SWOT analysis usage is both its strength and its weakness. For example, at the organizational level it at least requires the following assumptions to underpin its appropriate application:

- Clear knowledge of the organization's business scope. This provides the boundaries and the important context of its operations and includes understanding the organization's vision (why?), mission (what?) and organizational values (how?).
- In-depth knowledge of the organization's current and future customer needs as well as expectations.

On the other hand, SWOT limitations include:

- It is a cross-sectional analysis that pertains to a moment in time. The reality is that in today's volatile marketplace there are constant changes, which mean that the macro- and micro-environments are very difficult to predict. For example, who predicted the global economic crisis? How would your business be affected if a new competitor set up business next door to you tomorrow? Sales trends may explain the past, but to what degree of certainty may they predict the future?

■ A SWOT analysis may provide a very accurate picture of the current scenario, but the hardest part may be creating strategic alignment between competence and required provision.

PROCESS

There are two main components of carrying out a SWOT analysis – the internal environment analysis and the external analysis. Historically this has normally meant carrying out the following sequential steps:

1   Identify the strengths.
2   Determine the weaknesses.
3   Consider the opportunities.
4   Locate the threats.
5   Create a balanced and holistic SWOT analysis.

This entails systematically addressing each quadrant of Figure 2.1 by adopting different standpoints and perspectives and then viewing these findings holistically. Different standpoints could include the perspectives of the employee (manager through to the lowest level of the hierarchical structure), the long-term customer, the one-off customer, the current non-buyer, the direct competitor, the supplier and even the bank manager.

How these sequential steps are carried out, and by whom, is subject to budgetary constraints and organizational culture. Suffice to say that an organizational SWOT analysis will entail a minimum of three to four hours and can be achieved either for a group (ideally four to eight people) for a business- or unit-level SWOT or for an individual for a personal SWOT analysis. For the former, where departmental managers normally determine the SWOT analysis, it is recommended that an external facilitator be used so as to eradicate any potential conflicts of interest and bias.

Where group input is involved, the task is perhaps best achieved by individuals working on each quadrant and then sharing the information with others. This provides the opportunity for individual and original thought before collectively adapting and building upon other suggestions. Clearly

10

the overall aim of the SWOT is to create an objective, honest, meaningful and well-considered analysis where the organization or business, unit or individual is appropriately positioned within the operating environment.

APPLIED EXAMPLE

To demonstrate how to carry out these steps let us apply the generic process at an organizational level, for example as if we were the senior management team of the global brand of Nike Inc.

1 Identify the strengths

This stage involves identifying what your organization is recognized for. In other words, what does your organization do particularly well relative to your competitors? Typical answers should relate to your resources and capabilities, and these can be used as the basis for establishing or enhancing your organization's sustainable competitive advantage. For example, strengths could relate to a strong brand name or patents, exclusive access to highly valued expertise or resources, strong distribution networks, providing the 'best value' for money, or even simply to the organization being sited in an 'ideal' geographical location.

It may be worth you initially addressing the following questions, applying information gained from your internal marketing, financial, manufacturing, human resource and general organizational sources:

- What do you do better than anyone else?
- Why should people purchase from you relative to your competitors?

In the case of the premium brand of Nike, answers could for example relate to the identified strengths, in terms of claims with accompanying evidence, as illustrated in Table 2.1.

2 Determine the weaknesses

To determine your weaknesses, again the focus of attention needs to be targeted at your internal environment. However, it is important to realize that the source of this information is your market intelligence data, which are likely to derive from both internal sources (e.g. comparative monthly or

Table 2.1 Nike strengths

Claim	Evidence
Best high-quality 'sport'-focused products (footwear, apparel, equipment and accessories) across a diversified range of sports.	■ Elite athlete endorsement, e.g. world-ranked individuals and teams that include Tiger Woods (golf), Roger Federer (tennis), 140 NBA players including superstars Kobe Bryant and LeBron James (basketball), more than 20 gold medallists in the 2009 World Athletics Championships, and five times World Cup winners the Brazilian national football team (Nike, 2009a). ■ High-quality construction and innovative products are developed through cutting-edge research involving athletes, specialists from biomechanics, chemistry, exercise physiology, engineering, industrial design and related fields, and research committees and advisory boards (Nike, 2009b). ■ The Nike brand portfolio (contributing US$2.6 billion in 2008/09) includes the wholly owned subsidiaries of Cole Haan, Converse Inc., Hurley International LLC, Nike Golf and Umbro Ltd (Nike, 2009a).
Excellent retail presence and strong global distribution network.	■ Highly developed EKIN (personal sales) programme to support retail accounts (Nike, 2009b). Contracts with 700 shops; offices in 45 countries; and operations in 170 countries (Nike, 2009b). ■ Chain of Niketowns (e.g. 11 in USA) to showcase Nike products (Nike, 2009b). ■ Established 'futures' ordering programme that permits retailers to order five to six months in advance of delivery (Nike, 2009b). ■ Employs more than 34,000 staff across six continents (Nike, 2009b).
Distinctive and aggressive marketing communications.	■ Described as the 'goddess of marketing' (ICMR, 2001), Nike has established a long history of innovative and memorable taglines (e.g. 'There is no finish line', 'Just do it') and television commercials (e.g. World Cup football campaigns involving Eric Cantona). ■ Numerous marketing awards (e.g. Emmy awards for best commercial, 2000 and 2002; Cannes Advertising Festival advertiser of the year, 1994 and 2003; Nike marketing director won the coveted 2009 digital marketer of the year award) (Nike, 2009b). ■ Leads the sport industry in its breadth of imaginative marketing campaigns (e.g. Nike T90 – augmented reality treasure hunt in Hong Kong; Nike Zoom – Bluetooth stopwatch in China; Nike iD – interactive billboard in New York; viral marketing – NBA 'Most Valuable Puppet' campaign; and social media campaigns such as the 2009 Nike+ Human Race in 25 major cities across the globe).

12

Table 2.1 Continued

Claim	Evidence
Highly profitable business for over a decade (established on the principle of high quality and low costs).	■ Largest seller of athletic footwear and apparel in the world (Nike, 2009b). As an innovator and industry leader, Nike dwarfs its nearest competitor with a nearly 50 per cent market share of the athletic footwear market (Halpern, 2009). ■ Annually included in Fortune 500 companies (2009 – 136 ranking with profit of US$1,883.4 million) (*Fortune*, 2009). ■ In 2008/09 Nike reported total revenue figures of US$19.2 billion, a 3 per cent increase on the previous year (Nike, 2009b). ■ Nike possesses no manufacturing factories (i.e. does not tie up capital) and experiences very low manufacturing costs (independent overseas production) relative to its competitors (i.e. a very lean and flexible organization). ■ Has been established for over three decades, hence excellent economies and efficiencies of scale, with strong exclusive access to distribution channels.
Excellent level of global awareness and product use.	■ The global brand possesses instant recognition with its 'swoosh' logo (world number 2 'sports' brand – Ozanian and Schwartz, 2007; number 29 'global' brand – *Business Week*, 2008). ■ Very high levels of market penetration, with nearly everyone in the developed world having owned a Nike product at some time in their life.
Very strong innovative corporate culture rich in employee loyalty and team spirit.	■ Internally Nike has created its own 'way of life', developing its own rituals, terminology, values and team spirit. For example, swoosh ankle tattoos are common on its workforce; senior executives act as 'corporate storytellers'; and employees are called 'players', supervisors are called 'coaches' and meetings are referred to as 'huddles' (Ransdell, 2007). ■ Nike's strategy is driven by a board that consists of management and independent directors permitting outside and inside experience to think innovatively. ■ Nike has received numerous awards, e.g. in 2009 it was named as one of the 100 most sustainable corporations in the world (Innovest Strategic Value Advisors and Corporate Knights Inc.), one of the world's most ethical companies (Ethisphere Institute) and one of the 100 best companies to work for (Fortune award in 2006, 2007 and 2008) (Nike, 2009a).

annual reviews of your marketing, financial, manufacturing and human resource data) and external sources (e.g. derogatory media coverage). Typical weaknesses could for example relate to poor-quality product or service reputation or recall, poor financial ratios, a high cost structure, slow or unreliable supply chain services, lack of expertise, low morale or even areas of high staff turnover.

Since you are fundamentally trying to address the question 'What do you currently do badly relative to your competitors?', one good place to start is to look at your most recent customer complaint records as well as staff exit interview comments. While it is often difficult to be honest and critical about internal departments and activities (please note that no individuals should be cited or blamed in this process), the more truthful and objective you are the better the developmental outcome will be. With this in mind, further useful questions may include:

- What problems are frequently (re)occurring and possibly losing you sales?
- What could you improve that would directly affect your business performance?
- What are your financial weaknesses?
- What are your staff weaknesses relative to your strongest competitor?

Table 2.2 illustrates a typical applied outcome to this process.

Table 2.2 Nike weaknesses

Claim	Evidence
Heavily dependent upon others (e.g. overseas supply chain) to produce its high-quality products to meet strict deadlines.	■ Failure of its contractors to comply with its code of conduct, local laws, and other standards that could harm the business (Nike, 2009b). ■ While internationally Nike may plan globally, it must fully understand its overseas local production conditions and markets. For example, 'Nike continues to face a series of China-specific challenges in improving conditions in its contract factories. These include poor plant management skills, the inaccuracy of records and the difficulty of navigating an inconsistent regulatory environment' (EIU, 2007).
Endorsing elite athletes is a high-risk promotion strategy.	■ The future careers and performances of individual elite athletes are very unpredictable. Injuries, poor performances and negative publicity (e.g. alcohol, drug, rape, violence, dog-fighting, match fixing and gambling-related incidents) could seriously damage Nike's reputation.

14

Table 2.2 Continued

Claim	Evidence
	■ To reduce costs numerous up-and-coming athletes are sponsored, e.g. in 2009 more than 50 NBA basketball players. In hindsight, this is likely to create a poor return on investment on many contracts.
Nike's initial failure to accept and foresee problems in relation to its overseas production conditions resulted in negative media coverage from which it has been very difficult to recover.	■ Nike's overseas outsourcing model has received significant criticism relating to exploitation of child labour, poor working conditions, and violation of overtime and local minimum wage rate laws (Moore, 1998; Kenyon, 2000; Klein, 2000; *7 News*, 2008). ■ Being the number one sport success story and growing so quickly, Nike has been positioned as a subject of anti-globalization activist groups for more than a decade. With consumers calling for more 'socially responsible' organizations, it has taken numerous actions (e.g. a Vice-President position for corporate and social responsibility, and becoming a founding partner to the Soccer Homeless World Cup) and won many awards for leading ethical performance and corporate responsibility, but despite this proactive stance its manufacturing structure is still associated with human rights exploitation (Kenyon, 2000; Read, 2008).
Pockets of low staff morale exist largely owing to the effect of company redundancies.	■ While it was initially considered 'cool' to be associated with Nike, the bad publicity relating to overseas factory workers has meant morale has fallen since the highs of the 1990s. ■ Morale was further lowered when 1,750 redundancies were made in 2008 (Nike, 2009a).
Sometimes perceived as a male, arrogant and athletics-focused brand.	■ Historically the company has been known for its 'detached, determined, unsentimental' attitude (CFAR, n.d.), which together with its command-oriented tagline of 'Just do it' has been perceived by some as demonstrating an arrogant 'I don't give a damn' attitude (Sportretort, 2009). ■ With Nike's strong historical background from male athletic roots, some may question its expertise and understanding of other markets, e.g. the female fitness and golf markets.
Unsustainable and underperforming brands and products need to be appropriately managed.	■ In the case of the brand acquisition of Bauer 'an iconic ice hockey brand . . . Nike put the trademark swoosh on the Bauer skates and alienated loyal fans who thought of Nike more as a giant corporation than an innovator' (Thirdway, 2006). Nike acquired Bauer in 1995 and eventually divested itself of the company in April 2008. ■ In the case of products, continual analysis of internal sales data relating to product mix, width, lines and depth should determine specifically the product portfolio tactics of investment, harvesting or divesting.

As is evident from Table 2.2, some of your strengths may also be your weaknesses. For example, Table 2.1 revealed that one of Nike's strengths was that it owned no manufacturing factories, hence possesses excellent financial liquidity in times of rapid change. On the other hand, Table 2.2 identified that this could also be considered a weakness, because the company is highly dependent upon others to provide high-quality products to final users in a timely and reliable fashion. Such scenarios are common in the completion of a SWOT analysis, as they are in many aspects of management. Most management actions possess potentially positive and negative outcomes, but it is systematic, rational decision making that takes careful account of the risks, benefits and costs that makes actions appropriate to their specific context.

3 Consider the opportunities

As previously discussed, analysis of the opportunities and threats needs to make reference to the global through to the local, macro and micro, environmental changes that have an impact on your business. For example, these could derive from changes in the economic climate, lifestyle behaviours and attitudes, demographic patterns, new legislation and technological developments, as well as significant change in competitor activities or even the marketplace.

The aim in this phase of the analysis is to determine what your best opportunities are and where they lie. To accomplish this, questions such as the following need to be asked:

- What external environment changes can you best exploit?
- What are the competitor vulnerabilities that you can attack?
- What new markets could you enter or further penetrate?

Two contrasting yet popular approaches may be used to identify the most relevant opportunities to your organization, namely an 'outside-in' or an 'inside-out' approach. The former focuses initially on external market-oriented data such as general market trends or competitor activity. In the case of general market trends these are brainstormed and then screened for relevance by asking the question 'Which trends are most likely to affect our business in the next five years?' The downside of this approach is that trends, particularly future-oriented ones, are often notoriously difficult to predict. However, that said, in some cases future data can be very useful and considered with some degree of certainty. For example, in the case of Nike,

16

whose success has been founded on targeting the youth sporting culture, this could relate to the trend of changing demographic profiles in developed countries. Compared with a decade or two ago there are lower birth rates and people are living longer (see Table 2.3). This means that the future demographic market is already known, subject to no world catastrophe being imminent, and in five years time there will be an unprecedented lower percentage of youth and significantly higher percentage of elderly people. The obvious implication for Nike is whether it should start developing new product ranges for the elderly. An alternative outside-in approach could focus on competitor activities. This would entail profiling major competitors (e.g. Adidas) and, through appraising their current strategies, tactics, product ranges and actions, could lead to identification of which markets to compete in or conversely exploitation of gaps for new opportunities.

In comparison, the starting point of the 'inside-out' approach is from your previously identified strengths. From these you could determine any links or triggers that may be developed via externally generated opportunities and growth markets. For example, Nike's strength of globally recognized research laboratories and world best athlete input means that it can take advantage of its own cutting-edge research findings to capitalize on new or evolving technological developments. This could relate to developments in sporting materials (nanoshirts and bespoke equipment), coaching or management experiences (e.g. micro-chip managers, artificial intelligence performance improvements, interactive stadia and robotic officials) or even end-user marketing applications (e.g. holographic mobile viewing, fan ownership, and social networking technologies). By taking this approach you would logically be adopting a current time analytical framework based upon internal strengths before trying to locate external trend analysis data from which future predictions can be made.

Applying either approach to the Nike case study could reveal the opportunities as identified in Table 2.3.

4 Locate the threats

Again these are targeted at the external environment and focus on those factors that will have most impact upon your long-term future. It might be worth starting with you imagining the worst-case scenario. This might relate to dominant or innovative competitor activity that would decrease your market share, new legislation that may significantly increase your costs, highly embarrassing senior management publicity, or even some environmental

Table 2.3 Nike opportunities

Claim	Evidence
Demographic changes in developed countries mean that in comparison to the past there will be higher percentages of elderly people who are also likely to possess higher levels of disposable income.	■ There are unprecedented lower birth rates and increased longevity. For example, the United Nations predicts an increase in the number of over-60-year-olds in the world from 10 to 22 per cent by the year 2050 (MICA, 2002). ■ Michman and Mazze (2006) refer to the United States' affluent 'wealthier greying market' with no mortgage and significant disposable income.
The changing role and expectations of women both in sport and in life in general provide underdeveloped opportunities.	■ Blythe (2001) suggests that more women taking up paid employment positions has increased women's level of independence from men and created new forms of female need, attitude and spending patterns. ■ Increased commercialism and improved equality legislation have created new professional sport opportunities, e.g. netball, golf, tennis.
Technological developments have created 24/7 opportunities and improved geographical access to consumers.	■ Digital technologies and developments in mobile phone and computer communications mean that consumers can co-create rich multimedia experiences at a time and place convenient to them, e.g. the rapid increase in social networking practices via Twitter, Myspace and Facebook. ■ Consumer buyer behaviour can be tracked via technologies that allow more accurate targeting and customization (Blythe, 2001).
External growth opportunities (e.g. mergers, joint ventures and/or strategic alliances) have become more acceptable and mutually beneficial.	■ Westerbeek and Smith (2003) suggest that there is a trend to bring together complementary assets, defray costs and share risks by establishing new partnerships with strong brands and networks. ■ In Nike's case (Nike, 2009b) successful examples include: – Nike's wholly owned subsidiaries of Hurley International LLC (surfing, skateboarding and snowboarding brand) and Umbro Ltd (football brand). – Nike+ sport range, which includes a chip that is connected to iPod devices and technologies (Nike–Apple partnership). – Licence agreements that permit unaffiliated parties to manufacture and sell various items, such as swimwear, training equipment, eyewear, electronic devices and golf accessories.
The reduction and removal of many international trade barriers have created new overseas business opportunities.	■ Change in legislation relating to export and import duties, anti-dumping and safeguard measures, quotas, tax regulations, and reduction of other trade restrictions can open up new market development strategies, as has been demonstrated in large, populous countries such as China and India (Nike, 2009b).

18

Table 2.3 Continued

Claim	Evidence
Consumers have become more brand sensitive and possess more personal and discerning needs.	■ An individualistic, self-gratification, 'me, here, now', materialistic culture is common, with image association with particular brands being valued, e.g. sport team following (Westerbeek and Smith, 2003). ■ Equally Nike enjoys nostalgic loyalty to sport, and moments of success, to try to make a difference in the world. As explained in Nike's annual report, 'we can use the power of our brand, the energy and passion of our people, and the scale of our business to create meaningful change' (Nike, 2009b).

disaster such as a fire or earthquake. Typical questions that might be worth addressing include:

■ What external obstacles are you facing or might you face that could affect key elements of your business (e.g. supply chain, economic downturn)?
■ What new legislation might damage current profitable success (e.g. tax or superannuation employee provision or change in international trading barriers)?
■ How might your competitors be able to damage you (e.g. offering improved, substitute or cheaper products or services)?
■ What are your funders likely to do in the future (e.g. withdraw and reinvest their money elsewhere)?
■ Could any of your weaknesses or removal of one or more of your strengths (e.g. a particular person leaving to work for a competitor) threaten your long-term future?

Applying such questions to the Nike case study could result in the threats being determined as illustrated in Table 2.4.

5 Create a balanced and holistic SWOT analysis

Once stages 1 to 4 have been carefully brainstormed and a long list of sub-stantiated claims proposed, it is suggested that all of these ideas be transferred on to a whiteboard or blackboard. While the individual quadrants of Figure 2.1 have been considered in isolation, the overall SWOT analysis now needs to be more holistically considered. This means that balance needs to be created to ensure that one quadrant does not dominate the analytical process,

Table 2.4 Nike threats

Claim	Evidence
Nike competes in a very competitive and mature market.	■ There has for some time been an overcapacity and a market saturation of shoes in the world (Uchitelle, 1997). With retail margins low, established leaders Nike and Adidas face cut-throat competition from numerous brands whose aim is just to survive (e.g. Saucony). ■ New competitor and more specialist organizations are beginning to emerge, e.g. Ryka, Inc., which is meeting the very specific needs and demands of active 21- to 35-year-old women. ■ The intense nature of competition accompanied by rapid changes in technology and consumer preferences constitute significant risk factors to Nike (Nike, 2009b).
The global financial crisis has resulted in a significant slowdown in international trade (Nike, 2009b).	■ The global downturn has had a significant impact on individual disposable income spending levels, creating a recession in advanced, emerging and developing countries (IMF, 2009). ■ Multinational companies are exposed to typical eight-year economic boom and bust cycles (Blythe, 2001) and are constantly affected by exchange rate fluctuations, meaning that costs and margins do not have long-term stability.
Nike is exposed to the international nature of trade, and the business is affected by seasonality and volatile change.	■ Nike faces not only unpredictable macro- and microeconomic instability problems but also political unrest and terrorism incidents within certain countries (Nike, 2009b). ■ Similarly, as Nike is a branded consumer products company, sales are affected by the relative seasonal demand and fashion trends of various sports and fitness activities. For example, revenues historically are higher in the first and fourth quarters in comparison to those in the second and third fiscal quarters (Nike, 2009b).
Consumers increasingly expect corporations to create positive social impacts and reduce their environmental impact in the world.	■ While overseas exploitation of child labour and poor working conditions are frowned upon by anti-globalization groups, the use of global brand power to work with governments and communities to create meaningful change is held in high esteem. Examples of Nike success in this area include the establishment of the Lance Armstrong Foundation (the fight against cancer) and the 'Girl Effect' programme. In simple terms, this latter programme uses the power of adolescent girls to bring financial and social stability to communities of developing countries (Nike, 2009a). Demonstrating Nike's leadership in corporate responsibility, it provides an innovative solution to help break the cycle of inter-generational poverty around the world (Nike, 2009b).

20

Table 2.4 Continued

Claim	Evidence
	■ The textile industry is historically renowned for adversely affecting the environment (Textiles Intelligence, 2008), so Nike is permanently striving to maintain its eco-friendly reputation. Eco-friendly programmes that are beginning to reduce Nike's overall environmental footprint include the 'Reuse-a-Shoe' and 'Grind' programmes that eliminate and recycle waste; its first 'green' basketball shoe (the Air Jordan XX3); and its policy to adhere to Greenpeace's 'Commit or Cancel' principles (Nike, 2009a).
New legislation changes continually affect Nike's business success.	■ Change of governments, political parties and joint trading association agreements directly affects new legislation that affects overseas business activities. For example, many governments around the world are concerned about China's compliance with World Trade Organization rules. As a result, a wide range of legislative proposals has been introduced to address these concerns (Nike, 2009b).
	■ Examples of recent protectionist actions that affect Nike include the following:
	– In 2006 Turkey introduced a safeguard measure on all imported footwear into the country, the goal being to protect its local shoe manufacturing industry (Nike, 2009b).
	– Brazil and Argentina have initiated independent anti-dumping investigations against footwear made in China (Nike, 2009b).

e.g. 12 strengths and only 3 weaknesses. In the current applied scenario this has already been achieved, with each section containing similar quantities of claims and furthermore links being established between internal and external quadrants. For example, this can be demonstrated by reference to the negative publicity about overseas production practices (identified in the weaknesses section) and the linked positive outcome of 'trying to make a difference in the world', which recognizes the more personal and discerning needs of consumers over time (the opportunities section).

Once the audit is collectively considered to be an open and honest appraisal of the current environment, then it can be used for strategic planning purposes. The decision phase that directly follows could be enhanced by addressing more specific questions such as:

■ What strategies might we be able to implement to pursue opportunities that align with our strengths? (Strengths and opportunities comparison)

- How can we overcome our weaknesses to pursue high-ranked or high-weighted opportunities? (Weaknesses and opportunities comparison)
- How can we use our strengths to reduce the risk of threats? (Strengths and threats comparison)
- What mechanisms can we include to reduce the potential impact of our weaknesses, thereby avoiding the susceptibility to our most likely threats? (Weaknesses and threats comparison)

COMMON MISTAKES

While numerous examples of SWOT analysis exist both in practice and in the literature, many unfortunately develop an outcome that is either too basic or too weak to be of any meaningful use to a sport manager. Typical mistakes encountered include:

- Too much subjectivity, with superficial depth of analysis and reporting. Claims need to be substantiated, and it is suggested that evidence, typically in the form of two to five points as illustrated in Tables 2.1 to 2.4, be used for this purpose.
- Positive valuations are often given more emphasis than negative ones, which is often based upon a philosophy of 'Negative consequences will never happen to me.'
- Too few or conversely too many factors are included in each quadrant of Figure 2.1. Remember, there is unlikely to be a bottomless resource pit to properly address each factor. For the final published SWOT report it is suggested that there are between five and seven points per quadrant, and some would even argue that each of these should possess a ranked priority, thereby providing a clear focus and value upon which management decisions can be based.
- Opportunities are frequently written in a manner that is too vague (e.g. 'Overseas development') or alternatively focus on activities that take advantage of an opportunity (e.g. 'Promote products to female youth'). This is in effect the next phase of the planning process, where strategies and actions are developed from the SWOT analysis findings.

To overcome many of these weaknesses more advanced versions of SWOT analysis have been developed. For example, Koontz and Weihrich (2006) refer to a TOWS analysis, which focuses on the external before the internal environment, as well as considers the negative (threats and weaknesses) before the positive components (opportunities and strengths) of the analysis.

22

In addition, the Marketing Teacher (2000) makes reference to the acronym of POWER SWOT, where POWER provides a more critical and in-depth analysis and stands for:

P = Personal experience. The suggestion is to state your personal beliefs and perceptions, because these will directly affect the nature of your SWOT analysis.

O = Order. As for the TOWS analysis, the suggestion here is to change the order of the SWOT analysis, focusing on the uncontrollable external and negative aspects before considering the more controllable internal and positive factors of business operations.

W = Weighting. Too often claims are considered equal when in fact one is often likely to be considered more influential than others, e.g. Threat A = 15 per cent, B = 5 per cent, C = 60 per cent, D = 10 per cent and E = 10 per cent.

E = Emphasize detail. Too often reader knowledge is assumed by the use of the single words. The proposal is therefore to clarify the factor, and justify its significance through evidence.

R = Rank and prioritize. This particularly relates to the factors that will most affect the chosen strategy. For example, opportunities could be allocated a percentage (impact or likelihood of occurring) and then ranked, e.g. Opportunity B = 40 per cent, A = 25 per cent, C = 15 per cent, E = 10 per cent, D = 5 per cent and F = 5 per cent.

Furthermore to complete the depth of the strategic auditing process additional complementary analyses to the SWOT could include:

- five forces analysis (Porter, 1979);
- stakeholder and customer needs analysis (Change Factory, 2009);
- competitor analysis (Fleisher and Bensoussan, 2007);
- market opportunity analysis (Kotler and Keller, 2006);
- issue impact analysis (Sullivan, 2004) can be used, which 'seeks to analyse audit data (issues) by assessing influence (impact) on the environment' (p. 138).

INTERPRETATION AND MANAGEMENT DECISION

A SWOT analysis is a simple yet powerful diagnostic tool that determines situational baseline information through holistically appraising a work unit in its competitive environment. In its most rigorous form it can be used to better understand and appraise competitor offerings, but more commonly it is an annual activity providing management with an organizational audit from which strategic direction and plans can be formulated. It identifies opportunities to exploit as well as threats that, it is hoped, with rational decision making can be eliminated or at least appropriately controlled.

Being written either before or after a business has commenced, a SWOT analysis is a very flexible auditing tool, particularly as it can be used at the organization, unit and individual level. Its flexibility though is often its strength as well as its weakness. In the latter case, it has historically been prone to subjective reporting, and in this sense it should perhaps be best considered as a guide rather than a prescriptive tool.

Being supported by other complementary analyses (e.g. stakeholder and customer need analysis as well as an issue impact analysis), it should provide a realistic and honest assessment of your current position. From such important yet fundamental insights a better future can be planned matching or changing organizational capability to meet current as well as future market demands.

SUMMARY

Knowing your customer and competitor landscape, particularly in times of sensitive and volatile market change, is vital not just to grow a sport business but in many cases merely to survive. While large global organizations such as Nike expect to annually grow their financial bottom line, there are many local sports clubs whose sole aim is to survive each year. Whatever the sporting scenario, the SWOT analysis technique can help, as it potentially offers the following benefits:

- assesses your organization's current position relative to competitors and potential customer needs;
- provides insights into market opportunities, threats and trends to optimize returns on investment;
- reviews your dependence and value attached to your supply chain as well as the sustainable nature of your competitive advantage;
- increases the likelihood of successful new product or service launches, partnership developments and efficient outsourcing.

This chapter has suggested that, to effectively construct a SWOT analysis, five sequential steps are normally required, namely:

24

1   Identify the strengths.
2   Determine the weaknesses.
3   Consider the opportunities.
4   Locate the threats.
5   Create a balanced and holistic SWOT analysis.

However, it has also been identified that for a SWOT analysis to be useful it must be based on independent objective evidence to avoid the vague and subjective nature of so many past submissions. Furthermore, it is important to realize that the SWOT analysis is only the first phase of the strategic planning process. The next stage is to build on these situational audit findings in a systematic yet creative way to propose recommendations from which strategic and operational decisions and plans can develop.

Guides to further resources, useful web links and guideline answers to all the self-test questions featured in this chapter are available on a companion website at www.routledge.com/9780415491594.

SELF-TEST QUESTION

Carry out a SWOT analysis of yourself (individual-level SWOT) as if you are preparing yourself for an internal promotion opportunity.

CHAPTER 3

COMMENCING THE PLAN: SMART OBJECTIVES AND KEY PERFORMANCE INDICATORS

TECHNIQUE DESCRIPTION

The purpose of any sport manager is to improve performance. So, once the environment is understood (Chapter 2), it is then necessary to define the scope and direction of future activities. This is achieved by establishing mutually understood and agreed performance outcomes (objectives) written in very precise terms (SMART). The notion of SMART objectives, as well as what the acronym SMART actually stands for, has received numerous interpretations and developments over time. However, as Haughey (2009) and RapidBi (2009) suggest, it generally refers to:

S – Specific (significant, stretching or stimulating)
M – Measurable (meaningful or motivational)
A – Achievable (attainable, agreed upon, appropriate or action oriented)
R – Realistic (relevant, rewarding, reasonable or results oriented)
T – Time-based (timely, tangible or trackable)

The argument is that, the more detailed the way in which an intended outcome is written, the clearer will be its level of expectation, motivation and targeted resource usage. Collectively this increases the likelihood of its achievement. If one of these elements is neglected it is suggested that you are unlikely to achieve your objective.

Further performance-related terminology that will be introduced within this chapter includes:

■ Aims or goals – these create the general collective purpose and focus of an endeavour (the end), with the objective(s) being one element to goal attainment.

26

- Key performance indicators (KPIs) – these represent the most important quantifiable measures that indicate the progress or achievement towards the identified aims, goals or objectives.
- Critical success factors (CSFs) – these are the necessary elements that need to be in place for business success and could relate to factors such as essential expertise, finance, information, equipment and unmet demand.

To better understand performance alignment between aims, objectives and indicators, this chapter will first introduce you to their purpose, origin, theoretical underpinning and process of development, before demonstrating their practical use through a sport management example.

PURPOSE

The purpose of using SMART objectives and key performance indicators is that they can help sport managers to:

- establish focus, commitment and motivation towards individual or collective goal achievement;
- clarify objectively the priorities, standards and measurement of performance expectations;
- appropriately allocate resources to improve economy, effectiveness and efficiency in individual, unit and organization performance;
- measure performance and make adjustments in a timely and informed manner;
- identify and enhance developmental learning opportunities for individual staff.

In summary, business success commences by focusing on performance outcomes. These outcomes (ends) then act as planning targets from which the decisions of subsequent processes, systems and actions (means) are determined.

THEORETICAL OVERVIEW

The origin of SMART objectives is unclear, although Drucker (1954) through the publication of his book *The practice of management* is generally attributed as the father of the 'management by objectives' movement. Derived from the management function of planning and developed through Locke's (1968) motivational theory of goal setting, predetermined goals, or aims as they are more commonly referred to, became the cornerstone of management education and practice in the 1970s. However, whilst short- and long-term aims continue to provide useful general directions to pursue, greater specificity and meaning were always going to be needed to improve operational practice. Through Blanchard, Zigarmi and Zigarmi's (1986) *Leadership and the one minute manager* publication, the term 'SMART' became established in the management literature, and this has become one of the most recognized management acronyms in the twenty-first century.

More recently academic literature refers to the terminology of 'performance management' (Australian Public Service Commission, 2002) and the 'performance measurement system' (Varma, Budhwar and DeNisi, 2008). Performance management specifically refers to the planning and use of interrelated and aligned strategies and activities to improve individual, team and organizational outputs (Australian Public Service Commission, 2002), whereas performance measurement systems are linked to 'performance indicators' and the metrics of performance review. For example, on a national level the establishment of the Audit Commission in the UK in 1983 led to considerably improved public sector service accountability and includes the following six principles of an effective performance measurement system:

1 Clarity of purpose – it is important to identify who will use what information, how and why.
2 Focus – initially the priority and emphasis should be on information affecting the 'core' of the business, with managers needing to understand how appraised information will affect behaviour.
3 Alignment – any measurement system should be aligned with the organization's objective-setting and performance review processes.
4 Balance – the overall set of indicators should be cost-effective and provide a balanced picture of organizational performance.
5 Regular refinement – indicators need to be contemporary to meet the needs of changing environments, but they also need to be comparable over time.
6 Robust performance indicators – they should be reliable, valid and free from any bias.

(Audit Commission, 2000)

Performance management itself can be explained through systems theory and in particular by the input, throughput and output management model as portrayed in Figure 3.1.

28

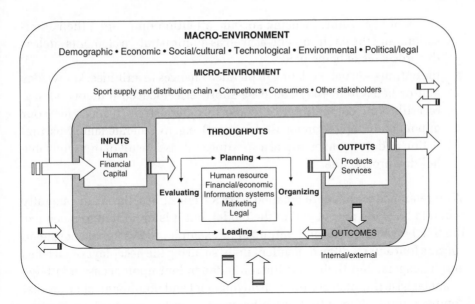

Figure 3.1 Systems model

Source: Adapted from Soucie and Doherty (1994).

In summary, systems theory maintains that management entails transforming inputs from the environment to outputs and outcomes via its throughputs – organizational processes and activities. Using a children's multi-sport coaching holiday programme to illustrate the theory, the first requirement could be considered to be competent staff, safe facilities, appropriate quantities and quality of equipment, and sufficient financial resources (inputs). Through carefully designed management policies, systems and activities (throughputs), the organizing body aims to produce a professional coaching service (outputs) that will ideally result in happy participants who on completion have improved their sporting attitudes, knowledge and behaviours (outcomes). This in turn, particularly if perceived to provide significant added value to the parent or guardian, is likely to lead to long-term sport participation, sustainable loyalty and repeat or even growth in the business (impact).

This model helps to explain that there are many types of general objectives, namely those that focus on:

- the inputs – 'what' you need, e.g. to attract five highly qualified and experienced staff members one month before the activity programme commences;
- the throughputs – 'how' you plan to develop specific values or attributes, e.g. to implement a staff training session that will elaborate on expected

codes of behaviour, focusing specific attention on people, their inter-actions and the environment, as well as administrative elements such as the processes of being paid;

■ the outputs – usually relating to planned changes in attitudes, knowledge and/or behaviour, they could be short-term focused (outcomes), e.g. regardless of competitive outcome to demonstrate respect for your opponent, or long-term focused (impact), e.g. to generate family partici-pation and/or membership of a sporting club as a result of this enjoyable holiday programme.

With reference to the more detailed SMART objectives, these are generally found to be at the output end of the model, but it is important to recognize the link between inputs and outputs. For example, professional sport team success (outputs) is often dependent upon securing the best players, coaches and managers, and their recruitment is dependent upon access to a large financial base (inputs). For this reason financial and non-financial ratios that compare inputs with outputs are often used in performance measurement.

Allied concepts to goals and objectives are the notions of key performance indicators (KPIs) and critical success factors (CSFs). These are related con-cepts but different. Whereas the former focus upon quantifiable performance measures, the latter relate to vital factors or elements that need to be in place to achieve the identified goals and objectives. KPI examples from the holiday programme scenario could include financial measures, such as profit per age group or sport, or be of a non-financial nature, such as the number of returning and new customers. On the other hand, CSFs could relate to factors such as high-quality employee attraction and retention, as well as issues of sus-tainability, e.g. an organization's ability to continue in business.

PRACTICAL APPLICATION

SMART objectives and key performance indicators are used to focus attention towards the achievement of intended outcomes, particularly in an environ-ment where scarce competing resources exist. Rather than employees and managers merely carrying out activities with little or no understanding of their purpose or how they contribute to broader organizational goals, objec-tives and indicators provide clarity, identifying what is important to an organization, unit or person. Their tried and tested application has been demonstrated in a variety of management settings ranging from orga-nizational strategic plans, departmental service, programme and project management delivery schedules, and field sports performance analyses through to personal annual performance appraisal schemes.

Performance outcomes are commonly used in contexts where quantifiable data are readily available and easy to measure. For example, in the multi-sport coaching scenario they could be defined in terms of measurable targets (e.g. a number – 50 enrolments; a percentage – 10 per cent time improvement in an 800-metre run; or a financial value – £250 profit) or adherence to independent standards (e.g. meeting defined threshold competencies or customer service standards). However, the use of performance indicators has also been used to value more difficult-to-measure activities such as the effects of leadership. For example, the Balanced Scorecard Designer (2009) suggests that leadership KPIs can be classified into professional success indicators, as well as people, collaborative and broad organizational initiatives. Furthermore each of these categories can be broken down as illustrated by the people initiatives category, which is subdivided and weighted according to reduced turnover, improved safety, succession planning, and coaching and development metrics (Balanced Scorecard Designer, 2009).

So what makes a good performance indicator? According to the Audit Commission (2000), to maximize the usefulness of performance indicators they must meet all of the criteria identified in Table 3.1. In other words each performance indicator needs to be able to influence behaviour, be quantifiable and comparable, be suitable for its intended audience and purpose, and be assigned to a dedicated committed owner.

Evidently, everything is potentially measurable and, without identifying the key performance indicators, directional targets and actions could be both numerous and meaningless. To focus attention on what is important to you, key indicators should be limited to those factors that are essential and provide most value to achieving the goals of your organization. This should also mean considering the breadth of user (internal and external stakeholders) and the likely use of the information extrapolated from the KPIs. As illustrated by Hoye, Smith, Nicholson, Stewart and Westerbeek (2009), in high-performance sport organizations there are likely to be many different stakeholder expectations to consider, and these might include:

- players – on-field success, low injury rates;
- employees – job security;
- sponsors – high association of positive benefits;
- owners or shareholders – return on investment;
- fans – high win–loss ratio;
- media – high level of interest.

Table 3.1 Criteria for robust performance indicators

Criterion	Explanation
Relevant	To avoid the mistake of using data just because they are readily available, performance indicators should relate to the strategic goals and objectives of the unit being analysed.
Clear definition	To ensure consistency of application, performance indicators should be written in a clear yet not too complex manner.
Easy to understand and use	Performance indicators should be constructed so as to be meaningful to the different users of the information.
Comparable	Indicators should be comparable on a consistent basis between organizations and over time.
Verifiable	The indicator also needs to be collected and calculated in a way that enables the information and data to be verified in terms of both data analysis methods and processes.
Cost-effective	The cost of collecting and analysing the information needs to be clearly balanced with its usefulness. Ideally it should be based on information already available.
Unambiguous	Performance change measurements should not be ambiguous.
Attributable	The performance indicator needs to be under the control of designated managers to ensure commitment and accountability prevail.
Responsive	A performance indicator should be significantly responsive to change measurement. Small changes will be of limited use.
Avoiding perverse incentives	It is important to consider what behaviour indicators encourage. Easy manipulation and transferring to others are to be discouraged.
Allowing innovation	Performance indicators should not be too prescriptive. They should permit innovation by focusing on outcomes and user satisfaction levels.
Statistically valid	Indicators should be statistically valid and therefore should use appropriate sample frames.
Timely	Up-to-date data need to be presented for timely performance management decisions.
Assessing the importance of the criteria	Single indicators rarely provide useful information on their own. Ideally a portfolio of indicators should be used reflecting both the context of use and the user.

Information sourced from Audit Commission (2000).

32

In some cases contradictory expectations may exist. For example, fans ideally would like ticket prices to a professional sports event to be low or ideally free, whereas shareholders would prefer ticket prices to be high to maximize their return on investment. For this reason a coherent yet balanced list of KPIs is usually selected to ensure that all stakeholder needs are represented.

Driven by accountability needs, broad but manageable KPI sets have been developed within and external to sport organizations. Known as 'benchmarks', they permit comparisons to the industry and other similar organizations, leagues, clubs, events and facilities. For example, Sport England has created a public sector sport venue (main halls and/or swimming pools) benchmarking frame of reference, as highlighted in Table 3.2. This performance management system proposes a portfolio of key performance indicators covering the four areas of access, utilization, finance and customer satisfaction. It is a national benchmarking exercise that uses 25 per cent through to 75 per cent standards, and performance comparisons can be made over time within an organization or between similar organizations and contexts.

ASSUMPTIONS AND LIMITATIONS

Constructing SMART objectives assumes as a minimum that desired behaviours or attitudes can be measured. For example, high levels of creativity or staff morale may be expected in an organization, but would be considered quite difficult behaviours to actually define and objectively measure in practice. One solution could be to define the SMART objective as an input, e.g. to host three creative yet developmental workshops within the next six months, as well as dedicate a follow-up week of work where everyone tries something new. Another solution alone or alongside input measurements could be a careful selection of a portfolio of output indicators. As exemplified in the staff morale example, this could include metrics such as low staff turnover, independent staff climate survey results, and voluntary attendance levels at social functions.

Any form of goal or target setting also assumes an appropriate level of resource to back its achievement. On the one hand this is dependent upon estimates being accurate, and on the other hand too many targets are likely to exceed resource constraints. To address the former, targets should evolve with time and not be set in stone. This should avoid the two ends of the spectrum, namely setting unchallenging or impossible goals. Regarding the

Table 3.2 Performance indicators for Sport England's National Benchmarking Service

1 Access

Key performance indicators
Percentage visits of 11- to 19-year-olds ÷ percentage catchment population of the same age group

Percentage visits from two of the lowest socioeconomic classes (UK classification) ÷ percentage catchment population of the same classes

Percentage visits of 60-plus-year-olds ÷ percentage catchment population of 60-plus-year-olds

Percentage visits from black, Asian and other ethnic groups ÷ percentage catchment population in same groups

Percentage visits disabled and under 60 years old ÷ percentage catchment population disabled and under 60 years old

Other
Percentage visits of 20- to 59-year-olds ÷ percentage catchment population in same group

Percentage of first visits

Percentage visits with discount card

Percentage visits with discount cards for 'disadvantage'[1]

Percentage visits female

Percentage visits disabled and 60-plus years old ÷ percentage catchment population disabled and 60-plus years old

Percentage visits unemployed

2 Utilization

Key performance indicators
Annual visits per square metre (of usable space, i.e. excluding offices and corridor space)

Other
Annual visits per square metre (of total indoor space, including offices and corridor space)

Percentage of visits casual, instead of organized

Weekly number of people visiting the centre as percentage of catchment population

3 Financial

Key performance indicators
Subsidy per visit

Other
Percentage cost recovery

Subsidy per resident

Subsidy per square metre

Total operating cost per visit

Total operating cost per square metre

Maintenance and repair costs per square metre

Energy costs per square metre

Total income per visit

Total income per square metre

Direct income per visit

Secondary income per visit

34

Table 3.2 Continued

4 Service attributes for customer satisfaction and importance (Likert scales)

Accessibility	Activity available at convenient times
	Ease of booking
	Activity charge/fee
	Range of activities available
Quality of facilities/ services	Quality of flooring in the sports hall
	Quality of lighting in the sports hall
	Quality of equipment
	Water quality in the swimming pool
	Water temperature of swimming pool
	Number of people in the pool
	Quality of car parking on site
	Quality of food and drink
Cleanliness	Cleanliness of changing areas
	Cleanliness of activity spaces
Staff	Helpfulness of reception staff
	Helpfulness of other staff
	Standard of coaching/instruction
Value for money	Value for money of activities
	Value for money of food and drink
Overall – satisfaction only	Overall satisfaction with visit

Note: [1] Disadvantage groups include over-50s, unemployed, single parents, disabled, students, exercise referrals and elite performers.
Adapted from Taylor and Godfrey (2003).

resource over commitment problem, this can be overcome by suggesting that any organizational department or unit adopts the rule of thumb of targeting between five and seven objectives and a maximum of ten KPIs per year. Anything more than this is likely to create insufficient focus and will probably prove expensive as well as too time-consuming to effectively improve performance.

PROCESS

Initially it may seem a daunting task to write very specific performance-oriented targets. While it is easy to understand the inherent logic of providing direction and priority, actually writing them can prove to be a challenge. To simplify the process, let us rephrase the task in hand, and suggest that defining outcome specificity is simply about deciding what is to be done, how and by when. Most organizations and individuals possess a good general understanding of what needs to be achieved; the hard part is putting it into words and then of course making it happen.

Simplifying it in this manner comprises a six-stage process that determines:

1   What do you want to achieve? (Specific) This should define clearly your intended outcomes or accepted levels of performance in jargon-free language. You may find that the degree of specificity increases as you become more informed as to what the exact nature of the objective entails and how it will be measured. This is common, so do not be alarmed if the initial focus is on the measurable, the achievable and the realistic elements of the SMART acronym.

2   How you will recognize it when it has been achieved? (Measurable) How do you measure its achievement and collect evidence of progress to this goal? Specific criteria need to be established. For example, the target could relate to an absolute number of active or new customers in a gym, a total monthly revenue amount or even a financial value of fortnightly sales made per person.

3   Is it achievable and realistic? As already mentioned, objectives need to provide an appropriate challenge in order to motivate staff, yet be achievable, given the resources, capabilities and time available. Management must attempt to remove obstacles that act as barriers to staff, and this includes providing them with appropriate levels of authority to deliver results. Unrealistic expectations, overconfidence and poor planning are often the main reasons for not achieving SMART objectives.

4   When do you want to achieve it by? (Time) Setting deadlines helps to protect you from procrastination and perfectionism. Deadlines or 'milestones' (see also Chapter 7) are therefore required to determine the interim deliverables as well as final completion dates. However, it is important to build in some flexibility, as plans are rarely implemented exactly as proposed. In many cases deadlines include a time variance of between 10 and 20 per cent to take into account unforeseen circumstances.

5   What happens when conflicts occur? Prioritizing objectives through a ranking system can sometimes prove useful, because conflicts can occur. If they do, trade-offs are required, particularly in public sector contexts, where complex accountability measures entail understanding social inclusion agendas alongside financial imperatives. For example, an increase in revenue may conflict with 'increase of disadvantaged group usage' and important 'customer satisfaction' measures. More recently this is also evident in commercial ventures, where financial profits are traded against the growing importance of corporate social responsibilities.

36

6   What will be the process of measuring completion or achievement? The first thing is to write the objectives down ('ink fades more slowly than memory') and place this list somewhere where you will constantly see it. The next stage is to establish the key performance indicators. These will determine the specific methods of measurement used to review your performance against objectives and ideally include a regularly updated visual display to motivate you towards their achievement. Using your preferred evidence-based monitoring system you will need to be aware of whether you are behind, on or ahead of schedule. If it is the former, rationally try to appraise your performance. Establish the reasons and factors why it is behind schedule, and then make appropriate adjustments as necessary. For example, should more resource or time be allowed or a lower-quality threshold be subsequently established? On the other hand, experiencing progress and being ahead of schedule boost commitment and confidence. Depending upon the nature of the goal, it is often a good idea to reward yourself where interim targets are achieved, and likewise celebrate your individual achievements appropriately when long-term objectives are exceeded or achieved.

APPLIED EXAMPLE

Since other chapters focus predominantly on organizational and work-oriented applications, let us demonstrate the application of this process to a personal and non-work specific task. For example, let us assume that you wish to use this process to plan next year's New Year resolutions, noting that equally it could be applied at the unit or organizational level of a business.

To establish a context in which to work, let us initially describe a scenario stating a variety of assumptions. Let us assume that you are a middle-aged person who never uses the stairs, is perceived to be overweight, and experienced a relatively boring last year of merely 'existing' rather than doing anything exciting. Motivated by a close school friend who recently died of cancer, you have decided to undertake and for once fully commit to some New Year resolutions.

Applying the six-stage process to this example, the following developments in undertaking this role could ensue:

1   After some brainstorming you determine that you want to achieve four general aims, namely:

- Lead a healthier lifestyle.
- Run a marathon.
- Raise money for a particular cause.
- Visit an overseas location.

These can then be arranged into higher-order goals and outcomes that ideally should be aligned and integrated. For example, the project goal could become 'to lead a healthier and more meaningful life', and two outcomes derived from this could be 'to run a sponsored overseas marathon' and 'to lose weight'.

2   Focusing at the outcome level, what is the level of expectation of 'gaining sponsorship', 'running a marathon' and 'losing weight'? Threshold standards of achievement are clearly demanded in the form of measurement criteria. For example, you might determine that your level of success will be to raise a minimum of £250 in sponsorship for Macmillan Cancer Support (forming a strong motivation towards personal achievement and a poignant memory of your close school friend), to complete a marathon in a time of 3 hours 30 minutes and at the same time to lose 20 kilograms in body weight.

3   Are these targets achievable and realistic? Remember that unrealistic goals are merely dreams and, for example, losing 10 kilograms in 10 days is not really possible or advisable. In reviewing your targets in consultation with others, you decide that, for a first-ever marathon attempt, particularly one located in a new country that you are not familiar with, your marathon target is perhaps too ambitious. With this in mind you decide to alter your targets to provide more appropriate challenges, assuming a lead time of about 9–11 months. The new targets therefore become a time of 4 hours 15 minutes; raising £500 in sponsorship (the other challenge was probably too easy); and a body weight loss of 17 kilograms, as you have now heard that muscle actually weighs more than fat.

4   As these objectives are being built they are becoming more specific and now require a time frame of completion and development dates. The limiting or determining factor of the measurable outcome must be recognized, and in this case it could for example relate to the marathon date. Having looked at the schedule of overseas marathons, determined flight availability and costs and got provisional approval from your employer for leave, you have decided to select the Shanghai International Marathon in China at the end of November, which gives you approximately 11 months to achieve your goal. Interim running events with target dates that act as a monitoring progress towards outcome achievement could include: a 10-kilometre race (to be completed in 55 minutes)

38

after two months; one half-marathon (to be completed in 2 hours 12 minutes) after four months; and a second half-marathon (to be completed in 2 hours) after nine months.

5   Of the two outcomes, it is already becoming apparent that the marathon completion is becoming a dominant driving force of personal achievement and excitement, and therefore you have decided to afford a higher level of priority to achieving the 'to run a sponsored overseas marathon' outcome over the 'to lose weight' outcome. Furthermore, within this outcome your number one priority will now be to complete a marathon in a time of less than 4 hours 15 minutes by 30 November 2011, with the second priority being to raise at least £500 of sponsorship for Macmillan Cancer Support. In summary, the prioritized SMART objectives in rank order (most important first) have now become:

- Objective 1: To complete the 2011 Shanghai International Marathon in a time of less than 4 hours 15 minutes.
- Objective 2: To pay into Macmillan Cancer Support more than £500 raised from sponsorship by 31 December 2011.
- Objective 3: To lose 17 kilograms in body weight as weighed on 1 January 2011 and 31 December 2011.

Since these objectives are written on SMART principles they are now unambiguous as compared to the vague general ideas proposed in stage 1 and therefore provide a shorter, clearer and more meaningful path to their achievement.

6   Specific objectives and performance measures should be inseparable (Hoye, Smith, Nicholson, Stewart and Westerbeek, 2009), and this is where key performance indicators become invaluable. So what needs to be measured and how? Achieving the primary objective of completing a marathon in 4 hours 15 minutes assumes the ability to be able to run at a certain pace (less than 9 minutes 45 seconds per mile) for the full marathon distance (26.2 miles or 42.2 kilometres). Ideally this would assume a capability of being able to run a mile once off in 7 minutes 45 seconds and feeling comfortable running at 8 minutes 45 seconds per mile for the first half of a marathon. In customizing the preparation for a first-time marathon runner, namely progressively building up cumulative running distances (miles or kilometres per week) and quality runs (high intensity mixed with appropriate recovery or tapering periods to avoid injury), the proposed schedule and KPIs for the primary objective of completing a marathon in 4 hours 15 minutes could be:

- KPI 1.1: To run the following progressive target distances per week, with the longest run (timing and distance) being identified in brackets:

Weeks 1–5   10 miles per week (Week 3: 4 miles)
Weeks 6–10   20 miles per week (Week 8: 6 miles)
Weeks 11–20   30 miles per week (Week 16: 10 miles)
Weeks 21–30   40 miles per week (Week 26: 14 miles)
Weeks 31–40   50 miles per week (Week 36: 18 miles)

- KPI 1.2: To undertake progressive challenging high-quality runs (distance and intensity identified) as per the following schedule:

Week 3   1 mile (8 minutes 15 seconds)
Week 10   5 miles (46 minutes 15 seconds, or 9 minutes 15 seconds per mile)
Week 15   10-kilometre race (1 hour, or 9 minutes 30 seconds per mile)
Week 25   half-marathon (2 hours 8 minutes, or 9 minutes 45 seconds per mile)
Week 30   1 mile (7 minutes 45 seconds)
Week 35   half-marathon (2 hours, or 9 minutes per mile)
One week before the marathon: training run of 3 hours 15 minutes (9-minute pace)

Incorporating the methods and frequency of measuring these KPIs will clearly determine whether you are behind, on or ahead of schedule to successfully complete your primary SMART objective. Furthermore, by entering a variety of competitive 10-kilometre or half-marathon events, you would in effect be contextualizing the measurement process, in this case by adapting physically and mentally to the challenging conditions encountered within the target task of completing the marathon.

This planning scenario has demonstrated the importance of aligning SMART objectives with KPIs and creating expectations that are both realistic and meaningful to the person concerned. Targets and methods that directly relate to personal beliefs and values can enforce strong commitment and drive individual motivation towards their achievement. Similarly, involving and sharing these targets with others can result in further benefits, such as objective feedback, team camaraderie, positive encouragement and support, particularly when and if problems do occur. With individual focus and collective commitment, there is every chance that the objectives will be achieved.

COMMON MISTAKES

So what are the common mistakes made when developing and using objectives and performance indicators? Typical errors include:

40

- Objectives are frequently too vague and meaningless. For example, what does the frequently cited objective 'serving the community needs' actually mean? This should be considered an aim rather than an objective. To avoid vagueness it is important that all elements of the SMART acronym are used and attention is given to the appropriate choice of verb in the objective. Verbs such as 'understand' and 'enjoy' provide little meaning and therefore become difficult to measure. Action verbs, such as 'acquire', 'identify', 'sell', 'produce', 'review' and 'measure', provide much clearer outcomes, particularly if they are free of jargon.
- Not involving appropriate stakeholders in the process of development and agreement to the outcome expectation. Without awareness, understanding and involvement, objectives similarly possess little purpose and hence commitment towards their achievement. The implication here is to fully understand user needs and to involve users in the development process so that they can share and take pride in their successful completion.
- Defining just the elements that are easiest to measure rather than those with the greatest potential value to stakeholders. Often the set of KPIs demonstrates a short-term financial skew and activity rather than an input, throughput, output performance focus, because the financial components are quantifiably easy to measure and conveniently adhere to annual accountability systems. The solution to these common problems is to use a balanced scorecard approach (see Balanced Scorecard Designer, 2009) so as to provide a more meaningful breadth of performance measures.
- Too many objectives and KPIs are proposed. The Audit Commission (2000) emphasizes the importance of focusing on the key 'need to know' versus the 'nice to know' performance targets. Successful organizations will try to prioritize objectives and limit KPIs to just a few; otherwise information overload and resource conflicts are likely to be encountered.
- Making inappropriate internal and external comparisons. Due regard needs to be given to comparing like with like, particularly where different measurements and systems are used or have changed over time. If not, feelings of unfairness and mistrust of performance measures are likely to ensue.
- Associating blame with outcome non-achievement. Judgements and sanctions are often publicly and personally encountered from performance measurements, resulting in manipulative practices used either to improve personal kudos or status or as a 'rod to beat someone's back' and apportion blame. To overcome the stigma associated with performance measurement, a supportive organizational culture and developmental learning process are required to optimize long-term performance.

INTERPRETATION AND MANAGEMENT DECISION

Performance management is achieved through the continuous cyclical process of analysing, planning, implementing and review. Being derived from tools from the analytical phase, SMART objectives and KPIs form an essential component of the planning phase, providing the key targets towards business success. In essence, their management function is to identify and align the organizational, unit and individual planning targets (ends) that 'engage focus, action, feedback and learning' (Berry and Thomas, 2009). They clarify management direction, identify current priorities and detail expected standards of performance. Ideally covering a broad and balanced perspective of outcomes, they can then be used to communicate the required ends from which the means can be designed. For example, once the 'what' is known, the 'how' (methods, systems and actions), 'who' and 'what other resources' can be determined so as to successfully implement plans into practice.

It must be remembered that planning is inextricably linked to all other phases of the management process, with the implementation and evaluation phases providing monitoring opportunities to refine and develop these targets as a more informed picture evolves. In this sense, SMART objectives and KPIs are used by management to determine whether the organization is on track to achieve its projected current and future performances. On tracking this progress, known as business activity monitoring, management can then make timely adjustments in an informed manner as to whether or not they want to continue along this path and if so at what speed. In the unpredictable and complex sport business environment, this makes planning and target setting a continuously live and active process.

CASE STUDY

Demonstrating the broader alignment of objectives and KPIs to strategic direction in the workplace, let us look at the sport organization of Tennis Victoria (2009a). As described by its own website, Tennis Victoria is:

> the representative body of all affiliated clubs, centres, associations, regions and their members throughout Victoria [Australia]. As the central administrative body of tennis in [the state of] Victoria, it is Tennis Victoria's role to manage, co-ordinate, promote, and unify the diverse facets of the sport.
>
> (Tennis Victoria, 2009a)

Tennis Victoria is linked to the umbrella and national sports organization of Tennis Australia (2009a), and therefore it operates in an environment where its organization plan must conform to the national governing body's vision, mission and values or strategic priorities. In other words, and as illustrated in Table 3.3, there is a hierarchical level of short- and long-term performance measures. (Please note that although these are initially based upon publicly available planning documents they have been adapted to meet the educational needs of this text and therefore must be considered fictitious.)

Once Tennis Victoria have agreed and established their performance indicators, the indicators can be measured and monitored graphically as illustrated in Figure 3.2. It is from these data that further management decisions can be made relating to changes in priority, resource allocation or refining of performance targets.

Table 3.3 Tennis Australia and Tennis Victoria performance criteria and measures

Organization	Performance criterion	Performance measure
Tennis Australia	Mission[1]	To make Australia the greatest tennis nation on the planet.
	Strategic goals[1]	1 To develop more champions and depth across all levels.
		2 To build and increase the number of better-quality tennis courts throughout the country.
		3 To provide an opportunity for all people to play tennis.
		4 To enable the entire tennis 'family' to work in unison towards common goals.
		5 To make prudent business decisions while still maximizing opportunities that ensure continued growth.
Tennis Victoria	Mission[2]	To make tennis a part of every Victorian's life.
	Values[2]	Will be known for:
		1 promoting the positive health, cultural, physical, mental and social benefits of tennis;
		2 creating and implementing innovative programmes and services;
		3 developing players to attain their potential;
		4 governance that is financially, ethically and socially responsible;
		5 fostering progressive and team-oriented administration.
	Strategic goals[2]	1 To grow and retain people's involvement through the promotion of tennis as a positive experience.

Table 3.3 Continued

Organization	Performance criterion	Performance measure
		2 To maximize the contribution to the sport of tennis by engaging the entire tennis community, current and potential.
		3 To promote a welcoming, sustainable and quality tennis environment.
		4 In partnership with our stakeholders to be the leader within Australia developing world-class junior players.
		5 To motivate excellence in staff performance and to ensure that a high standard of corporate governance is delivered.
	SMART objectives (selected examples relating to strategic goals 1 and 4 above)[3]	*Strategic goal 1*
		1.1 To increase community awareness of Tennis Victoria and the opportunities to play tennis by 10 per cent as measured by the annual and independent Tennis Australia Survey.
		1.2 To develop four new participation programmes that bridge current demographic gaps by 1 December 2011.
		1.3 To recruit and retain 85 new Junior Development Coaches by June 2011 and within one year of this date have at least 15 per cent of them sitting the Club Professional Coach examination.
		1.4 To develop and implement strategies to increase the 20 per cent conversion rate of participants into the membership, club and coaching network.
		1.5 To establish and utilize a state-wide database that provides measurable statistics by 15 April 2011.
		Strategic goal 4
		4.1 To create a player development pathway by December 2011 to recognize and reward highly ranked junior players in Victoria who are not yet eligible for the National Academy.
		4.2 To investigate and identify at least five new opportunities to broaden competitive opportunities to enhance player development in 2011.
		4.3 To develop and implement a strategy to enable communication with all player development stakeholders by 15 April 2011.

44

Table 3.3 Continued

Organization	Performance criterion	Performance measure
		4.4 To identify, upskill and promote 10 per cent of coaches dedicated to player development by July 2011.
		4.5 To increase the number of Australian Money Tournaments in accordance with Tennis Australia's 2011 strategy.
		4.6 To increase the income derived from commercial player development programmes by 8 per cent by 23 December 2011.
	Key performance indicators (selected examples relating to strategic goals 1 and 4 above)[3]	*Strategic goal 1 examples (ranked in order of importance)*
		■ 100,000 participants per year accessing the programme opportunities by 2011.
		■ 10 per cent of programme participants converted to membership or coaching by 1 June 2011.
		■ To exceed 2011 access and programme targets.
		■ At least 40 media releases through a structured publicity schedule in 2011.
		■ To average at least 500 tennis enquiries per month over 2011.
		Strategic goal 4 examples (ranked in order of importance)
		■ 10 per cent annual increase of players (boys and girls) ranked in ITF 1 – 800 by 1 December 2011.
		■ 35 per cent of male players and 25 per cent of female players in the top 20 Australian ranking in each junior age group (12, 14, 16 and 18) by 1 December 2011.
		■ 25 per cent of the Tennis Australia National High Performance Academy allocated positions will be Victorian athletes by 1 December 2011.

Notes:
[1] Derived from Tennis Australia (2009b).
[2] Derived from Tennis Victoria (2009b).
[3] Adapted from Tennis Victoria (2006).

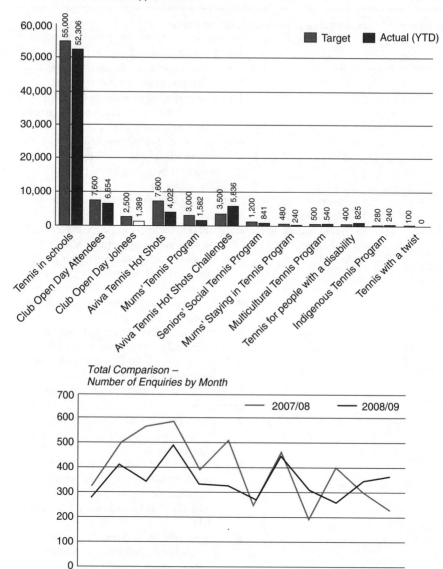

Figure 3.2 Tennis Victoria performance comparisons

Source: Tennis Victoria (2009b).

commencing the plan

SUMMARY

In conclusion, the main benefit of using SMART objectives and KPIs is that they act as targets that can engage and motivate individual and team performance towards measurable achievement. Furthermore they determine what is important to an organization in both the short and the long term and enable feedback and hence learning to take place at the individual, unit and organization level. In essence, in a complex sport business environment they provide a focus of attention and highlight the commitment required towards business sustainability.

The process of writing clear performance-oriented targets involves answering six questions, namely:

1   What do you want to achieve?
2   How will you recognize it when it has been achieved?
3   Is it achievable and realistic?
4   When do you want to achieve it by?
5   What happens when conflicts occur?
6   What will be the process of measuring completion or achievement?

It must be remembered that this chapter has been directed at just one element of the planning stage as applied to the performance management system. The previous chapter covered the auditing stage, and other components of planning are introduced in subsequent chapters. Planning must therefore be considered in a broader context, avoiding the common mistakes of focusing entirely on easily measurable targets, being skewed towards the needs of just one stakeholder, or not being linked to the management processes of planning, implementation and evaluation. To this end a portfolio or balanced breadth of SMART objectives, written as outcomes and monitored through performance indicators, must not only be planned but additionally implemented, monitored and reviewed. This means that ideally performance outcomes need to be compared with independently established benchmarks as well as internal organizational data, so that ongoing effective management decision making can logically follow.

Guides to further resources, useful web links and guideline answers to all the self-test questions featured in this chapter are available on a companion website at www.routledge.com/9780415491594.

SELF-TEST QUESTION

Please complete Table 3.4 to identify the limitations of the following 'not so SMART' objectives and provide an example of how it could be improved in the 'SMART objective' column.

Table 3.4 Non-SMART objective improvements

Non-SMART objective	Current limitation	SMART objective
1 Improve business performance next year.		
2 Understand customer needs.		
3 Develop internal communication by 31 March 2011.		
4 Increase gym club membership by 5 per cent.		
5 Achieve an Olympic gold medal in every sport at the London 2012 Olympics or else cut the elite funding to that sport.		

CHAPTER 4

MANAGING RISK: WHAT IF?

TECHNIQUE DESCRIPTION

Sport and the notion of risk are inseparable concepts (Elliott, 2004). With a sport industry history that includes fatalities (e.g. the Lahore cricket shootings, the Sydney to Hobart ocean race drownings, the Bradford fire and the Hillsborough football spectator deaths) as well as recent ticketing, financial, legal and weather-related incidents, risks potentially have an impact on the success of every organization, large and small.

Risk management has become a legal requirement in many countries and is of primary concern to all sport managers, but what exactly is it? According to the Institute of Risk Management (IRM), the world's leading international professional and training body in the subject matter, risk management is 'the process which aims to help organizations understand, evaluate and take action on all their risks with a view to increasing the probability of their success and reducing the likelihood of failure' (Institute of Risk Management, 2010).

Applied to all levels of your organization, risk management historically constitutes a protection mechanism that focuses attention on what could stop you achieving business success. In today's contemporary sport industry, risk management is considered to be a central part of an organization's strategy, involving forward, lateral, responsible and balanced thinking (Office of Sport and Recreation Tasmania, 1999). More specifically it entails an ongoing systematic and rational analysis of an organization's exposure to risk, leading to the development and implementation of plans to avoid, reduce or transfer the potential impact of such risks.

To this end this chapter will introduce you to the risk management process, which includes:

- risk assessment – the overall process of risk analysis and risk evaluation;
- risk treatment – the process of selecting and implementing risk reduction plans;
- risk control – the mechanisms of reporting, communication and review.

Furthermore it will describe key risk analysis techniques and provide a framework to ensure that you understand the complexity of contemporary risk, as well as are able to identify, assess and appropriately manage risks found in the sport industry.

PURPOSE

Purely from an occupation health and safety perspective a cursory review of accident ratios reveals that for every serious injury there are typically ten minor injuries and 600 near misses (Morrison, 2008a). Even in this limited sense the aim of risk management can be seen to be at minimum about eradicating negative incidents such as the occurrence of serious injuries and reducing the near misses. More generally though, the purpose of risk management is to identify a broad range of risks that could affect organizational performance and then develop and if necessary invoke risk reduction plans, so as to mitigate such adverse impacts before they occur (Government of Western Australia, 2007). This has been largely driven by accidents or disasters occurring, followed by litigation, media amplification and subsequent regulation. Collectively these have affected sport management practice all round the world. For example, at the corporate governance level, the Turnbull Report (1999) in the UK and the Sarbanes–Oxley Act (2002) in the USA have introduced risk management at the strategic level, whilst the universal 'duty of care' principle has now become commonplace in most national occupational health and safety workplace acts and hence operations.

However, risk management is not merely a self-preservation, moral or compliance-related activity. In this litigious and economic-driven society and particularly in light of the events of September 11, 2001, it has become an important component of business success and consequently developed into a well-researched and multidisciplinary profession. Providing a forward-looking and early risk detection system, effective risk management potentially saves an organization considerable disruption, time and money, as well as adding value to an organization by:

- engaging stakeholders in safe behaviour that complies with relevant health, safety and security legislation;

50

- optimizing operational efficiency through proactive, transparent prioritization and planning techniques, leading to more reliable and objective decision making;
- establishing systems to monitor and document incidents, preparing for emergencies, and assisting you in obtaining appropriate insurance cover;
- developing and supporting people as well as the organization's knowledge base;
- protecting and enhancing an organization's image, thereby providing stakeholder confidence and organizational resilience in frequently encountered volatile market conditions.

In summary, risk management 'supports accountability, performance measurement and reward thus promoting efficiency at all levels' (Institute of Risk Management, 2010). Sport managers who appropriately manage their risks will be able to spend more time on strategic rather than firefighting activities, and recognize the fact that you will have more chance of possessing a sustainable future, relative to managers who adopt the 'It will never happen to me' approach.

THEORETICAL OVERVIEW

Every activity involves some level of uncertainty and risk, whether this be merely crossing the road, betting on a horse race or even managing a stadium development project. Risk must therefore be considered a ubiquitous concept, with a completely risk-free sport environment being unattainable (Office of Sport and Recreation Tasmania, 1999).

But what is meant by the term 'risk'? Derived from the classical Greek term to signify unfavourable activities or potential danger, it is now a word commonly used by managers to describe either the probability of loss (Det Norske Veritas, 2010) or the chance that a hazard could occur (O'Toole and Mikolaitis, 2002).

According to Toohey and Taylor (2008) the study of risk and risk assessment originated from gambling activities in the seventeenth century and maritime insurance premiums in the eighteenth century, and since the twentieth century has been associated with the discipline of economics. For example, risk assessment techniques are used in financial markets either for insurance purposes or for investment strategies (e.g. mean variance portfolio optimization; see Markowitz, 1987) to illustrate the trade-offs between financial risk and returns. Comparing different options and valuations usually involved complex mathematical modelling and formulae (Black and Scholes, 1973), and rather than propose just one ideal scenario it was refined to include hedged positions involving two or more parameters (e.g. short- and long-term investments and/or between a 30 and a 70 per cent chance of occurring). As global markets have become more volatile, risk management techniques and instruments have similarly become more sophisticated and common. Value-at-risk adaptations developed (see YiHou Huang, 2009), and in the last decade the general principle of allocating risk to management decisions has transferred to a number of other applications, including the dominant one of health and safety.

Being subjective in nature and associated with harm (e.g. injury to spectators) and detriment (e.g. loss of money or a championship), risk is typically classified in the literature according to the level of probability of occurrence and the severity of likely impact (Klinke and Renn, 2001). Using qualitative measures to assess these two categories, organizations have then applied their own classification scheme to assign quantitative data to evaluate their perceived risks. For example, the Government of Western Australia (2007) has developed its own sport- and recreation-related risk reference tables as illustrated in Tables 4.1 and 4.2.

Allocating each risk to a quantifiable level (first column of Tables 4.1 and 4.2) and then multiplying the two figures together provides a numeric measure from which management can make a decision on how to treat the risk (see Table 4.3).

For example, it would be considered more important to develop a risk management strategy for a risk assessed with a magnitude 12 rating (such as a heart attack in Table 4.3) than for a risk evaluated at 5 (such as blisters and cramp). Note also that the nature of the injury is dependent upon the circumstance, with the likelihood of a heart attack occurring at a marathon (Table 4.3) being considered a higher probability than that of a heart attack occurring in a sport centre (Table 4.1).

Such quantifiable risk analyses have became common around the world, and in light of a rapidly developing international discipline a universal risk management standard was established in 2002 (AIRMIC, ALARM and IRM, 2002). Developed in line with international ISO/IEC standards (e.g. ISO/IEC 73 and 31010), this universal standard, which has been translated into 17 languages, proposed a risk management process of best practice as highlighted in Table 4.4.

Offering flexibility in application, this process provides a formal auditing risk management tool that initiates the ongoing cyclical risk management process.

52

Table 4.1 Qualitative measures of probability

Level	Descriptor	Description	Frequency of occurrence	Sport centre injury example
1	Rare	The incident may occur in exceptional circumstances.	Less than once in 15 years.	Death or paralysis.
2	Unlikely	The incident could occur at some time.	At least once in 10 years.	Heart attack or concussion.
3	Moderate	The incident should occur at some time.	At least once in 3 years.	Broken bones and convulsions.
4	Likely	The incident will probably occur in most circumstances.	At least once per year.	Bleeding and sprains.
5	Almost certain	The incident is expected to occur in most circumstances.	More than once per year.	Blisters, nose bleeds, nausea and headaches.

Source: Adapted from Government of Western Australia (2007).

Table 4.2 Qualitative measures of severity

Level	Rank	Financial impact	Injuries/death	Reputation and image	Sport centre injury example
1	Insignificant	Less than 570	No injuries.	Unsubstantiated, low impact, low profile or no news item.	Bruises through being struck with a tennis ball.
2	Minor	570 to 5,700	First aid treatment.	Substantiated, low impact, low news profile.	Cuts and lacerations through swimming pool tiles.
3	Moderate	5,700 to 28,700	Medical treatment required.	Substantiated, public embarrassment, moderate impact, moderate news profile.	Concussion through collapse of football goal posts.
4	Major	28,700 to 86,180	Death or extensive injuries.	Substantiated, public embarrassment, high impact, high news profile, third-party actions.	Young child drowning in swimming pool.
5	Catastrophic	More than 86,180	Multiple deaths or severe permanent disablements.	Substantiated, public embarrassment, very high multiple impact, high widespread multiple news profile, third-party actions.	Terrorist or shooting incident.

Source: Adapted from Government of Western Australia (2007).

Table 4.3 Sample risk criteria

Risk level	Criteria for management	Health and safety example at a marathon
1–3	Acceptable	Wasp sting: 1* × 2** = 2
4–5	Monitor	Blisters and cramp: 5* × 1** = 5
6–9	Management control required	Dehydration: 3* × 3** = 9
10–14	Urgent management action	Heart attack: 3* × 4** = 12
15–25	Unacceptable	Terrorist attack prediction: 3* × 5** = 15

* = Probability; ** = Severity
Source: Adapted from Government of Western Australia (2007).

Table 4.4 Risk management process

Process	Description
Organizational context	The uncertainty encountered by the organization as well as the scope and culture established towards managing this uncertainty.
Risk assessment:	
– Risk analysis	Provides a risk profile by identifying, describing and estimating an organization's exposure to uncertainty.
– Risk evaluation	Compares risk level estimates to established organization criteria.
Risk reporting	Internal and external reporting of threats and opportunities.
Decision	The course of action chosen.
Risk treatment	The process of selecting and implementing measures to modify risk.
Monitoring	The feedback mechanism to ensure the effectiveness of the current system as well as to make continuous improvements.

Source: Adapted from AIRMIC, ALARM and IRM (2002).

Evolving from a broad range of management disciplines and applications, this standard constitutes what Piekarz (2009: 145) suggests is the third age of risk culture, namely where risk is 'characterised by its complexity in origin, and seen to create both opportunities/up sides as well as the more familiar threats/down sides, which are generated by the complex interaction of forces'. Rather than just relate to the negative consequences of the natural environment (first-age risk culture) and people-generated risks (second-age risk culture), the third age introduced a broader understanding of risk that included positive benefits (upside risks) as well as negative ones (downside risks). For example, what might be the positive and negative consequences of over-demand at a New Year's Eve sports event? The benefits may include improved atmosphere, greater financial profit, happier sponsors and more media coverage, but these may be accompanied by downside risks that include overcrowding, delays, public scuffles, or even fatalities due to limited emergency service access.

PRACTICAL APPLICATION

Reflecting the organizational culture and managerial mindset of an organization or individual, the scope of risk and hence management practice varies considerably. At one extreme it could be very broad and focus on organization growth or survival relating to a significant capital investment decision, whereas at the other extreme it could be very narrow and merely relate to obtaining personal luggage insurance for an individual one-off flight.

Regardless of scope, it must be recognized that risk assessment is both relative and value laden, being very subjectively appraised in practice. For some, losing £30,000 on a business deal may be a daily occurrence and a completely acceptable risk to undertake. For others, losing this absolute amount might lead to considerable embarrassment, loss of employment or even bankruptcy. Equally, personal decision making and perceptions are often inconsistent, particularly when engaging with non-work and voluntary activities. Whereas you may be very risk aware at work, risk evaluations of voluntary activities outside work, such as gambling, do-it-yourself tasks and adrenalin-related sports, are rarely undertaken. As a result, the consequences of losing large sums of money or your house, sustaining serious injuries or even losing your life owing to participation in such activities unfortunately are too common.

Ironically risk also presents opportunity, benefits and rewards. Indeed Morrison (2008b) suggests that business innovation involving creativity and risk taking is now considered essential in management. He elaborates: 'the trouble is if you don't risk anything, you risk even more' (Morrison, 2008b). The important point is that businesses now recognize that they need to balance their opportunities and risks, since risks have the potential to affect all strategic, operational and project-oriented activities (Government of Western Australia, 2007) in a positive and negative way.

This has led to organizations using risk management applications to manage business, compliance, financial, knowledge management and operational risks. For example, AIRMIC, ALARM and IRM (2002) cite compliance applications, such as health and safety, environmental applications, trade descriptions, consumer and data protection regulations, and financial applications that include credit availability, foreign exchange rates, interest rate movements and other competitor activities.

56

ASSUMPTIONS AND LIMITATIONS

Risk identification and assessment, the key foundations of effective risk management strategies, are not an exact science. Whereas they aid forward thinking and judgements towards certain hazards, they are often clouded by individual perceptions and subjectivity. For example, which risks and eventualities should be considered and which should not? Too often they assume normal occurrences, and extremes are barely considered. For example, who would have ever predicted the incidents of September 11 or believed that the scale and scope of recent natural disasters involving fires, earthquakes, tsunamis or even sport-specific crowd disasters would ever happen to them?

To help guard against complacency, bias and inconsistency, the Office of Sport and Recreation Tasmania (1999) proposes that sport organizations should clearly define their own acceptable levels of risk from the outset. For example, unacceptable consequences according to the Office of Sport and Recreation Tasmania (1999: 29) could be framed by the following criteria:

- injuries requiring hospitalization;
- financial loss exceeding a stated cost for one occurrence;
- a significant drop in participation ('significant' to be organizationally defined);
- legal proceedings against the organization.

In addition it suggests that the baseline standards for unacceptable likelihoods could be classified in terms of:

- frequent minor injuries ('frequent' and 'minor' to be defined by the organization);
- events that frequently interrupt the organization's activities ('frequently' to be defined);
- frequent small financial losses ('frequent' and 'small' to be defined).

In practice there are also likely to be conflicting risks and ethical tensions, so a balance involving risk trade-offs is frequently encountered. For example, Elliott (2004) cites the trade-off between driver safety and revenue streams in Formula 1. In particular he refers to the pit stop scenario, where the act of high-pressure petrol being blasted into the car fuel tanks was reintroduced for television entertainment value, despite the obvious danger and previous incidents of fuel spillage and ignition. Trade-offs can additionally exist in the consideration of different risk reduction strategies. Elliott (2004) again makes

57

reference to Formula 1 when he asserts that the action of a safety car being used to slow down the cars after an accident could in itself create another accident by dramatically reducing the driver speed, the car tyre pressure and its steering capacity.

Piekarz (2009) reports other significant risk management issues and potential technique limitations as:

- communication problems – confused terminology around the world and perceptions that are often distorted by media reporting;
- new hazards or risks – new generations bring new problems and methods of acceptability, e.g. different acts of terrorism in the twenty-first century;
- probability levels being difficult to accurately quantify;
- the difficulty of establishing causality;
- the lack of consideration of aggregate risks in the evaluation process.

Furthermore, the focus of this chapter is on the single organization managing its own risks and limitations. In comparison, major and mega-sports events typically involve managing complex risks and processes across multiple stakeholders, covering significant expertise and resources. This demands the establishment of a multiple-stakeholder crisis management team and culminates in the production of a very sophisticated incident management plan, the details of which are beyond the scope of this text.

Despite such limitations, the techniques of risk management introduced in this chapter possess international acceptance and do serve as excellent sources of focusing management attention on key variables from which realistic and contextual plans can be developed.

PROCESS

Simplifying the international standard process (AIRMIC, ALARM and IRM, 2002), the Government of Western Australia (2007) proposes a systematic and logical risk management process involving five key activities, namely:

1 Establish the context.
2 Identify the risks.
3 Assess the risks.
4 Treat and control the risks.
5 Monitor and review.

58

1 Establish the context

Given that any risk is relative and situational, defined by parameters such as local legislation as well as an organization's purpose, strategic objectives and capability, it is vital initially to establish the scope of application. This defines the comprehensive nature and extent to which risk management is undertaken, as well as the risk acceptance criteria of the activity. In the sport management context, the Office of Sport and Recreation Tasmania (1999) suggests that you achieve this by establishing the boundaries and expectations of:

- the external influences on the organization, e.g. recognizing the current trends of litigation, increasing expectations of service quality, less personal responsibility, and a blame culture;
- the organization and its operations, e.g. the assets at risk and the historical risk culture, involving policy, structure and established norms of behaviour;
- the risk profile of the activity under review, e.g. strategic, operational or project level or nature of risk(s) being considered.

Clearly the context and unit of analysis will directly influence the specifics of your process, namely the stakeholders that need to be included, the resource commitment required and the defining parameters of the risk exposure(s). For example, is this consideration of the risk of personally losing your mobile phone or at the organization level losing your health club's computer data? Is it focused on one area, a health and safety review of a renovated sport club canteen, or a more comprehensive review of the organization, such as the financial and succession risks of a professional sporting team? The purpose of this stage is therefore to articulate what the risk management process is applied to, as well as to establish the general level of risk exposure and the key stakeholders affected.

2 Identify the risks

Having established the scope of the risk management process, you need to determine the range and types of risks to be identified. Risks typically entail a source or hazard (e.g. flammable materials), an event (e.g. someone dropping a match or lit cigarette) and a consequence (e.g. the Bradford fire disaster). Analysis of any one of these elements may initiate the forward- or backward-looking process of risk identification, which involves determining potential risks as well as their cause, effect and means of impact.

Focusing upon the questions of what could happen, when, how and why, each function or activity should be carefully appraised for likely risks. A disciplined and streamlined approach to risk identification and categorization can be achieved through using techniques such as:

- in-house group brainstorming (e.g. likely threat or 'What if?' scenario analyses, and reviews of the organization or industry's previous accident and injury logs);
- scenario-based activities (e.g. examining incidents or lessons from the past);
- flowcharting or systems analysis (e.g. a sequential diagram of key activities and critical points);
- seeking expert advice (e.g. fire health and safety experts);
- industry-established audits, taxonomies or checklists.

An example of the latter could for example include generic risk source lists that typically categorize common sources of risk, what is at risk and the likely consequences (see Office of Sport and Recreation Tasmania, 1999: 26), or sport-specific risk categorizations, such as Leopkey and Parent's (2009) 13 risk issue categories pertaining to large-scale sporting events.

However you choose to identify the risks, they should all be defined and clearly documented at this stage. This commences the process of producing a risk register or profile. Formats for this vary considerably, but normally risks are individually numbered, their influences identified, and their likely consequences if untreated stated (see the example of the first four columns of the risk analysis and evaluation form in Table 4.5).

This forms the analytical basis of the next stage of the process, risk evaluation, and further demonstrates to external stakeholders that some level of risk management has taken place, particularly in the event of potential litigation in the future (Office of Sport and Recreation Tasmania, 1999).

On the subject of legal expectations, it is important to realize that legislation does not usually require you to eliminate all risk, but as illustrated by health and safety legislation you are 'required to protect people as far as is "reasonably practicable"' (Health and Safety Executive, 2009). In other words, not every risk is necessarily to be considered. Some are indeed very improbable, such as a terrorist attack on a small voluntary table tennis club in Switzerland. This means that each organization should establish its own baseline for comparative purposes so as to identify its unique vulnerabilities to realistic downside risks (threats) as well as upside risks (opportunities). Ideally,

60

Table 4.5 Risk analysis and evaluation form

Risk number and type	Source of risk	What is at risk?	Consequence	Probability	Severity	Level of risk
1.1 Relationship	Commercial – salary cap fraud	Players, sponsors and spectators	Damage to reputation; loss of sponsorship, best players and membership income			
2.1 Human factor	Negligence – pitch preparation	Officials and players	Injury, litigation, damage to ground or club reputation			
2.2 Human factor	Anti-social crowd behaviour	Players, sponsors and spectators	Damage to reputation, loss of sponsorship and membership income, and in some cases could trigger violence leading to panic and death			

describing and categorizing such risks should initially involve in-house personnel, as this permits a knowledgeable and locally driven mechanism for ensuring appropriate management scrutiny, ownership and attention to the organization's potentially unique hazards and impact.

3 Assess the risks

This activity is the fundamental backbone to an effective risk management strategy. It involves you applying common and consistent criteria to evaluate and prioritize your risk management activities.

As previously mentioned in the 'Theoretical overview' section of this chapter, risk analysis and evaluation (the final columns of Table 4.5) are largely based on the applied assessment of the risk's probability of occurrence (likelihood) and the severity of the impact (consequence) to the local context. Using prior knowledge, experience and often anecdotal evidence, a collective decision with key stakeholders needs to be made as to where each of the previously identified risks should be classified on these two parameters. By means of either a five-point (see Tables 4.1 and 4.2) or a three-point (e.g. high, medium, low) classification system, these qualitative data are converted to numerical values, and the multiple of these parameters provide the quantifiable matrix criteria on which management actions are determined. For example, using the information contained within Table 4.3, a wasp sting at a marathon (probability rating of 1 × severity rating of 2 = 2 on a 5 × 5 matrix) is perhaps likely to be considered an acceptable risk, with no additional management action planned – suffice to say that access to basic first aid provision is assumed at every sporting event. Conversely, if the weather forecast for this marathon was predicted to be over 30 degrees Celsius on the race day, the risk of dehydration (probability of 3 × severity rating of 3 = 9) would be expected to require a coordinated management plan of action, including triggers (measurable thresholds), towards implementation.

This stage of the process therefore assigns particular values to each risk and when compared with organizational and/or industry standards (e.g. IAAF marathon standards in this case) establishes whether the risk is acceptable or unacceptable. Where it is considered unacceptable the risk needs to be treated by management intervention.

62

4 Treat and control the risks

Risk treatment and control involves you determining, selecting and implementing pertinent risk mitigation actions with alternatives. Management decisions should be based upon a critical appraisal of evidence, and you should consider amongst other things the required resources, benefits and legal requirements of different implementation options. Such interventions, according to the Office of Sport and Recreation Tasmania (1999), include:

■ risk avoidance (e.g. do not undertake the activity);
■ risk acceptance (e.g. do nothing);
■ risk reduction (e.g. minimize the likelihood or severity to an acceptable level);
■ risk monitoring (e.g. deferment);
■ risk transference (e.g. legally allocate the risk to someone else);
■ risk financing (e.g. cover the actual cost).

In the case of the marathon example, the options available to treat the risk of dehydration, ideally in combination rather than alone, could be:

■ to change the race date or start timing to another season or an earlier or later start time (avoid);
■ to acknowledge that part of the joy of marathon running is to challenge yourself physically and mentally, so protecting the participants too much might compromise the participant experience (accept);
■ to provide additional drinks stations, first aid centres and personnel along the route, make use of areas of shade, and make a variety of health and safety public announcements before, during and after the event (reduce);
■ to establish monitoring systems (e.g. measure temperatures around the route) to re-evaluate the risk level and determine threshold triggers for action (e.g. if the event temperature exceeds 35 degrees Celsius the event should be immediately postponed) (monitor);
■ to insure against death and/or cancellation of the event in extreme weather (transfer);
■ over time to set aside finance to cover the cost of the risk occurrence (finance).

Where it is difficult to mitigate the risk, contingency plans must be developed, formalized and invoked. For example, what will be the procedure in the case of an emergency for hospitalization or in the worst-case scenario that someone dies whilst running on the course? More specifically, what will be the process of communication, by whom and how, to the deceased's next of kin as well as to the media?

Management equally can choose to accept rather than treat the identified risk, particularly where risk reduction is too complex and formal mitigation is most unlikely. If this is the case, it is once again advisable to document the reasons why you have made this decision, so that a trail of thought can be established should there be a legal investigation. Remember, you are only accountable to the information available to you at a moment in time, so make sure that you document the sources of evidence to substantiate your decision(s).

Regardless of the intervention strategy chosen, further courses of action should also be readily determined and included in the action plan (e.g. staff being assigned to the location of a crowd-related incident at the marathon and, if this escalates into further danger, the event being temporarily suspended or ultimately cancelled).

5 Monitor and review

Clearly regular consultation and communication throughout the risk management process are vital to ensure commitment to this important ongoing process. This entails strong leadership of relevant stakeholders in an inclusive and open environment. The culmination of this work is the production of an in-depth risk management plan that documents the context of the review, identifies the specific risks, their consequences, ratings, risk levels, position accountabilities, training and support mechanisms, appropriate controls, treatments and courses of action, and monitors strategies, detailing the intervals of review.

Such a plan then needs to be converted into action. This involves documenting and communicating risk mitigation actions to all affected stakeholders, as well as testing their effectiveness in practice. In the case of evacuation procedures, unfortunately these are too often tested in very limited conditions, such as before the public have arrived at an event and by giving the key stakeholders knowledge of the exact time of the emergency practice. The reality though, as seen by the Hillsborough disaster, is that evacuation procedures in a packed sport stadium are very different from those in an empty one in which key individuals can fully prepare.

Formal and informal controls and periodic reviews should be regularly undertaken, and this often involves revisiting various stages of the process.

64

Where accidents or incidents of non-compliance to the plan occur, they should be formally reported and trigger other procedures. This could for example include an investigation into the reasons for non-compliance, procedural and system improvements, or further staff training or support as appropriate.

Where recommended changes are agreed to, documentation updates are required in the plan, and once again these should be communicated to all relevant personnel. New incidents and accidents will naturally occur and, in the light of evolving levels of expectation and risk treatment, the process of risk management will always be a continuous activity. The important point is that, at any one time, an organization should have in place a current and comprehensive risk management framework, plan and set of procedures that are constantly reappraised. Without this, the sustainable value and future of an organization or unit within it may be severely at risk.

COMMON MISTAKES

The Health and Safety Executive (2009) suggests that it is important not to over-complicate the analysis (too much detail and control) or at the opposite extreme totally ignore or simplify the process too much. To this end it is suggested that only reasonably foreseeable events and behaviours should be considered, and earthquakes for example be considered only if you live in or around an active fault line.

Similarly the nature of voluntary participation in the activity must be duly recognized, since certain sports and outdoor activities naturally face more hazards or risks than others. For example, there are few hazards associated with crown green bowling, as compared with the activities of parachuting, rock climbing, ski jumping, rugby or trampolining. In the latter cases, individual participants are likely to be aware of and be willing to accept the levels of risk inherent in these activities or even abstain from participation if full-body protective padding was a necessary condition to engage in the activity. As mentioned by the Office of Sport and Recreation Tasmania (1999: 25), it is essential 'to rationalise our risk management and not strive for risk control beyond the expectations of participants'. In such cases reference to the sport's national governing body regulations and guidelines of best practice should as a minimum be endorsed.

However, this does not mean that risk management should adopt a mini-malist approach and become merely a mechanical paper exercise to comply with regulations (Piekarz, 2009). For some, unfortunately, this has proved to be the case, with the risk management process being considered purely on a theoretical and generic one-off basis. For example, a physical inspection, rather than merely carrying out the process from an office, is recommended, as is the consideration of different weather conditions. A marathon run in hot, cold, windy, icy or even very wet conditions brings with it very different risks to manage in each scenario.

Furthermore risk management is about risk identification and prudent consideration of appropriate management actions. It is not the responsibility of just one person, nor is it about apportioning blame, appraising individual performance or deliberately being alarmist. Whilst personal accountability towards individual actions is recommended, to ensure personal ownership and proper resource allocation, individuals making important decisions should not be compromised or pressured by political outcomes or the consequence of cancellation. In essence, effective management of risks is only possible through open and honest discussions and a collective commitment and responsibility to the process.

INTERPRETATION AND MANAGEMENT DECISION

Organizations that proactively identify, evaluate, categorize and prioritize their risks are better informed than those that do not, and can therefore establish thresholds that trigger either management actions to control specific risks or acceptance of the consequences. Software such as RiskSense (particularly used in venue and event industries) and ModelRisk (which provides some of the most advanced modelling software) can further assist managers to produce a number of visual interfaces that aid in the understanding and interpretation of the risk management process.

Informed decision making in managing risks is only possible where proactive systems identify the broad range of risks that cover strategic, operational, financial, and health and safety settings. Once risks are identified, preventative and reactive treatments need to be carefully planned and balanced against likely costs. On the one hand, 'It is obviously foolish to spend vast sums of money on a negligible reduction in risk' (Office of Sport and Recreation Tasmania, 1999: 15), but on the other compliance with legal requirements, regardless of cost, must be considered mandatory.

The volatile nature of sport, with its potentially high emotional content and often significant media attention, means that early warning signs need to be clearly identified and appropriate tried and tested action plans implemented.

66

In some cases incidents may occur at some distance from key decision makers, so information and decision-making channels need to be clearly established and important decisions speedily executed. For example, verbal confrontations between fans can quickly escalate into violent brawls if they are not properly contained at the face-to-face location of occurrence.

Risk management must therefore be fully integrated into your organization's culture, with senior management assigning clear levels of responsibility and decision making for urgent action. Whilst continuous incident prevention is the main aim of the risk management process, effective reactive strategies and tactics become vital to increase the likelihood of success and reduce the probability of failure in achieving your organization's objectives (AIRMIC, ALARM and IRM, 2002).

CASE STUDIES

Fortunately there is a variety of different risk assessments or management plans available and accessible from the internet. They demonstrate different levels of detail, and include the following sport examples:

■ Australian Communications and Media Authority (2005). As a service provider of the 2006 Commonwealth Games, the Australian Communications and Media Authority (ACMA) (the national broadcasting, internet, radio and telecommunications regulator) demonstrates its commitment to risk management by placing an extract from its own risk management plan at http://www.acma.gov.au/webwr/_assets/main/lib299/appen%204%20-%20risk%20management%20plan.pdf.
■ Vicsport Triathlon Sport (2003) uses the format of a three-by-three matrix of assessment and considers weather, medical, security and miscellaneous risks to protect the organizing committee from legal action. See http://fulltext.ausport.gov.au/fulltext/2003/vic/Help_Sheet7.pdf.
■ London 2012 Olympic and Paralympic Games. Examples include:
  – Formal risk assessment and management documentation related to the preparations for the London 2012 Olympic and Paralympic Games (House of Commons, 2007, http://www.publications.parliament.uk/pa/cm200607/cmselect/cmpubacc/377/377.pdf; National Audit Office, 2007, http://www.nao.org.uk/publications/0607/preparations_for_the_olympics.aspx).
  – Flood Risk Assessment (Olympic Delivery Authority, 2007), located at http://planning.london2012.com/upload/publicaccessodalive/07-02-06%20vol14a%20flood%20risk%20assessment%20(387).pdf.

Further risk assessment examples of a general nature that could be applied to local sport club facilities can be seen at:

- Health and Safety Executive (2006a) – an office-based example, http://www.hse.gov.uk/risk/casestudies/pdf/office.pdf.
- Health and Safety Executive (2006b) – a village hall-based example, http://www.hse.gov.uk/risk/casestudies/pdf/villagehall.pdf.

SUMMARY

Whilst it is inevitable that sport organizations will always encounter some risk, owing to the hazardous nature of their activity, effective risk management ensures that this does not result in significant loss, harm or liability. It is about responsible management and should be embedded within your organization's culture and policy. Through a transparent decision-making process, risk management provides a variety of benefits, which include reducing the chance of unexpected and costly surprises, reducing insurance premiums, protecting your organization's assets and optimizing your strategic outcomes.

As an ongoing activity of continuous improvement, this chapter has outlined a five-step risk management process that involves:

1 Establish the context.
2 Identify the risks.
3 Assess the risks.
4 Treat and control the risks.
5 Monitor and review.

Whilst each step can and should be revisited at any stage in the process, this all-encompassing risk management process covers risk assessment, treatment and control techniques. Risk assessment is usually measured in terms of consequence severity and probability of occurrence, whereas treatment and control strategies have been seen to include risk avoidance, acceptance, reduction, monitoring, transference, and financing options.

Entailing a methodological approach of overt, forward and responsible thinking, the process of risk management culminates in the production of clearly documented live frameworks, policies, plans and procedures that need to be appropriately implemented. Even though limitations include conflicting and subjective interpretations, multi-stakeholder complexities

68

and causality issues, cost-effective risk management benefits all sport orga-nizations, as well as begins to fulfil your duty of care.

Failure to identify, monitor and manage your unique risks can lead to cata-strophic circumstances and in extreme cases the demise of your organization. Are you prepared to take that risk?

Guides to further resources, useful web links and guideline answers to all the self-test questions featured in this chapter are available on a companion website at www.routledge.com/9780415491594.

SELF-TEST QUESTIONS

To gauge your understanding of risk management terminology, process and applied practice, please work through the following two tasks.

Task 1

1   A risk is classified as anything that has the potential to cause harm.
    ❑ True
    ❑ False
2   Risk assessment is the process of selecting and implementing risk reduc-tion plans.
    ❑ True
    ❑ False
3   Which of the following can be considered benefits of managing risks?
    a.   Less time firefighting
    b.   Justification of a health and safety position
    c.   More efficient use of resources
    d.   Determining levels of insurance cover
    e.   Compliance with regulations
    f.   Improved team cooperation and communication
4   Place the following risk management activities in sequential order of implementation
    a.   Assess the risk
    b.   Establish the context
    c.   Identify the risk
    d.   Monitor and review
    e.   Treat and control the risks

5   In health and safety terms, what is so important about 'reasonably prac-
    ticable', and how might it be determined?

Task 2

Using the London Organising Committee of the Olympic and Paralympic
Games (2007) 2012 *Changing places programme* documentation for
contextual information, located at http://www.london2012.com/documents/
locog-publications/changing-places-toolkit.pdf, briefly define the scope of
your project and then complete the risk assessment form on pages 9 and 10
as if you were organizing such a project to improve your own locality. What
practical problems did you encounter, and how might these be resolved?

70

CHAPTER 5

WHO WILL DO THE WORK? IDENTIFYING THE PEOPLE REQUIREMENTS

TECHNIQUE DESCRIPTION

As sport organizations are service industry based, their survival is highly dependent upon effective employment, development and deployment of their human capital. No senior manager would disagree with the time-honoured cliché that people are your most important asset (Pearson and Thomas, 1991). It is as valid today as it was two decades ago. Yet hiring and firing of staff are regarded as being among the most difficult decisions that managers make. As elaborated by American Express (2010), 'Successful hiring can be expensive and time consuming. Unsuccessful hiring can be disastrous to a company's health.'

Influenced by legal imperatives, union pressures and an organization's strategic objectives, the cornerstone to any employment decision is depen-dent upon understanding and clearly articulating your workforce needs. To this end, this chapter introduces you to the integrated and conventional foundation stages of the human resource management recruitment process, entailing:

- the job analysis – the initial process of identifying and determining the general requirements of the job, leading to the more detailed promotional and selection documentation of the job description and person speci-fication;
- the job or position description – the document that determines and communicates what the job involves, typically detailing its role, duties, performance standards, accountabilities and reporting relationships;
- the person specification – the document that provides a profile of the ideal person, in terms of the minimum essential criteria necessary to carry out the job.

Whereas job analysis initiates the process of gathering data to define what that the incumbent will actually do, its outcome is to produce a detailed job description and person specification that act as communication tools to inform the recruitment and selection process.

Once these are in place, further recruitment, selection and induction techniques are implemented to ensure that there is a strong foundation for the building of an effective and efficient workforce.

PURPOSE

The purpose of the job analysis and description stage of recruitment is to challenge, establish and document the job-related employment activities, procedures, development and performance appraisal process of an individual's work (hr.guide.com, 2001). By breaking the job down into its essential components, you are in effect challenging the assumptions on which the job is based and thereby attempting to avoid discriminatory practice (Department for Business, Innovation and Skills, 2009).

Affecting different elements of the organization's human resource plan, job analysis and description provide a multi-purpose function depending upon their specific application. For example, HR Management (2009a) suggests that job analysis and description are important because their potential benefit relative to human resource management application includes:

■ Recruitment, selection and placement:
  – determine and communicate the organization's cultural and required person fit, as well as the job expectations of vacant positions;
  – establish appropriate salary levels, where the employee fits into the organization, and the minimum requirements for applicant screening, and provide the focus for selection instruments or questions;
  – create equitable promotion and transfer opportunities through establishing detailed and transparent baseline criteria.
■ Job evaluation and design:
  – appraise the relative worth of jobs and establish fair compensation rates;
  – streamline work processes, increasing productivity and enhancing employee satisfaction levels.
■ Compensation:
  – identify skill levels, compensation factors, responsibilities and minimum standards of the work environment.

72

- Performance appraisal, training and development:
  - provide focus on duties to be evaluated, performance standards and future goals;
  - determine training content, method and assessment for career advancement.
- Compliance with legislation:
  - identify strengths and weaknesses of current practice as well as illegal labour-related practices.

THEORETICAL OVERVIEW

Recruitment practices in the sport industry are comparable to those in most other industries; hence this section will draw heavily from generic human resource management and industrial psychology literature (Minten and Foster, 2009).

At the organizational level there should exist a human resource planning process. This is defined by Bratton and Gold (2003: 191) as the 'process of systematically forecasting the future demand and supply for employees and the deployment of their skills within the strategic objectives of the organization'. Anthony, Kacmar and Perrewé (2006) suggest that the human resource plan, which is derived from the strategic corporate plan, is likely to determine the objectives, policies, programmes and activities of the following human resource functions:

- recruiting;
- selecting;
- placing;
- training and developing;
- health and safety;
- compensating;
- appraising;
- promoting;
- retiring;
- laying off;
- terminating.

To elaborate further on just the first three stages of the recruitment process, job analysis or formulation is the starting point to establishing the general content, requirements and context of the position (Smith and Stewart, 1999).

To compile this entails understanding the different hierarchical levels and general terminology of work classification activities, as summarized in Table 5.1.

To eradicate potential bias in the job analysis process, as well as to meet employment law requirements, a number of different methods have been developed to determine the work activities, tasks and responsibilities of the position. HR Management (2009b) suggests that these methods either alone or in combination include:

- observation methods (e.g. direct observation; work methods analysis, including time and motion study and micro-motion analysis; and the critical incident technique);
- interviews (e.g. structured or unstructured interviews; and open-ended questionnaires with incumbents and supervisors);
- questionnaires (e.g. position analysis questionnaire – PAQ; functional job analysis; work profiling system – WPS; common metric questionnaire – CMQ; Fleishman job analysis system – FJAS);
- a task analysis inventory;
- the diary method;
- competency profiling;
- analysis of manuals and other reference material.

Table 5.1 Hierarchy of work activities

Category	Explanation	Example
Job family	Category of similar occupations.	Management.
Occupation	Similar jobs across an industry.	Sport event manager.
Position	Combination of the duties assigned to one person covered by one job description.	Finance and sponsorship manager.
Duty	A unit or subdivision of work tasks that is normally performed by and the responsibility of an individual.	Budgetary analysis.
Task	One of the work operations of a duty, defined by its method and implementation context.	Planning and preparing the annual budget by integrating statistical data and administrative requirements to achieve the department's goals.
Element	Smallest component of a task.	Printing out the income data for the month under review.

Carrying out such methods objectively determines the complexity of tasks and levels of authority, which provides a clear rationale to establish the relative remuneration scale of the position (Smith and Stewart, 1999).

Derived from this information are the job description and personnel specification. These documents are used to inform prospective candidates of the position details, as well as clarify and provide management with the criteria for selection or cases of dispute. Whereas the former commonly details the job's primary role, its duties, performance standards, account-abilities and reporting relationships, the latter provides an objective outline of the person required, usually written in terms of the essential and desir-able skills, knowledge, experience, personal attributes and qualifications (Minten and Foster, 2009). Without clarity of such detail it is not possible for individuals either to commit to or to be held accountable for specific roles of a position.

In essence, focusing upon the first three stages of this recruitment process provides an objective and very strong foundation to an optimum person–task–environment fit. When accompanied by additional appropriate human resource management practices, this can create a psychological working climate that enhances employee motivation and long-term commitment towards achieving organizational goals (Chelladurai, 2006).

PRACTICAL APPLICATION

Recruitment opportunities occur either through someone leaving or through business expansion. Recruitment techniques are therefore used in the employment of staff to new or existing positions in both paid and voluntary sport settings. As suggested by Watt (2003), the sort of ad hoc appointments that historically exist in voluntary sport clubs, involving the least unwilling people accepting secretarial or treasurer positions, need to be vehemently discouraged. For sport organizations to perform optimally, individual competence needs to match position requirements; in other words, the right people need to be recruited to the right jobs.

As previously mentioned, the techniques of job analysis, job description and person specification are in practice used for many different pur-poses and do not solely relate to recruitment purposes. Their practical use includes establishing the need for a position, increasing productivity levels, determining baseline standards for selection, training and career planning, and evaluating compensation claims or even vocational rehabilitation programmes. Clearly such systematic analysis facilitates the detailed examination of performance management for a variety of needs at both the position and the personal levels.

ASSUMPTIONS AND LIMITATIONS

Any new position created assumes first that there is a need for the position and second that appropriate funds are available (Smith and Stewart, 1999). Alternative arrangements suggested by Torrington, Hall and Taylor (2005) could include:

■ Reorganize the work.
■ Use overtime.
■ Stagger the hours.
■ Offer the work on a part-time basis.
■ Subcontract the work out.

With the often seasonal nature of sport, employing some of these strategies alone or in combination may prove attractive even to current staff, where job enrichment, enlargement or promotion opportunities are frequently sought.

Assuming though that there is a need for the new or existing position, what level of detail is required to describe the position? On the one hand job descriptions need to have sufficient detail to ensure some level of accountability, but on the other hand they should not include too much detail that will prove to be constraining. Tasks will change over time, and too much detail, particularly relating to procedures, means that the job description will need numerous rewrites and approvals. To maintain some degree of flexibility, procedural detail should be contained within the regularly updated operational manuals. The job description can merely make reference to a catch-all clause such as 'in accordance with the agreed procedures of the operational manual or plan'. Similarly one catch-all responsibility clause is frequently included in job descriptions to permit additional flexibility, such as 'Perform other related duties as required'.

However, Torrington, Hall and Taylor (2005) suggest that this is insufficient. They argue that, despite job analysis, description and person specification being the most conventional approaches to recruitment, such techniques are too prescriptive and inflexible. As a viable alternative, they propose that the recruitment process should be framed by asking the following four questions relating to the vacancy:

76

1 What does the job consist of?
2 In what way is it to be different from the job done by the previous incumbent?
3 What are the aspects of the job that specify the type of candidate?
4 What are the key aspects of the job that the ideal candidate wants to know before deciding to apply?

One further limitation relates to the historical practice of focusing on current needs. For example, Anthony, Kacmar and Perrewé (2006) make reference to traditional versus future-oriented job analysis techniques, suggesting that, in environments that change rapidly, job analysis and the resulting documentation can become dated very quickly. While this is a valid criticism, uncertainty and unpredictable futures seem inevitable, even if one were to adopt a future-oriented approach in practice.

PROCESS

From job analysis through to completion of the person specification, the recruitment documentation process (adapted from HR Management, 2009c) consists of the following five steps:

1 Identify the purpose of the job analysis.
2 Select the analysts.
3 Select the appropriate method and process of analysis.
4 Collect the data.
5 Develop the job description and person specification.

1 Identify the purpose of the job analysis

Applying to both new and existing positions, the first stage of recruitment is to clearly understand the scope of the analysis, since it determines the people to carry out the analysis (who), the method (how) and the specific data to be collected (what). For example, recruiting to a chief executive position of a national sport governing body is likely to involve a very different process and stakeholder involvement when compared to the recruitment of a treasurer at a local voluntary rugby club. Similarly and as previously mentioned, a job analysis may not actually be used for recruitment purposes. It may be used to inform the basis of an organizational restructure (e.g. downsizing or a merger), evaluate the equitable nature of employee salaries

77

(e.g. comparison of different positions) or even be used as a rehabilitation programme (e.g. establishing the extent of injury and current capability), which all have very different analytical purposes.

Regardless of application, the purpose and nature of the job analysis need to be clearly identified from the outset. Given the focus of this chapter on recruitment, let us exemplify the approach relating to the recruitment process for an existing position, more specifically for a public sector aquatics manager position where the previous incumbent has just been internally promoted to lead a lottery-funded community project.

2 Select the analysts

Once the boundaries and purpose of the job analysis have been determined the question of who carries out the analysis arises. Should it be external, such as an independent consultant as in the case of a rehabilitation evaluation, or internal, involving the human resource (HR) department, the reporting line manager and the current incumbent in the case of the aquatics manager appointment? If internal, do such persons have the competence and experience to carry out the task, or should they be trained in the use of selected methods? In the case study of the aquatics manager position, let us assume that, since the internal HR manager has been employed with this council for more than a decade, the line manager wrote the job description three years ago when the centre opened and the current incumbent will still be employed within the council workforce, there is no need for specific training for these analysts.

3 Select the appropriate method and process of analysis

Once it has been agreed which personnel are to be involved in the recruitment process (an HR representative, the line manager, the current incumbent and, specifically for the selection process, the often included local authority requirement of an independent department representative and three councillors), the next stage is to fully understand the needs of the position. The Chartered Institute of Personnel and Development (2010) suggests that this means thinking about not only the content (such as the tasks) making up the job, but also the job's purpose, the outputs required by the job holder and how the job fits into the organization's structure. It is important as well to consider the skills and personal attributes needed to perform the role effectively.

78

If the position already exists, this is an ideal opportunity to see whether the nature of the position or its particular outcomes need to be changed in any way. To meet future needs, should the position be restructured, or a succession strategy of performance management be considered? Regardless of whether the existing position remains or is changed, the following questions need to be addressed:

- What are the required duties (current and future) of the position?
- How will the person be expected to perform these duties to achieve unit and organizational outcomes?
- How do we document the position requirements (e.g. in terms of outcomes, measurements, responsibilities, etc.)?

To help address these questions, job analysis templates (see examples provided at Rothman, 2004 and Service Canada, 2010) are commonly used and adapted to local contexts. Furthermore, other publicly available checklists or questionnaires can be used to inform completion of these templates (see examples of new job clerical or management responsibilities questionnaires available at SmartBiz, 2010).

The methods to collect these data can be sought from a variety of desk research sources either from within the organization (e.g. organization charts, process analyses, job descriptions and customer feedback logs) or external to it (e.g. job recruitment websites and industry examples of best practice). Where information is still lacking, field research methods can be used as identified in the 'Theoretical overview' section of this chapter (greater explanation and detail can be found at HR Management, 2009b, and Anthony, Kacmar and Perrewé, 2006). In the aquatics manager example, the current post holder could be observed for a day and then followed up with an interview or questionnaire to elaborate on questions such as:

- Was this a typical day?
- If not, how would it change over a month and over a year?
- What do you consider to be the main and other duties of this position?
- What are the frequency, duration, skill and equipment demands of these duties?
- What improvements and future practices would you suggest to optimize the position outcomes?

Additional or alternative approaches could include carrying out a time log for a month or even chronologically appraising a sequence of tasks using the critical incident technique methodology (see Bacal and Associates, 2009, for further details).

Ideally, though, a variety of different analytical methods should be selected involving more than one person (e.g. human resource staff, managers who take on people for similar positions, the incumbent, and team members of the established position). One method in isolation and a viewpoint from just one perspective are likely to prove unreliable, accentuating potential method-ological weaknesses and some degree of personal bias. Multi-methods, on the other hand, permit cross-checking and identify cases of discrepancy, particularly relating to overvaluing position detail and interpretations of what individuals like doing as opposed to what the actual needs and duties of the job are.

Clearly the context will dictate the detailed nature of this activity. For example, a new position in a new structure will involve considerably more work and an in-depth consultation process as compared with an established position with a job description that is only three years old.

4 Collect the data

Before the data are collected the process and purpose of the job analysis should be coherently communicated to the relevant people in the orga-nization, namely the people that the analysis directly affects, such as the holders of comparative positions as well as the union(s). As determined by Anthony, Kacmar and Perrewé (2006: 209) such stakeholders 'should be informed of who will be conducting the analysis, why the job analysis is needed, whom to contact if they have questions or concerns, the schedule or timetable of events, and their role in the job analysis'. Without such infor-mation, employees may feel perturbed or anxious, perhaps even perceiving that their roles and positions are under threat. Involvement in the process, particularly in the job analysis stage, helps to reassure individuals of their value, helps others to formally understand what you do, and establishes personal ownership and commitment to the employment process.

Once the data collection plan has been determined, it then needs to be appropriately implemented, giving due consideration to the availability of the participating people.

The collected data then need to be organized, reviewed and verified. To confirm that this information is valid and complete, the Commonwealth of Australia (2009) suggests asking yourself as well as the current incumbent the following questions:

80

- Given the identified accountabilities of the job, are the duties and tasks, and the knowledge, skills and abilities listed against each, really the most critical ones?
- Are the tools and equipment listed really necessary to perform the job?
- Have all necessary special considerations been included?
- Have I missed any key duties, tasks, tools or equipment?

Having made the necessary amendments this completes the job analysis phase.

5 Develop the job description and person specification

The job description and person specification are the documents that evolve from the job analysis data collection phase. Whilst the job or position description details the position scope, describing the responsibilities, activities and working conditions of the position, the person specification summarizes the human characteristics, personal qualities, knowledge, experience and skills required to successfully perform the job.

Job or position description

An effective job description articulates what the incumbent is expected to do, in a concise, clear and well-structured manner (Chelladurai, 2006). This entails a logical format that is normally based upon the previous job description or, if unavailable, a generic in-house or external template with headings, such as that provided in Table 5.2.

Such a template provides the key categories to consider, and you merely write the job-specific detail into the open cells. The expectations of each element need to be clarified:

Table 5.2 Job description template

Element	Description
Job title	
Reporting relationships	
Department or location	
Work context	
Main purpose or role	
Responsibilities and duties	
Salary and benefits	

- Job title – a clear and meaningful gender-neutral name that accurately reflects the main purpose of the position.
- Reporting relationships – how the position interacts with different internal and/or external stakeholders.
- Department or location – the geographical location(s) and the unit within the organization structure where the position is located.
- Work context – this element provides an introductory description of the unit of work and is an opportunity to promote recent achievements to potential candidates.
- Main purpose or role – a brief yet concise statement of the function and scope of the position to address the questions 'Why does the position exist?' and 'What is the incumbent expected to achieve?'
- Responsibilities and duties – normally the main section of the job description, as it clearly defines the core responsibilities, the likely duties to be undertaken and often the key outcomes of the position. This section also forms the basis of the incumbent's training and development plan, as well as commonly being used for performance appraisal reviews.
- Salary and benefits – employers often wish to keep this flexible to extend the pool of interest, hence suggest statements such as 'Competitive salary plus superannuation'. Potential applicants on the other hand would prefer to see the inclusion of a salary range (including or excluding superannuation) to determine whether it meets their level of expectation.

This descriptive detail should avoid jargon, acronyms and conscious or subconscious bias. Bias not only reduces your access to the recruitment talent pool but in addition puts you at risk of legal action (Department for Business, Innovation and Skills, 2009).

The hardest and most important section to write is generally the responsibility and duties section, so let us focus a little more on the expected norms of best practice here.

Whilst some job descriptions do include a task list, it is preferable to cluster tasks into a few broad responsibility and duty statements that reflect the position outcomes. The reasoning for this is that individual tasks and their processes commonly change, unlike broader all-inclusive responsibilities. This in effect could lead to long, tedious and unnecessary processes of rewrites and approvals. In this sense responsibilities or, as they are sometimes referred to, accountabilities or duties are commonly clustered around occupational standards involving a combination of general statements (e.g. leadership, decision making, teamwork, communicating, planning, monitor-

82

ing and evaluating) and specific statements (e.g. technical, such as pool plant management, and software usage).

These responsibility statements are normally written in the present tense and start with an action verb, followed by an object and an explanatory phrase. For example, one of the aquatic manager duties might be: Monitor (the action verb) on a day-to-day basis the filtration, reticulation and chemical dosing equipment (the object) to ensure its ongoing operation (the explanatory phrase). To permit easier readership, try to avoid overusing the same action verbs. In addition, omit unnecessary articles ('a', 'the') and vague subjective modifiers ('several', 'occasional', 'high-level') that are usually open to misinterpretation.

Finally, to provide some level of relative importance, individual responsibilities are sometimes assigned estimated percentages. Determined in minimum blocks of 10 per cent of job time, these are then listed sequentially in importance on the job description.

Examples of some of these practices can be found at Businessballs.com (2010), including the use of common expressions pertaining to different general management positions, namely directors, import and export managers or business development managers, and account managers.

Through analysis of these responsibilities and duties, you will be able to more clearly identify the person requirements to ensure the goals of the position, work area and organization are achieved.

Person specification

The person requirements contained within the person specification are derived from the job description and normally relate to the skills, knowledge, experience and personal qualities identified as necessary to perform the duties of the position (Chartered Institute of Personnel and Development, 2010). As illustrated in the person specification template of Table 5.3, these are normally stated in terms of the essential and desirable requirements of the position, and further defined by how they might be measured.

Each of the requirements in Table 5.3 can be briefly elaborated upon:

■ skills – something that a person can do (e.g. competence in preparing a profit and loss statement, using a particular booking system, or speaking fluently in two identified languages);

Table 5.3 Person specification template

Requirements	Essential	Desirable	Method of assessment
Skills			
Knowledge			
Experience			
Personal attributes			
Other, e.g. qualifications or licences			

- knowledge – something that a person knows (e.g. employment law, up-to-date filtration processes, current issues in local authority pricing structures);
- experience – an instance of observing, encountering or personally undergoing something (e.g. change management, conflict handling, dealing with the press);
- personal attributes – a distinguishing property, quality, or feature of the position (e.g. able to work as a team member or routinely lifts 25 kilograms or more);
- other – elements not covered by the other categories, such as legally required occupational and professional licences, or working with children, as well as other health or safety certifications, or reference to specific work conditions (e.g. a driving licence, but only if the position necessitates travel to a location where public transport or other forms of transport are unavailable, or work that involves unsociable hours such as weekends, bank holidays and all night shifts).

As the name suggests, 'essential' equates to the minimum requirements to perform in the position, without which the person would not be able to carry out the job (Minten and Foster, 2009). For example, this may relate to legal requirements such as a national working visa, the possession of a full driving licence if applying for a player chauffeur position at the US Open, or a teaching qualification for a secondary school physical education teacher position. 'Desirable', on the other hand, must be understood to mean those criteria that enhance a person's capacity to perform in the job. In other words, it should specifically relate to those elements that the employer would ideally like the candidates to possess but are not critical to performing the tasks of the job. For example, a sports-related degree or proven leadership skills in the voluntary sector may often be deemed desirable but not essential. To assist in determining what is essential and what is desirable, the Commonwealth of Australia (2009) proposes the following factors need to be considered:

- the difficulty or criticality of the tasks being performed;
- the impact on job outcomes;
- the impact on the performance of other employees;
- the consequence of error if they are not performed effectively;
- how frequently the tasks are performed.

Once the essential requirements have been established it is good practice both to try to justify why these elements are essential and to ask your equal opportunity experts to view and amend the list as necessary.

In the case of the aquatic manager position, the essential and desirable criteria might consist of the following:

- Essential criteria:
  - well-developed communication, negotiation and dispute resolution skills;
  - ability to work to deadlines in a fast-changing environment;
  - proven ability to manage swimming centres and associated facilities;
  - knowledge of aquatic industry standards (e.g. pool plant equipment use, safe handling and storage of chemicals, pool supervision requirements);
  - demonstrated ability to undertake a risk management approach to pool safety;
  - experience in accurately handling and reconciling cash and credit transactions;
  - current qualifications in lifesaving and first aid (including advanced resuscitation).
- Desirable criteria:
  - proven ability in leading a small aquatics team;
  - ability to carry out ongoing asset and equipment maintenance;
  - competence in the use of information technology including Word, Excel and PowerPoint;
  - knowledge of crowd management techniques;
  - experience in working with multicultural communities;
  - qualifications in sport and management.

Note the common use of expressions such as 'ability to', 'knowledge of' and 'experience in', and the fact that each criterion contains only one idea – more than one constitutes a separate criterion. Also be aware of overstating the essential requirements of a position, as these can seriously limit the size of the recruitment pool. In some instances the desirable criteria may even be more extensive than the essential, particularly if a limited pool of applications is anticipated and a broader range of applicant is being encouraged to apply.

For each requirement identified, the method(s) of assessment should similarly be determined, including reasonable adjustments to include people with impairments. Criteria that cannot be objectively assessed should simply not be included in the list of essential requirements. Assessments may vary from viewing and photocopying original certificates (e.g. a current first aid certificate) through to implementing certain tests (e.g. graduate recruitment communication and numerical skills tests) or even undertaking certain tasks (e.g. teamwork under time pressure) as components of the recruitment process.

Once approved, the person specification and its accompanying methods of assessment should be free from discriminatory practice and thereby provide the information from which the recruitment panel can objectively shortlist and judge each applicant.

CASE STUDIES

The breadth of sport industry practice can be demonstrated by selected extracts from three sport management job descriptions that include person specification detail, from New Zealand. As illustrated in Tables 5.4, 5.5 and 5.6, the style varies considerably with the nature of the position as well as the norms of the local organization. For example, some adopt a more concise style of writing than others, and there exist different headings to convey the position requirements and duties sections. In the latter case organizations sometimes choose to focus more on inputs, detailing task-oriented activities through to outputs such as performance outcomes. To complete the picture, some even align these accountabilities with quite specific performance measures, as illustrated in the Netball Western Australia Development Manager position extract in Table 5.7.

Table 5.4 Sport Taranaki Programme Manager job description

Title of position: Programme Manager	Business unit: Core Business Unit	Reports to: General Manager

Purpose of the role

- Ensure programmes are operated effectively and efficiently.
- Manage the programme facilitators.
- Develop and maintain key stakeholder relationships.

Key responsibilities

1 Programme management
- Manage, in conjunction with the General Manager, all human resource issues associated with the programmers.
- Provide effective leadership for programmers.
- Manage reporting, including monitoring and evaluating responsibilities for the programmers.
- Provide appropriate plans and direction to programme staff.

2 Organization development
- Liaise with the Executive Team on future planning for the programmes and the organization.
- Provide the General Manager with strategic directions that will allow the programmes to grow and expand.
- Meet weekly with the General Manager to plan and review operations and provide regular work plans.

3 Relationship management
- Ensure positive working relationship with all stakeholders through efficient communication.
- Market and promote all programmes with assistance from the Marketing Manager.
- Build and develop new relationships with stakeholders and key funding providers.

4 Human resources
- Liaise with the Executive Assistant to develop and update job descriptions for Sport Taranaki programmers.
- Manage day-to-day human resource for the programmers.
- With the General Manager conduct six-monthly performance appraisals for the programmers and develop their personal development plans.

5 General
- Fully support the philosophy and culture of Sport Taranaki, including the Regional Sport and Physical Activity Strategy.
- Act in accordance with the corporate values of Sport Taranaki (professionalism, passion, honesty and *manaakitanga*).

Table 5.4 Continued

Delegations of authority	Capital expenditure – N/A. Operational expenditure – within budgets. Authorization to hire staff – no. Authorized to sign contracts – no.
Responsible for	No. of staff – 15. Budget Programme staff budget management in consultation with designated others.
Professional and technical capabilities	Professional: – Proven planning and management skills. – Proven experience in providing leadership and direction to staff, as well as specific groups within the community. – Proven understanding of relationship building to successfully work with providers and community groups. – Proven experience in administration, with strong computer skills. – Proven ability preparing and implementing plans with an outcome-based focus. – Familiarity with a wide range of sports and health-related programmes. – Qualifications and/or experience in sport, recreation and health, or similar. Technical: – Excellent organizational, time management and people skills. – Excellent oral and written communication skills. – Decision-making skills. – General knowledge and understanding of the structure of sport. – Ability to operate as part of a team. – Ability to work flexible hours including weekends and evenings.
Qualifications	Preferred: – Tertiary qualification or equivalent preferred.

Source: Sport Taranaki (2009).

Table 5.5 Tennis Auckland Chief Executive Officer position overview

The Tennis Auckland Inc. Board now seeks a Chief Executive Officer to lead the organization, driving and delivering the strategic and operational plans. Given the profile of the sport of tennis and Tennis Auckland, this role is one of the most highly prized sport-business positions in New Zealand.

Reports to	The Tennis Auckland Board. The Chief Executive Officer interacts with the Chairman on a regular basis.
Remuneration	A competitive/attractive remuneration package will be available to the successful candidate. The composition of the package will be a matter of discussion and agreement with the Tennis Auckland Board.
Key duties	1 Leadership. Provide effective leadership and direction to the Tennis Auckland staff and family of stakeholders ensuring future development and promotion through well-executed commercial, sport and event-related programmes. The Chief Executive Officer will lead, manage and administer all staff employed by Tennis Auckland, including overseeing the training and professional development of personnel, and supervision of HR strategies, including recruitment goals, job design, selection of personnel and performance management. [Points 2 and 3 omitted.]
	4 Management. Assume the overall responsibility for the management of the day-to-day operations of Tennis Auckland, including all the human and financial resources, driving and developing the business consistently with the agreed strategic direction. Ensure Tennis Auckland meets regulatory requirements, including building compliance, OSH and ACC. The Chief Executive Officer is responsible for the management of the insurance and foreign exchange requirements of Tennis Auckland.
	5 Planning and policy. In conjunction with the Board develop, implement and achieve the agreed Tennis Auckland Strategic Plan. The Chief Executive Officer will implement a corporate vision for Tennis Auckland to achieve the stated goals and aims across the whole of the business.
	6 Revenue. Develop stable and diverse revenue streams, underpinning the delivery of Tennis Auckland programmes, services and activities. The Chief Executive Officer will ensure appropriate processes are in place, and relationships managed, to achieve funding support from available funding agencies.
	7 Financial. In conjunction with the Board, manage Tennis Auckland's operations in a transparent, efficient and profitable way. The Chief Executive Officer will prepare in a timely manner each year an operational budget, consistent with the Strategic Plan, and when approved by the Board of Directors manage the operations of Tennis Auckland activities to achieve the stated budget objectives, and is therefore intimately involved with all aspects of financial management including cash flows and monthly account monitoring.

Table 5.5 Continued

8	Promotion and marketing. Ensure the optimal development and promotion of all Tennis Auckland activities, services and programmes while building the profile of Tennis Auckland through strong brand and communication programmes and robust marketing alliances. The Chief Executive Officer will coordinate the marketing and operation of the hospitality boxes at the ASB Tennis Centre and ensure positive relationships are maintained with sponsors (current and potential) so that there is support to enable Tennis Auckland to carry out planned activities, both currently and into the future.
Desirable attributes	■ Strong, effective leadership skills with the ability to inspire others to achieve the identified strategic objectives of Tennis Auckland while building a shared interest in the Tennis Auckland business goals.
	■ The ability to work successfully with a wide range of people including but not limited to volunteers, staff, sponsors, tennis club officers and players, local authority staff, professional tennis players and their organizations.
	■ A strong, energetic, inclusive, decisive and down-to-earth manager of people, with the ability to both identify and harness the specialist knowledge of the Tennis Auckland stakeholder family for the benefit of Tennis Auckland as a whole.
	■ Superior presentation and communication skills, a strong personal presence and the ability to act eloquently and confidently as the public 'figurehead' of Tennis Auckland.
	■ An open personality, assured, persuasive, with a balanced ego, a sense of humour, unquestioned integrity and the ability to make a credible and positive impression on others.
	■ A practitioner of modern business practices, with the capacity to think, plan and prioritize at the strategic level; the ability to grow an organization through steady and continuous improvement against established performance objectives; and the capacity to quickly respond to hands-on situations.
	■ Experience in dealing with government agencies (e.g. SPARC), particularly in development funding.
	■ Strong marketing and brand skills, with the ability to identify and nurture commercial and marketing opportunities for Tennis Auckland, delivering stable and diverse revenue streams; a good balance of commercial acumen (including events and facilities management) within a not-for-profit service organization context.

	■ Solid financial acumen, including the capacity to interpret and report on financial accounts. ■ The ability to effectively manage complex and competing priorities, within an often dynamic and changing work environment. ■ Strong computer skills with demonstrated ability to use Microsoft Office™ products including Word, Excel and Outlook or similar products. ■ Sport management or business management background, preferably in tennis, will be highly regarded.
Decision making and authority	The Tennis Auckland Chief Executive Officer will have designated decision making and authority for and on behalf of Tennis Auckland, to include: ■ Financial and budgetary delegation: The position will be involved in developing and overseeing all programme budgets within Tennis Auckland. The position will incur expenditure within the delegations provided by the Tennis Auckland Board. ■ People management: The position is responsible for the overall performance of all Tennis Auckland staff and contractors. ■ Stakeholders and Tennis Auckland Board: The position involves considerable interaction with the Tennis Auckland Board, stakeholders and other business units. There is a need to provide sound advice to the Tennis Auckland Board on all aspects of Tennis Auckland business.
Hours of work	The nature of the position requires out-of-hours work, and domestic and some international travel. No time-in-lieu arrangement exists for additional hours worked, as the remuneration package will reflect the extent of commitment.

Source: Tennis Auckland (2009).

Table 5.6 Rugby World Cup Accreditation Manager position overview

Role	Critical to the success of RWC 2011 is an accreditation programme that effectively manages the secure access at each venue for the thousands of people who will be working to make Rugby World Cup 2011 a success. The Tournament Management System (TMS) that will underpin the accreditation programme is currently being scoped, and the Accreditation Manager will come on board in time to refine the TMS to ensure it will meet the demands of such a large-scale and multi-venue event. Once this is completed, the Accreditation Manager will work with the extended team to determine the appropriate accreditation zones and then work with the venues to determine how these zones will be applied at each location. In 2010 the role will focus on scoping, establishing, testing and trialling of accreditation centres at each venue and putting in place the related structures, processes, policies and procedures. Come Tournament time, the role will be based at the Main Operations Centre, overseeing up to 15 accreditation centres around the country supported by the Tournament workforce, including RNZ 2011 staff, provincial union support and volunteers.

Key results areas and expected performance outcomes	**Strategic direction and planning:**
	■ Lead and participate in the development and implementation of the RNZ 2011 strategy for the operation of an effective accreditation system.
	■ Assist in the identification of key issues and relationships related to accreditation that are relevant in achieving strategic and operational goals.
	■ Assist in the annual budget process relating to accreditation.
	
	Planning and development:
	■ Scope and develop an appropriate accreditation system that:
	  – provides for approximately 15 accreditation centres;
	  – maintains and does not compromise the secure working environment required;
	  – establishes appropriate accreditation zones within each venue used throughout the tournament.
	■ Develop and manage a standard Tournament-wide accreditation policy that includes consideration for the unique challenges each venue will bring.
	■ Develop appropriate training and educational programmes to ensure the accreditation programme is understood and the policing of the zones is managed in a professional manner.

Testing and training:

- Deliver training on the Accreditation Programme for Provincial Union (PU) staff and volunteer staff.
- Successfully complete the test events relating to accreditation that will be held in the lead-up to the Tournament as part of an overall testing programme.

Systems management:

- Manage the alignment of operational requirements for accreditation to RNZ's existing TMS.
- Manage the processes and procedures to centrally maintain accreditation information in TMS.

Delivery:

- Deliver a smooth and seamless accreditation process that allows approved Tournament personnel to receive the appropriate level of Tournament access dependent on their approved needs through:
  - overseeing the system delivery and roll-out of the accreditation programme;
  - working closely with PUs and volunteers to facilitate the effective Tournament delivery of the accreditation programme in approximately 15 accreditation centres.

Team management:

- Ensure all accreditation staff receive the training required to enable them to carry out their responsibilities in a professional and efficient manner.
- Ensure all accreditation staff are fully aware of the obligations of all venues, provincial unions and other key organizations.

Other:

- Carry out other duties as required by the management team to help meet either organizational or team objectives.

Experience and qualifications:

- Proven experience and success in a similar role, with at least five years' experience at a senior level.
- Project leadership experience.
- Considerable experience with successfully developing and maintaining computerized accreditation systems that encompass a multitude of sites and areas.
- Experience in large-scale event management.

Attributes, qualifications and experiences considered desirable for the role

Table 5.6 Continued

Personal attributes:

- Rugby empathy.
- A bias towards action.
- Ability to work with diverse stakeholders and build successful win/win working relationships.
- Willingness to take ownership and be held accountable.
- A willingness to challenge and be challenged; able to listen.
- Ability to communicate effectively, both written and verbal.
- Strategic capability and an eye for detail.
- Ability to work independently with little supervision.
- Sound business judgement and decision-making capability.
- Attention to detail.
- Ability to cope under pressure and maintain a sense of humour.
- Willingness to go the extra mile when required.

Remuneration   The remuneration package will be structured to attract high-quality candidates. At the time of applying candidates are invited to indicate their current remuneration package and remuneration expectations.

Source: Adapted from Rugby World Cup 2011 (2009).

Table 5.7 Netball Western Australia Development Manager position description

Major accountabilities	Performance measures
Management of budget and oversight of all activities of Development Unit, as Unit Leader, including coordination of Development Unit members to achieve required outcomes.	Effective management of people and activities in accordance with budgets, and comprehensive understanding of Development Unit programmes, activities and plans.
Coordination and promotion of accreditation and development of coaches and umpires through delivery of Netball Australia accreditation programmes and additional initiatives.	Numbers of accredited coaches increased by 5 per cent per annum and badged umpires by 5 per cent per annum.
Development, implementation and acquittal of funding and/or grant applications, to support programme or resource development to benefit affiliated member regions, associations, clubs and individuals.	Effective funding and/or grant applications developed as required, with a minimum 50 per cent success rate, and implemented and acquitted to the satisfaction of programme objectives and funding providers.
Maintenance of relevant records, statistics and information relating to the Development Unit, including for reporting purposes.	Records, statistics and information maintained in an efficient and effective manner.
Assistance with relevant enquiries from affiliated member regions, associations, clubs and the public, as required.	Accurate and timely assistance provided, with all enquiries resolved (or at least acknowledged) within 48 hours of receipt.
Contribution of information for inclusion in the *Eye on the Ball* newsletter and the website.	At least one new development-related article regarding each of player, coach and umpiring per issue of *Eye on the Ball* and appearing on the website per month.

Source: Netball Western Australia (2009).

INTERPRETATION AND MANAGEMENT DECISION

Recruitment practices need to be socially inclusive and value diversity for social justice (legal) as well as business reasons (Minten and Foster, 2009). As explained by Cox and Beale (1997: 13), 'Valuing diversity is a philosophy . . . [and] represents a distinct organizational resource that, properly leveraged, can bring a competitive advantage against organizations that either are culturally homogeneous or fail to utilize their diversity.'

Objectively applying job analysis, job descriptions and person specifications in an inclusive and transparent manner helps to eradicate conscious or subconscious discriminatory practices. This in turn can lead to a clearer decision-making process and more effective appointments, and reinforces a culture of openness, trust and fairness that is likely to inspire employees to achieve organizational goals.

Equally the use of such tools must not be used as a straitjacket to the recruitment process. Where equivalents of essential criteria may have been overlooked, for example previously unknown overseas qualifications, or where an applicant possesses exceptional competences that could significantly enhance organizational performance, flexibility should be adopted. This means that job descriptions and person specifications should not be cast in stone, and flexibility in decision making is permitted providing that it is implemented in a fair, open and consistent manner. For example, if the applicant is the best candidate on merit, and in addition is a retired Olympic medallist, the original position may be changed to include a percentage of corporate hospitality duties, subject to applicant acceptance and the decision being passed through the organization's recognized approval process.

Job analysis, descriptions and person specifications clearly provide a mutual function of determining person fit to the organization and vice versa. However, it must be remembered that organizations as well as people change over time. With this in mind, management should set a periodic programme of documentation review and not just wait for certain triggers such as a resignation before updating it. Significant changes, such as introduction of new equipment or procedures, restructuring of a department, or staff turnover becoming higher than in other sections of the organization or industry, should be used to initiate the review process (Anthony, Kacmar and Perrewé, 2006). In addition, if considerable change is anticipated then the job description should attempt to identify responsibilities in both a general and a future orientation rather than provide a current or largely prescriptive task list to achieve.

96

COMMON MISTAKES

Mistakes potentially can occur within and between each stage of the job analysis, description and person specification processes. For example, HR Management (2009d) suggests that typical mistakes apparent at the job analysis stage include:

- lack of top management support;
- lack of training of the analyst and incumbent;
- use of only one method and a single source of data;
- insufficient time allowed for the process;
- intentional or unintentional distortion from the incumbent;
- failure to review the job periodically.

Similarly, it is found that job descriptions frequently contain jargonized, clumsy and superfluous language. To avoid these mistakes, try to use clear English in a well-structured and succinct manner. Do not overstate the position's responsibilities or include criteria that are not relevant to the position. Promising more than can be realized can lead to poor retention, and stating more than 12 responsibilities usually proves to be ineffective and unwieldy for incumbents to focus on in practice.

Person specification errors on the other hand normally relate to issues of bias. Too often recruiters try to appoint on the unsubstantiated premise of 'like-minded' individuals. Furthermore, try to avoid the inclusion of attributes that cannot be tested, such as 'a sense of humour' or 'generally physically fit', or relate to personal circumstances, such as 'willingness to work irregular hours' or 'required to relocate'. Such expectations may disadvantage those with caring responsibilities and constitute indirect discrimination, particularly in circumstances of 'unjustifiable age limits or requesting qualifications which are not essential for the post' (Minten and Foster, 2009: 90). However, it must also be noted that in certain situations direct or indirect discrimination can be permitted, namely when the criterion can be objectively justified as a genuine occupational requirement. The case of a religious minister's require-ment to practise that religion or the appointment of a female at a women's rape centre can be entirely justified.

SUMMARY

In conclusion, whilst each organization, position or potential candidate is different, the first stage of the recruitment process is a constant. This entails carrying out a job analysis to define what the incumbent will actually do, and then documenting this information via a job description to describe the role and responsibilities of the position, and a person specification to communicate the required person profile.

In the contemporary climate, fully engaging with the techniques of job analysis, job description and person specification is considered to be 'a good business investment because it can be used to support most HR functions: recruitment, selection, orientation, training, work plans, compensation, performance reviews and legal defence' (Service Canada, 2010).

The recruitment documentation process has been seen to comprise five steps, namely:

1   Identify the purpose of the job analysis.
2   Select the analysts.
3   Select the appropriate method and process of analysis.
4   Collect the data.
5   Develop the job description and person specification.

Competition and equal opportunity legislation have made job analysis a mandatory activity, and through clearly articulated job descriptions and person specifications these collectively establish the foundations of a more effective and diverse workforce (Anthony, Kacmar and Perrewé, 2006).

By identifying the boundaries, responsibilities and requirements of positions, they provide important communication tools to prospective candidates, recruitment agencies, work colleagues and management, and serve to inform the recruitment, selection, and individual career planning and development processes. Their organizational benefits include:

■   identifying the cultural fit between the incumbent and the organization and the relative position fit within the organization's structure and remuneration scales;
■   clarifying job purpose, responsibilities, performance expectations, and accountabilities of a position;
■   determining the requirements of the incumbent and providing the criteria for selection or promotion to appoint fairly on the basis of merit, which in turn minimizes subjective judgements and legal compensation claims (Chartered Institute of Personnel and Development, 2010).

On the other hand, the strengths of their formalization and descriptive clarity have sometimes been classified as also being their weaknesses. Limitations,

98

for example, have been suggested to be their level of prescription, inflexibility and focus on current or past responsibilities. However, with an open mind, inclusive and transparent communication, periodic review, and a driving principle of equal opportunity, such weaknesses can easily be overcome.

Job analysis, description and person specification are the first, yet important, underpinnings to effective recruitment practice. Human resource management activities that evolve from these stages include selection, induction, training, appraisal, and support and development of professional attributes, through to career planning and exit. Indeed, in the service industry of sport, management must commit to recruiting and developing their most valued assets, their staff, if they wish to improve their organization's operational performance and productivity now and in the future (Smith and Stewart, 1999).

Guides to further resources, useful web links and guideline answers to all the self-test questions featured in this chapter are available on a companion website at www.routledge.com/9780415491594.

SELF-TEST QUESTION

Identify the weak elements of the job details presented in Table 5.8, which fictitiously represents a position in a national fitness chain. Propose an improvement for each weakness identified.

Table 5.8 Poor job description and specification

Job element	Detail
Job title	National Member Manageress.
Reporting relationships	Line managr.
Department or location	Currently in the sport membership department, but this is likely to be restructured in the future. Could quite literally be located at any fitness centre in the country dependent upon specific problems to be resolved and the company's business needs.
Main purpose or role	For several years I have assisted the CFO to improve centre memberships, devlop new BAF schemes and progressively create just-in-time turnkey solutions.

Table 5.8 Continued

Job element	Detail
Responsibilities and duties	Process reports. Process complaints. Manage communications. Develop a variety of systematic responses to allow each centre manager to increase their membership numbers and work out why so many members are currently failing to renew their annual membership.
Key selection criteria	25–35 years old. Personally very fit and high-level sport achievements expected. Five years of high-level sport management experience. English, Chinese and Indian language fluency, as plan to expand the brand internationally. Computer experience. Driving licence. Creative team and individual player. Excellent communication skills. Pleasant personality and emotional stability. Undergraduate sport management degree.

CHAPTER 6

APPRAISING THE ORGANIZATION'S PORTFOLIO: WHAT STRATEGIC BUSINESS UNITS SHOULD WE FOCUS ON?

TECHNIQUE DESCRIPTION

Sport organizations exist to provide something of value, usually in the form of different products and services to meet and hopefully exceed customer needs. Collectively these outputs constitute your organization's product mix or business portfolio. Within this portfolio some products as well as product lines will naturally be more profitable than others, currently and/or in the future. So the frequent management dilemma arises: how do you balance the conflicting demands of different products and services competing for often scarce organizational resources? What level of priority and balanced investment risk should you adopt to ensure a sustainable future?

Addressing such questions requires the application of strategic marketing analysis tools of business portfolio analysis. Applying the ubiquitous concepts of the product life cycle (the time period between the inception of a product and its discontinuation in the marketplace – Johnson, 2009) and strategic business units (autonomous operating businesses or departments, product lines, or products or brands that are sold to a well-defined market or segment – Kotler and Keller, 2006), this chapter will introduce you to two of the most effective and popular diagnostic marketing techniques:

1   Boston Consulting Group (BCG) matrix – a graphical approach to strategic business unit analysis of a multi-segmented organization, classifying strategic business units according to relative market share and market growth;
2   General Electric (GE)/McKinsey multiple factor matrix – a more sophisticated portfolio management tool that adopts a nine-cell matrix of analysis based upon industry attractiveness and business strength.

To achieve the strategic aim of maximizing profit from competing products across different life cycles, this chapter will describe the key principles and evolving theory of portfolio models. Having identified their purpose, their assumptions and typical applications, you will be provided with an applied sport example in which to understand the process of construction, analysis and appropriate management interpretation.

PURPOSE

The purpose of using business portfolio analysis techniques is twofold, namely to map the current position of the business units of an organization and to inform decision making towards establishing future strategies that will maintain or improve organizational performance. For example, knowledge of the product life cycle stage can provide valuable insights into appropriate as well as inappropriate marketing activities that can directly influence profit and cash flow. Similarly, the visual displays of complex product data, the outputs of portfolio analysis, permit sport managers to:

- classify product portfolio development, collectively and individually, hence providing a management framework for product optimization, e.g. to help to manage the risk, cash usage and generation of launching a new product;
- provide a platform for multi-stakeholder dialogue that can establish cleaner and more sustainable strategic product processes and practices (Life Cycle Initiative, 2010);
- determine different product market strengths, weaknesses and growth potentials, so as to prioritize which strategic business units (SBUs) receive more attention or resource allocation or should be divested;
- identify portfolio weaknesses so as to be able to add new products or SBUs to balance an organization's portfolio.

In essence, portfolio analysis provides management with an important analytical tool to evaluate an organization's diversified product lines, from which more strategic and sustainable management decisions can follow.

THEORETICAL OVERVIEW

Predicated on the principle of the biological clock, products are believed to experience a life cycle of birth, growth, maturity and death. Introduced by

102

Levitt (1965) in his article 'Exploit the product life cycle', product life cycles are now a well-recognized and established concept in management literature, where product sales or profits (vertical access) are plotted against time (horizontal access). As illustrated in Figure 6.1, the revenue/sales path (continuous line) of a typical new product follows a bell shape (Morgan and Summers, 2005) and normally is suggested to consist of the four developmental stages of introduction, growth, maturity and decline.

The profit path, as indicated by the dotted line in Figure 6.1, understandably lags behind the sales line, owing to the need to cover initial costs before break-even point is reached (Chapter 8) and the business starts to return a profit.

According to Kotler and Keller (2006) this product life cycle (PLC) principle recognizes the common features of most products and services today, namely that:

1 they possess a limited lifespan;
2 their sales pass through a number of distinct stages, each of which has different characteristics, challenges and opportunities;
3 their profits are not static but increase and decrease through these different stages;
4 the financial, human resource, manufacturing, marketing and purchasing strategies that products require at each stage in the life cycle vary.

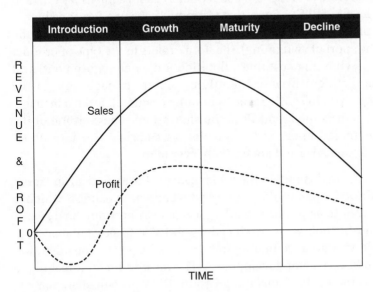

Figure 6.1 Stages of the product life cycle

More specifically the characteristics of each stage are elaborated upon in Table 6.1 and presented with appropriate strategy implications.

However, it is important to realize that, in the same way that each human is unique, so is a product. In reality each product is likely to possess its own life cycle and be affected by its own macro- and micro-environment. This means that the PLC may vary between months and years, or as in the case of humans it is even possible to move from birth to death in a matter of days. In marketing terms this gives rise to fads (e.g. Christmas or fitness gimmicks), fashions (e.g. seasonal replica kits), slow or fast adoptions (e.g. Wii Fit), and recycled PLC paths (e.g. established events such as the Olympic Games), which makes PLC stages in sport quite difficult in practice to predict (Shilbury, Westerbeek, Quick and Funk, 2009).

If the model is used as a guiding framework, effective and timely management activities can be planned to influence consumer demand and hence sales across PLC stages (Summers, Gardiner, Lamb, Hair and McDaniel, 2003). Table 6.1 illustrates this point by suggesting that promotion awareness strategies are common in the introduction stage of the PLC. In contrast, to maintain the high profit levels of the maturity stage, revitalization or extension of this stage can be achieved through more appropriately implementing the market penetration and development strategies of Ansoff (1957).

Similarly the literature (Thompson, 2002; Shank, 2009) sometimes refers to three different levels of PLC, namely that of product category, form and brand. Whereas the 'product category' relates to the more generic nature of the product (e.g. the sport of swimming), the 'form' refers to the type of product variations (e.g. swimming costumes, flotation aids, pool equipment) and the 'brand' the distinguishing or identifying feature of each form in the marketplace (e.g. Speedo's LZR Racer swimming costume). From a management perspective, it is the brand PLC, the shortest and most erratic of the three, that it is most important to consider, as category and form PLCs frequently last for decades and are unlikely ever to die.

Evolving from this single product life cycle theory is the analytical and more strategic process of appraising the multi-product mix of a business, which is sometimes referred to as product, market or business portfolio analysis. A variety of diagnostic tools was introduced in the 1970s to assist managers to balance cash flows among competing products, taking into consideration their respective PLC stage of development. The most influential technique has proved to be the Boston Consulting Group (BCG) growth-share matrix. As illustrated in Figure 6.2, this plots market share (the control you have

Table 6.1 Typical product life cycle stage characteristics and strategies

PLC stage	Characteristics	Strategies
Introduction	■ *Customers* – initially unaware of product and its benefits. First market entrants are known as 'innovators'. ■ *Competition* – few or no competitors. ■ *Costs* – high per unit costs owing to expensive research, development, promotion and distribution costs. ■ *Sales* – low volume and growth until demand is established. ■ *Price* – dependent upon short- or long-term goals and market position strategy, but usually high (price skimming) to recover costs. ■ *Profit* – negative or at best very low.	■ Prospecting strategy emphasizing product development and testing, market distribution, and promotion strategies to stimulate levels of awareness, trial and demand.
Growth	■ *Customers* – public awareness increases through word of mouth from 'early adopters', which directly influences 'early majority' consumers. ■ *Competition* – increases with more entrants as the stage progresses. ■ *Costs* – declining on a per-unit basis owing to longer production runs and potential economies of scale. ■ *Sales* – if quality product, sales increase rapidly owing to greater levels of awareness, interest, trial and adoption. ■ *Price* – different product versions, which may lead to slight price reductions. Often priced to penetrate the market. ■ *Profit* – begins to grow. At mid-stage, rises rapidly and significantly; the highest it is ever likely to be.	■ Strategic action to create growth via rapid market acceptance, high sales volume, cost reduction and high profitability. ■ Stage strategies include: – product strategy: improve product quality and features; – promotion strategy: develop product interest, preference and repeat purchase behaviour through aggressive brand promotion; – distribution strategy: engage new channels and long-term relationships.

Table 6.1 Continued

PLC stage	Characteristics	Strategies
Maturity	■ *Customers* – approximately 60 per cent of market entrants have now either purchased or already tried the product – this is followed by the 'late majority' customers. ■ *Competition* – at its most intense period, which drives the changes in profit and costs. ■ *Costs* – initially lowered as a result of production volumes increasing and experience curve effects. However, costs are then likely to increase owing to intensity of competitor activity. ■ *Sales* – volume continues to grow but at slower rate than previously. Sales eventually peak and plateau when market saturation reached. ■ *Price* – tends to drop owing to the proliferation of competing products. ■ *Product* – well known and established. Brand differentiation and feature diversification become important as market segments. ■ *Profit* – high and then at saturation level begins to go down.	■ Longest phase of the PLC and most products currently located in this stage. ■ Stage extension strategies include: – modify, develop or revitalize the product and its lines, e.g. a child's version or add technological features; – develop new uses and attract new users by promoting to underdeveloped segments; – enter new markets, e.g. overseas; – repackage and create more frequent use programmes, e.g. promote new rules or offer ticket discounting schemes; – extend distribution network, e.g. sell through additional outlets.
Decline	■ *Customers* – primarily are 'laggards' who are most risk averse and price sensitive. ■ *Competition* – significant number in early stage of decline, but in the latter stages there are just a few who are likely to be the more entrenched with significant market share. ■ *Costs* – costs become counter-optimal, e.g. large costs on more refined promotion will not necessarily increase sales volume. ■ *Sales* – volume declines or stabilizes. Without changes in strategy or market conditions sales will not recover to previous peaks. ■ *Price* – reduced price as discounts expected. ■ *Profit* – diminishes considerably.	■ Supply exceeds demand as product outgrows its usefulness. Supporting a product with little demand is unprofitable. ■ Since the product is likely to be losing market share the dominant strategy becomes one of managing production and distribution efficiency rather than increasing sales. Where products cannot be economically repackaged a cost-effective retrenchment strategy should be quickly adopted.

Information sourced from Brassington and Pettitt (2003); Summers, Gardiner, Lamb, Hair and McDaniel (2003); Kotler and Keller (2006).

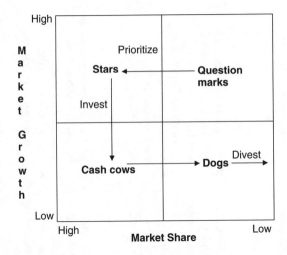

Figure 6.2 Boston Consulting Group growth-share matrix

over a market) against market growth (the attractiveness and potential future sales of a market).

With market growth (cash usage) being linked directly to the PLC paradigm it is argued that this indicates in principle the cash requirement needed by a product or SBU to generate high cash returns. Relative market share (cash generation) on the other hand is chosen rather than profit, as it includes more information than just cash flow.

This then provides a four-cell matrix in which to map an organization's current SBUs, which are represented by individual circles. As the industry matures, successful SBUs are likely to follow a natural cycle of progression from question mark, to star and then through to cash cow and dog (Kotler, 2000). As with the PLC concept, each stage or in this case cell is said to possess its own unique characteristics and hence strategy implications. These are elaborated upon and applied to contemporary Nike examples in Table 6.2. In general summary:

- Question marks possess low market share and high growth potential. Due to cash limitations only a limited number of these can be selected for investment but which ones?
- Stars are the emerging businesses and cash cows of the future. To maintain market share against strong competition they can become heavy users of cash.
- Cash cows encounter a dominant share of the market but possess low growth potential. Since they usually generate more cash than they use,

Table 6.2 Boston Consulting Group matrix cell characteristics and strategies

Cell	Characteristics	Strategies to provide a balanced portfolio	2010 Nike examples
Question marks	■ Low market share and high market growth. ■ PLC stage – introduction; high failure rate. ■ Investment – heavy expenditures owing to high early development costs. ■ Earnings – negative to low. ■ Cash flow – negative, as they are a net cash user.	■ These are the unknowns and must be appraised carefully to determine whether to invest or divest. Whilst they do not generate much revenue, they possess long-term potential to grow and make money. ■ Invest in attractive and stronger long-term SBUs. Aim: to dominate the segment and invest aggressively to obtain market share. ■ Withdraw the unattractive and weaker SBUs.	■ Attractive SBUs include: – electronic products such as the Nike+ range, which includes the iPod Sport Kit; – 'The Chance,' a global search project for talented footballers to join the Nike Academy.
Stars	■ High market share and high market growth. ■ PLC stage – growth. ■ Investment – develop the capacity to expand. ■ Earnings – low to high. ■ Cash flow – negative, as they again are a net cash user.	■ Aim: to increase market share at the expense of short-term earnings. These provide the potential for the most profitable long-term opportunities and are likely to become self-sustainable. ■ Strategy: to invest by aggressive promotion and expanding the product or service range.	■ Nike golf equipment, such as Nike One Tour golf balls, which have been strongly endorsed by Tiger Woods. ■ Nike product lines such as the Kobe and LeBron basketball collections.
Cash cows	■ High market share and low market growth. ■ PLC stage – mature. ■ Investment – maintain capacity. ■ Earnings – high.	■ Aim: to own as many as possible, as these are well established and provide high profit margins. ■ Since the market is not growing, investment is not advisable; instead	■ Established running footwear brands such as Nike's Air Max and Air Force 1. ■ The Air Jordan and the Livestrong product ranges,

- Cash *flow* – positive, as they are a net cash generator.
  - Strong cash cows – hold and defend market position to maintain market share and cost leadership.
  - Weak cash cows – harvest, i.e. generate as much short-term cash flow as possible by milking their cash generation capacity.

Brazil replica jerseys, and the All Star Classic Chuck Converse sneakers.

Dogs
- Low market share and low market growth.
- PLC stage – decline.
- *Investment* – gradually reduce capacity.
- *Earnings* – high to low.
- Cash *flow* – low positive net cash contributor.

- Weak market presence and growth potential; therefore difficult for them to make a profit even with investment.
- Limited future, with unlikely economies of scale.
- Focus on a short-term strategy of orderly withdrawal and divestment, i.e. sell or liquidate unless affected by other benefits such as providing jobs, completing a product line or enjoying other SBU synergies.

- Nike's Bauer Hockey and the Exeter Brands Group subsidiaries were sold off in 2008 and 2007 respectively.

Information sourced from Blythe (2001); Lussier and Kimball (2004); Asia Pacific Marketing Federation (2010); Nike (2010).

they are important to fund the development of other question marks and stars.

■ Dogs are your loss makers offering virtually no long-term potential and therefore need to be sold or liquidated.

Labelling individual SBUs in this manner indicates where the brand is positioned relative to its competitors and where it is likely to go in the future. Such information can assist corporate analysts to determine specific strategies to build (invest in), hold, harvest or divest themselves of each SBU, so as to maintain a balanced business portfolio (Kotler, 2000; Asia Pacific Marketing Federation, 2010).

Whilst BCG proposes a two-by-two analytical matrix of one single variable, the General Electric (GE)/McKinsey attractiveness–competitive position matrix provides a more complex multi-factorial model with nine cells to apportion SBUs to, as illustrated in Figure 6.3.

In the matrix's original format GE used a variety of industry attractiveness sub-categories or factors (size, growth, competitive structure, relative market share, profit, and technical, social, environmental, legal and human impacts) as well as business strength factors (size, growth, market share, profit, margins, technology position, strengths and weaknesses, image, environmental

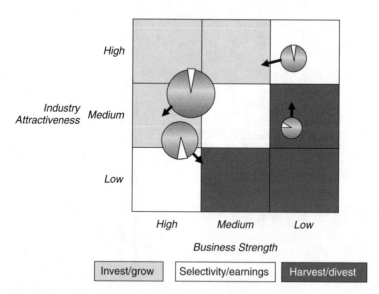

Figure 6.3 The General Electric/McKinsey attractiveness–competitive position matrix

110

impact and management) to support its analytical base (Kotler, 2000). These factors or drivers could then be selected, weighted and rated individually so as to be adaptable to local conditions (Johnson and Scholes, 2002).

Once local needs of what constitutes industry attractiveness or business strength were determined, each circle could then be used to represent an individual SBU. Similarly to what happened in the BCG analysis, the relative size of each circle was determined by the market size, and in more sophisticated drawings the identified segment contained within the circle acted as a pie chart to convey the organization's profit contribution at a moment in time. Future direction and predicted movement of the SBU across the matrix could additionally be highlighted by drawing an arrow from each circle.

In other words, potentially complex business information could be visually presented in a relatively simple manner so that marketing planners could recognize the different performance capabilities of each SBU and then plan future strategies across a balanced portfolio of SBUs (Elliott, Rundle-Thiele, Waller and Paladino, 2008).

Over time numerous other developments in portfolio models and strategic management tools evolved from BCG or GE principles, and these include:

- Little's industry maturity/competitive position matrix (Patel and Younger, 1978) (considers the strength of competitive position relative to the life cycle of the industry);
- Shell directional policy matrix (Robinson, Hichens and Wade, 1978) (refinement of the GE business screen matrix, which contends that for each cell a different strategy is preferred);
- Barksdale and Harris's (1982) portfolio analysis (introduces a pioneering category, an infant, as well as two additional negative growth classifications to BCG, namely warhorses and dodos);
- Porter's (1985) industry/market evolution model (focuses on three evolution stages of the industry as well as five forces of competitive rivalry that influence market attractiveness);
- BCG's advantage matrix (see Mercer, 2001) (recognizes economies of scale and competitive differentiation);
- parenting and relatedness matrices (see Johnson and Scholes, 2002) (takes in consideration synergies between SBUs);
- Sonfield and Lussier's (1997) entrepreneurial strategy matrix (applies the BCG matrix to small business and limited product lines);
- action priority matrix (see TimeAnalyzer, 2006) (aids in selection of projects that legitimately provide the quickest and highest returns);

- profit impact of marketing strategies (PIMS) (Strategic Planning Institute, 2010) (uses cash flow and return on investments and compares these with a large database of industry benchmarks to create effective business strategies);
- strategic position and action evaluation (SPACE) matrix (determines what strategy an organization should use) and the more sophisticated and high-level strategic management quantitative strategic planning matrix (QSPM), which permits choice between viable strategies (Maxi-Pedia, 2010).

To elaborate briefly on just one of these developments, the Shell directional policy matrix is presented in Figure 6.4.

Each cell in Figure 6.4 provides classification as well as implications for strategic investment, namely:

1 = Leader: invest major resources in these SBUs.
2 = Growth: grow the market by focusing some resources here.
3 = Cash generator: milk the resources to invest elsewhere.
4 = Try harder: beware; these SBUs could be vulnerable later on.
5 = Custodial: treat as a cash cow, milk and do not commit additional resources.
6 and 8 = Phased withdrawal: move cash to SBUs with better returns.
7 = Double or quit: gamble and select some of these SBUs for future investment.
9 = Disinvest: liquidate or sell these as speedily as possible.

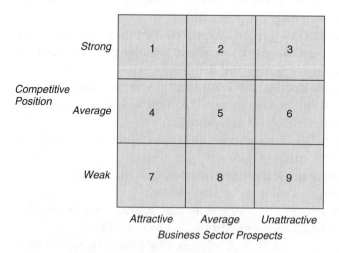

Figure 6.4 Shell's directional policy matrix

Focusing on strategic decisions derived from GE matrix mapping and the Shell directional policy matrix suggests that those SBUs attributed as being situated in the top left of the GE matrix (high market attractiveness and high business strength) should be invested in and grown. In contrast, those mapped in the bottom right (low market attractiveness and business strength) should generally be harvested, got rid of or repositioned, as they offer few prospects to the organization, and those that reside in the middle diagonal should entail further investigation and some degree of selectivity (Johnson and Scholes, 2002).

The results from such analyses assist management to determine where to allocate their limited resources and clarify which strategic direction their SBUs should take for organizational sustainability.

PRACTICAL APPLICATION

The product life cycle concept was, as the name suggests, originally applied to better understand the marketing requirements of different phases of a broad range of physical products. For example, proactive use was typically seen by market pioneers such as Coca-Cola or 3M that introduced not just new products but also new markets. Launching products in such a scenario is potentially high in both risk and expense, and knowing the characteristics of each stage permits management to better plan cost-effective strategies to maximize sales and profit across the PLC. In particular, organizations aim to prolong the growth stage of a product and revitalize it in the maturity stage of the PLC. On the other hand, retrospective use of PLC analysis can be seen when managers are deciding when to enter an existing market with a new product. Knowing that there is an established yet relatively untouched niche market can influence differentiated products and accompanying promotional strategies to make significant inroads, such as that seen by Dell in the computer market and Nike in the sports footwear market.

However, over time the PLC concept has been extended to a variety of other services and applications. Shank (2009) for example, in referring to sport applications, highlights the unique scenario of managing elite performers, whether these are at an individual level or a collective entity such as a national team or professional league. This can be illustrated at the individual level, where unique PLCs can be seen to exist for retired athletes who reintroduce themselves, such as Lance Armstrong and Michael Schumacher, or athletes such as Tiger Woods who quickly fall from grace owing to publicized off-field transgressions.

Similarly PLC analysis underlies all types of portfolio matrix and management decisions. Originally applied to strategic business units of large organizations, the BCG matrix has more recently been applied to divisions, brands, product lines and any other form of cash-generating entity (Elliott, Rundle-Thiele, Waller and Paladino, 2008). Evaluating these individual entities with regard to market growth, share, competitive position, industry attractiveness and other parameters that affect financial return helps a manager to balance their risk and resource allocation. BCG and GE matrix applications have been broad, with the analytical tools being used for general product management, brand marketing, strategic management, and portfolio analysis within and between organizations (Lussier and Kimball, 2004). No more is this apparent than with the developments of the Boston Consulting Group (2010), which is now a world leader in strategic business consultancy and is one of the exclusive partners of the London Olympic Games 2012, advising them on ticketing, merchandising, sponsorship and revenue strategies (London 2012, 2009).

ASSUMPTIONS AND LIMITATIONS

Every management tool possesses assumptions and limitations, and the PLC and portfolio matrices are no exception. According to Blythe (2001) and Morgan and Summers (2005), the product life cycle concept assumes that:

- changes in consumer preference are only one-way;
- all products exhibit the archetypal life cycle, passing through each stage before death naturally occurs;
- it is easy to determine which part of the life cycle specific product lines are currently operating in.

In practice not all products pass through each stage nor follow such a prescriptive life cycle. Some return to a previous stage, as evidenced by the relaunch of some of Adidas's nostalgic fashion lines, and some move from the introduction phase to decline within a couple of weeks, as was the case with the introduction of the XFL sport in America (Lussier and Kimball, 2004). Whilst management can directly influence the stage of PLCs, for example price-cutting long-established products can quickly move them from maturity to the decline stage, unpredictable events, such as a serious career-ending injury or a car or plane crash, can immediately end a product's life cycle. At the opposite extreme, certain products, such as the popular sports and pastimes of athletics, skiing or swimming, are never likely to die or become obsolete.

114

Clearly the length of each stage as well as the duration of the PLC is an enigma that can and does vary enormously between several weeks and hundreds of years in the case of athletics. This means that each PLC is likely to be unique, making stage predictability very difficult in practice. In essence, constant short-term fluctuations will naturally be encountered, and these could if misinterpreted lead to the implementation of inappropriate strategies and ultimately business failure.

For this reason life cycle analysis is generally to be considered a largely explanatory and descriptive product development management tool. These inherent limitations and weaknesses similarly have an impact on the BCG matrix, which additionally assumes (Blythe, 2001):

- that market share can be enhanced through investing in promotion and that it will generate surpluses;
- that financial surpluses will be generated in the maturity stage of the PLC;
- that the most appropriate opportunity to build a dominant market is in the growth phase of the PLC.

Whilst the BCG provides a simple means of appraising current activity, along with a relatively straightforward method of developing future strategies, it is not without its problems. For example, limitations include its ambiguity and sensitivity in classifying the market as well as high and low share, and its over-simplification in emphasizing cash flow and just the two factors of market growth and share. In practice market growth is not the only indicator of market attractiveness (see Porter, 1985, and his industry/market evolution model). Similarly, low-share or niche businesses can be profitable, and performance criteria such as return on investment, economies of scales and experience curve effects are ignored in the original form of the matrix.

For these reasons multiple factor portfolio techniques such as the GE matrix were developed, providing a more complex and comprehensive level of analysis. However, the GE is similarly not without its limitations. For example, aggregation of the weightings and ratings of each dimension is both difficult and subjective, only broad strategy guidelines are proposed, and the model largely neglects the core competencies leading to value creation.

Such criticisms led Kotler (2000) to conclude that portfolio models should be used, but used cautiously, as they potentially:

- place too much emphasis on the future, emphasizing entry into high-growth businesses at the expense of current businesses;

- are sensitive to the selected underlying ratings and weightings;
- fail to delineate SBU synergies, particularly in decentralized settings.

PROCESS THROUGH AN APPLIED EXAMPLE

To illustrate the practical process and use of portfolio analysis techniques in a sport setting, let us use the globally emerging sport of cricket as the product of analysis. Sanctioned by the international governing body of the sport, the Indian national governing body the Board of Control for Cricket in India (BCCI) introduced the DFL Indian Premier League (IPL) to the world in 2008. The IPL brand has quickly developed into a highly financed, telegenic and annual Twenty20 cricket tournament between competing Indian cricket teams that possess a mix of both local (such as an icon player – a player from the home Indian city as well as players aged under 22 from the region) and the very best overseas cricketers from around the world. The IPL is founded upon marketing forces and financial auction principles rather than player nationality. Ownership of one of these franchises started at US$67 million (Rajasthan Royals in 2008), but with the two new additions to the league this quickly escalated to US$333 million (Kochi in 2010) and US$370 million (Pune in 2010) (Ravindran and Gollapudi, 2010). The success and growth of this iconic brand, even at a time of global recession, has simply been unprecedented in the history of the sport. For example, the estimated brand value has increased from US$2.01 billion to US$4.13 billion in just one year (*Times of India*, 2010); it is the most watched television programme in India, drawing audiences of up to 40 million (NDTV, 2009); the Airtel Champion's League – the grand finale of world Twenty20 cricket teams – has evolved from such success; and it still possesses considerable potential for further growth (*Times of India*, 2010).

Using such a scenario, although predominantly using hypothetical data since the IPL does not have to publicly declare its annual financial performance, we will first apply the Boston Consulting Group matrix to the eight established IPL franchised clubs (two will be added in 2011), as these constitute the collection of strategic business units of the IPL. To complete a more in-depth analysis we will then demonstrate the process of applying the General Electric market attractiveness–competitive position model to one of these business units, Chennai Super Kings, the market leader and 2010 winner of the tournament.

Boston Consulting Group (BCG) matrix

The generic process of undertaking the BCG analysis entails the following steps:

1 Determine the nature of a strategic business unit (SBU).
2 Identify the relative market share and market growth of each SBU.
3 Draw and appropriately label and scale a BCG matrix.
4 Plot each SBU on the BCG matrix.

1 Determine the nature of a strategic business unit

Each of the cricket clubs of the IPL is a strategic business unit, as it constitutes an autonomous operating business of a geographically segmented cricket market. For example, all teams are located in India and are specifically linked to key cities, such as the Daredevils to the city of Delhi (north of India), the Indians to the city of Mumbai (west), the Royal Challengers to Bangalore (south) and the Knight Riders to Kolkata (east). Collectively these SBUs form the professional Twenty20 Indian cricket market.

2 Identify the relative market share and market growth of each SBU

Since high relative market share indicates position dominance and a stronger likelihood to develop cash, each SBU or club needs to initially be appraised for its relative share of the market. Different measures of market share may be used for this purpose, although normally market share is extrapolated from publicly available sales figures. However, in light of the fact that some IPL franchises have failed to submit annual reports, including balance sheets (*Economic Times*, 2010), we will use estimated brand values, since they are readily available and have been annually reported in the *Times of India* (2010). Summarized in Table 6.3, these brand values are based upon revenue streams that include broadcasting, IPL sponsorship, team sponsorship, merchandising and gate receipts, as well as the effect of performance, the catchment population of the city, the capacity of the stadium and the presence of iconic players (Brand Finance, 2009).

As illustrated in Table 6.3, the 2010 brand values of the eight original teams vary from US$34.4 million (Hyderabad Deccan Chargers) to US$48.4 million (Chennai Super Kings). The two new entrants being launched possess no market share and therefore cannot be included in this analysis. These data, which will be used later in the analytical process, reveal that the breadth of SBU ratios varies between 0.71 (US$34.4/US$48.4) and 1.0 (US$48.4/US$48.4) and

Table 6.3 Indian Premier League club brand values

Team	2009 brand value (US$ million)	2010 brand value (US$ million)	Brand value percentage change	2010 market share ratios
Kolkata Knight Riders (KKR)	42.1	46.0	+9	0.95
Mumbai Indians (MI)	41.6	40.8	−2	0.84
Rajasthan Royals (RR)	39.5	45.2	+14	0.93
Chennai Super Kings (CSK)	39.4	48.4	+23	1.0
Delhi Daredevils (DD)	39.2	40.5	+3	0.84
Royal Challengers Bangalore (RCB)	37.4	41.9	+12	0.87
King's XI Punjab (KXB)	36.3	36.1	−0.6	0.75
Hyderabad Deccan Chargers (HDC)	34.8	34.4	−1	0.71

Information sourced from Brand Finance (2009) and *Times of India* (2010).

the 2010 market growth rates between plus 23 per cent (Chennai Super Kings) and minus 2 per cent (Mumbai Indians).

In general, business organizations want to invest in rapidly growing SBUs in rapid growth markets so as to provide sustainable future opportunities for themselves. However, the unique nature of sport and in particular professional leagues requires cooperation, competition and unpredictability. Sport spectators rarely want to see leagues that are dominated by one market leader and few competitors; instead they crave unscripted excitement and entertainment derived from outcome uncertainty (Stewart and Smith, 1999). So ideally the BCCI as well as each SBU wants the IPL market to grow, as well as all SBUs within it. Naturally though, in the introduction and growth stage of the IPL life cycle both the league and individual SBUs require substantial investment. Normally market growth rates are not expected to exceed 10 per cent per annum. However, such has been the international success of the IPL that in the third season of operation the collective brand value of the IPL doubled in 2010 (*Times of India*, 2010). This has largely been due to international market development strategies by BCCI, as well as individual strategies and tactics by each SBU. The former can be exemplified through switching from a pay-to-view to a free-to-view television channel in 2009, which increased viewership in the United Kingdom tenfold (IPL, 2010). An example of a successful SBU tactic can be seen in the Kolkata Knight Riders team, where the celebrity co-owner implemented hard-sell tactics of the team brand to counteract the team's very poor on-field performances (calculated to equate to 6 per cent growth) and managed to return an increased brand value of 9 per cent (Brand Finance, 2009).

118

3 Draw and appropriately label and scale a BCG matrix

Once the maximum and minimum of each range have been determined, the axis can be constructed, labelled and scaled accordingly (see Figure 6.5). Using relative market share or in this case 'relative brand value share' as the x axis, and market growth rate as the y axis, the range and division of each axis are arbitrarily classified as high and low. Normally the horizontal axis is logarithmically presented as a ratio (see the final column of Table 6.3), which is determined by comparing each SBU with the largest market competitor. For example, King's XI Punjab's brand value in 2010 was US$36.1 million. Comparing this value with that of the market leader, the Chennai Super Kings (US$48.4 million), gives a ratio of approximately 0.75.

The y axis on the other hand relates to absolute market growth rates and is usually expressed as a percentage. This growth rate may relate to product, product line, market segment, business or as in this case study the SBU growth rate. Equally this unit of analysis could include comparison to other benchmarks such as the national inflation rate or gross national product performance. In the case of the IPL, India experienced an inflation rate of 13.73 per cent in 2010 (*Trading Economics*, 2010), and this can be included in the matrix so that below average inflation (e.g. King's XI Punjab) and above average inflation (e.g. Chennai Super Kings) categorizations can be made.

At the mid-point of both the horizontal and the vertical axis, a line is drawn vertically and horizontally respectively, so as to provide a four-cell matrix in which to allocate SBUs and assess above- and below-average performances.

4 Plot each SBU on the BCG matrix

Once the matrix has been drawn to scale the information from each SBU can be systematically plotted, as illustrated in Figure 6.5.

The exact location of each circle, which indicates both the market growth rate and the relative market share of each SBU, is plotted on the BCG matrix and usually ends up being allocated to one of the four quadrants. However, it is not a problem to have some circles that cross two or more cells, as has occurred with King's XI Punjab (the two-toned circle in Figure 6.5), as there is nothing particularly 'magical' about where the intersecting lines are drawn (MindTools, 2010). In practice, there may be very little difference between a 'dog' and a 'cash cow'.

The area of each circle of the BCG needs to be proportionally drawn to represent the relative difference between each SBU. If the ratio for example was calculated at 0.5 then one circle would be twice the size of the other.

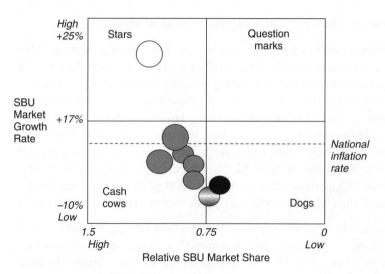

Figure 6.5 Boston Consulting Group matrix applied to Indian Premier League clubs

As depicted in Figure 6.5, the market leader, currently Chennai Super Kings (which moved from fourth rank to first in one year – *Times of India*, 2010) is always displayed on the left of the chart. In this case it is the stand-out and healthy performer, being the only SBU to be classified as a star (high market share and growth) and one of just two SBUs that gave growth returns higher than inflation. In comparison Hyderabad Deccan Chargers is the only clear dog, although King's XI Punjab appears to be in very close proximity, with both clubs recording a negative brand value return relative to the previous year. The other five teams represent cash cows, and all appear to have produced similar brand value performances in the 2010 season.

General Electric (GE) matrix

The GE process is similar in nature to the BCG process. Application of the GE technique typically requires you to carry out the following steps:

1 Determine the nature of the strategic business units.
2 Identify the factors that contribute to the dimensions of market attractiveness and business position.
3 Establish the methods of measuring market attractiveness and business position.
4 Score and weight each SBU driver.
5 Plot each SBU on the GE matrix and interpret the findings.

120

1 Determine the nature of the strategic business units

Since all of the IPL SBUs operate in the same product market, namely cricket, the GE matrix can be applied to any of the SBU business portfolios as well as those of the BCCI. With this in mind let us hypothetically apply this model to just one club, namely the market leader and 2010 winner, Chennai Super Kings, and more specifically to three of the four commonly encountered business areas of professional sport, namely spectator services, sponsorship services and licence rights (Westerbeek and Smith, 2003). Note that television rights will not be considered here merely because in the IPL these are managed and revenues allocated centrally by the BCCI.

2 Identify the factors that contribute to the dimensions of market attractiveness and business position

To illustrate the process of identifying the factors or drivers that affect both market attractiveness and business position, let us use the component of team sponsorship services. Whereas the first dimension indicates the growth potential of the sponsorship market, the latter relates more specifically to the relative competitive strength or competitive advantage of the club. For example, is sponsorship considered to grow in the cricket market, and if so what are some of the drivers that will influence this growth?

In the applied scenario where teams are very young, many sponsors were probably not too keen to become involved in the first or second season of operation, owing to the league's unknown value and spectator following. However, with excellent attendance figures and a global interest being established through a ten-year broadcasting deal, the potential to grow Chennai Super Kings' two club sponsors and eight partners is now immense. The market attractiveness to sponsors will be dependent upon the overall market size and the annual growth rate of popularity, as well as factors that relate to Porter's (1985) competitive forces, such as barriers to entry and intensity of competition. These become the unique and applied value drivers of the market attractiveness dimension in this scenario (see Table 6.4).

The market may offer growth potential, but are you as one competitor in this sport market able to take advantage of it? If we were considering Hyderabad Deccan Chargers this might not be the case, but as we are applying this analysis to the Chennai Super Kings, the current on- and off-field market leader, their business strength is considered extremely high. The Chennai Super Kings are led by Mahendra Dhoni, the captain of the Indian cricket team in all forms of the game. The parameters of the business strength dimension could relate to drivers such as market share, growth, product

121

quality, financial backing, distribution network, promotional capability and management competence (see Table 6.4).

3 Establish the methods of measuring market attractiveness and business position

Once these individual drivers have been identified for each dimension they need to be accurately and reliably measured. This requires selecting methods that are appropriate to their purpose. For example, tracked independent market analysis of growth rates to measure market attractiveness, such as that carried out by Brand Finance (2009), is much stronger than in-house subjective opinions. Similarly, business or competitive strength in the sport industry has been notoriously biased towards emotional fan opinions and unquestioned loyalty. In the current scenario, fit-for-purpose business strength measures could relate to on-field performance win–loss ratios (product quality), sponsorship accrued (managerial competence) or increases in membership and merchandising profit sales (promotional effectiveness) relative to competing IPL teams. From these more objective data sources, SBU proportions can be more reliably assigned meaningful values.

4 Score and weight each SBU driver

The next stage requires you to calculate via a numerical rating system a weighting for each of these individual drivers. As illustrated in Table 6.4, this

Table 6.4 Weighted factors underlying market attractiveness and competitive position of sponsorship services for Chennai Super Kings

	Factors	Weight	Rating (1–5)	Value
Market attractiveness	Overall market size	0.4	5	2.0
	Annual market growth rate	0.3	4	1.2
	Barriers to entry	0.1	2	0.2
	Competitive intensity	0.2	3	0.6
	Total	**1.0**		**4.0**
Business strength	Market share	0.1	2	0.2
	Share growth	0.1	2	0.2
	Product quality	0.3	4	1.2
	Financial resource	0.1	1	0.1
	Distribution network	0.1	2	0.2
	Promotional effectiveness	0.1	3	0.3
	Managerial competence	0.2	5	1.0
	Total	**1.0**		**3.2**

122

involves allocating a relative importance weighting to each factor, which cumulatively should total 1.0 for both marketing attractiveness and business strength dimensions. For example, in the present sponsorship scenario it is suggested that the overall market size (0.4) is considered to be twice as important as the competitive nature of the industry (0.2). Whilst this is subjective it does provide a much stronger basis and greater depth of modified analysis than the BCG matrix, which simplifies the process to market growth and relative market share.

Once the factors for each dimension have been weighted, each driver is scored or rated in terms of market attractiveness or current level of competitive position ranging from 1 to 5 (e.g. 1 = very unattractive, very weak competitive position; 5 = very attractive, very strong competitive position). For example, in Table 6.4 financial resource availability is deemed a weakness, recording a rating of 1. In comparison, managerial competence (e.g. they have just employed the industry sponsorship leader) is now considered to be a strength, and hence the allocated rating of 5. These ratings are then multiplied by the importance weightings, and summed so as to provide a cumulative market strength (4.0) and business strength value (3.2).

Similar processes can be carried out with reference to each component under review, in this case spectator services and licence rights.

5 Plot each SBU on the GE matrix and interpret the findings

From the resulting data a visual portfolio can be plotted, in the same manner as the BCG matrix was constructed earlier, but this time against low, medium or high values. Using hypothetical data, Figure 6.6 highlights a GE matrix as applied to an IPL club.

Figure 6.6 indicates that at least fictitiously the selected club is relatively strong in two areas of business, sponsorship services and licence rights. Furthermore, they both are considered to be attractive areas in which to invest and grow and, assuming available funds, these are the areas they should actively pursue. On the other hand, the component of spectator services is not considered to be one of the club's strengths. While they must be provided, as they are the lifeblood of the club's revenue-earning stream, they currently offer limited potential for growth, perhaps because they already operate at full-house capacity. In this sense, management should be selective as to whether or not to invest resources in this area or even consider subcontracting it out to more specialist service providers.

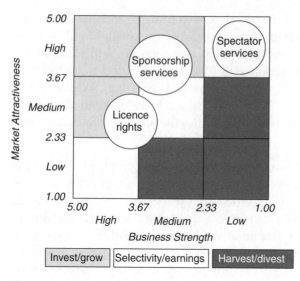

Figure 6.6 General Electric matrix applied to an Indian Premier League club business portfolio

INTERPRETATION AND MANAGEMENT DECISIONS

Whilst PLC and portfolio matrix tools are not able to predict the duration of individual life cycles, stages or cells, they can assist marketers to appraise current offerings, focus on future events and propose appropriate strategies (Lamb, Hair and McDaniel, 2006). More specifically, integrating all SBUs and products into one matrix allows you to categorize each unit according to future cash contribution as well as current requirements (Elliott, Rundle-Thiele, Waller and Paladino, 2008).

Interpretation and management decisions entail contextual analysis followed by strategic choice and implementation. For example, the type of the market needs to be considered and differences between consumer and industrial markets as well as products and services duly recognized. Similarly, the scope of analysis and nature of competition need to be fully understood. In the IPL example used, individual teams compete with one another, but their individual success is also dependent upon cooperation, a facet that is not always shared in many other business settings (Stewart and Smith, 1999). Because of this, it is not in anyone's best interest for IPL teams to be unsuccessful on the field or off it. Whereas multi-product businesses such as Nike are likely to target dogs to divest themselves of, the BCCI does not necessarily wish to take such a decision and may prefer to develop strategies to grow such SBUs.

124

Furthermore, market analysis and sport performances need to be considered in the context of competing markets as well as the macro-environmental influences at a moment in time. In the IPL example, this might include competition from the growth of other major sporting codes, one-off events such as the 2010 Commonwealth Games or even national team participation in shared cricket locations. Conversely, negative macro-environmental factors that could affect strategic IPL decisions could include recent cricket-related incidents of player security, match or spot fixing or on a general level even the long-term impact of the global financial crisis.

While understanding the local context, you need to make decisions that will build a balanced portfolio within your organization. This provides you with sufficient positive net cash flow to ensure a sustainable future. This is simple to say, but what is actually meant by the term 'balanced'? Should you just focus on cash cows, the most profitable SBUs of the portfolio? The answer is no, as managing too many cash cows places your future profitability at risk. Similarly, too many stars could lead to a cash crisis, and too many question marks have an impact on current profitability. In a multi-product or multi-division organization you are likely to need a cross-section of SBUs, where high and low growth opportunities will provide short-, medium- and long-term returns. The major lesson or implication drawn from the PLC concept is that you need to plan for new products to replace those that will eventually fade and die. In other words, you require the money generated from the cash cows to fund the stars and selective question marks, to ensure you have a future.

In recognizing the relationship between the PLC and SBUs in the BCG matrix, the Asia Pacific Marketing Federation (2010) suggests that typically there are three decision paths to future success, namely:

1 Continuously aim to generate cash cows (cash generators) so that you can invest in non-self-sustaining question marks (net cash users).
2 Stars (cash neutral) require reinvestment so that in mature markets they can become cash cows and dominant market leaders.
3 Segment the market for dogs (low cash contributors) and either nurse them to health or manage them for cash.

Similarly, the Asia Pacific Marketing Federation (2010) suggests three paths to failure, and warns:

1 Do not over-invest in cash cows and under-invest in question marks – this is a short-term approach to profit.

2   Do not permit competitors to gain share in a high-growth market – invest in your stars.
3   Do not over-milk your cash cows – they will eventually become very low cash earners.

In terms of GE matrix decision making, three broad strategy guidelines are recommended: maintain investment in or preferably grow the SBUs with high or medium market attractiveness and business strength scores; harvest or divest yourself of or at least do not invest in low/low or low/medium SBUs; and selectively invest in the high/low or medium/medium SBUs to maintain or increase your earnings.

By appropriately understanding the market in which you operate and the information provided by BCG and GE matrices, you can better plan your general directional organizational strategy. In the case of the IPL, the BCCI has already released growth and expansion plans by granting additional licences and establishing contractual agreements until at least 2017 (NDTV, 2009). Endorsing Ansoff's (1957) product development strategies (e.g. CSK currently possesses only two merchandising product lines; the introduction of the World Twenty20 Champions League), market penetration strategies (e.g. consumer loyalty and discount schemes) and market development strategies (e.g. new IPL team franchises and overseas broadcasting contracts) will allow the development of coherent and integrated marketing action plans for the sport, league, clubs and individuals.

COMMON MISTAKES

Portfolio models prove very useful in a multi-division organizational setting where profit is a key consideration, as they help to determine where money is made or lost and draw attention to the development of new products. However, common mistakes relate to their inappropriate application, misinterpretation and subsequent poor strategy selection of action.

Johnson and Scholes (2002) for example suggest that particular market settings and drivers need to be carefully understood before such models are blandly applied to all applications. Guesswork about driver selection, method of measurement and apportionment of weighting, which is frequently encountered, can lead to very subjective decisions of extending what should clearly be 'dead' lines. Similarly, what constitutes a high and low market growth and share in one industry may be very different from another. Fast-moving consumer goods often possess very slow growth rates, such as

126

less than 1 per cent per annum (Mercer, 2001), but this does not necessarily make them unprofitable ventures.

The BCG matrix is predicated on the assumption that money is both the critical resource of production and the primary performance indicator of value. In some sport instances, innovative management competence or mental strength may be preferred over financial backing. Furthermore, some private sector and public sector sport organizations are not necessarily driven by money and growth motives, placing higher values on field performances and political imperatives. In such scenarios the BCG matrix may be considered inappropriate and adapted versions of the GE matrix preferred, as they better understand the complex interrelationships that exist in practice.

Other portfolio model application errors include applying the analysis to too broad a range of products or market segments. Kotler (2000) argues that, owing to the effect of averaging, this often leads to locating the SBU in the wrong cell, thereby compromising the strategies selected for what could be two or more very differently performing products. However, that said, individual SBUs and products should not be considered in isolation. As highlighted in Figure 6.7, a portfolio means that each SBU contributes different sales and hence profits over time. In particular, at time point 1, only A and B contribute to earnings, whereas at point 2 A, B, C and D create sales, but at point 3 only C and D contribute to profit and these are in the decline stage of their respective life cycles.

In addition, the synergistic effects of SBUs must be recognized in strategic management decisions. Individually some products may be low financial performers but act as loss leaders or low-quality versions, encouraging further sales in high-premium and profitable product lines.

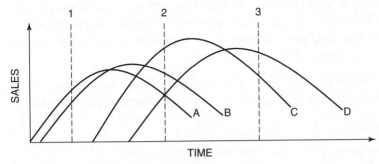

Key:
A, B, C and D = Individual strategic business units
1, 2 and 3 = Moments in time

Figure 6.7 Multi-SBU life cycles

Clearly understanding and interpreting the idiosyncrasies of the sport industry are vital if effective interpretation and strategy implementation are expected. In the context of the BCG this may relate to specific strategies of managing dogs, which are often misunderstood in the sporting arena. For example, a poorly performing professional sports team (financially and on the field) may actually benefit from its position owing to early draft selections. Likewise a poorly performing local authority swimming pool should not automatically be closed, as it may create additional community issues and be entwined with significant political ramifications. Furthermore, what may be considered a dog for one organization may prove to be a cash cow for another. No more was this apparent than when Nike bought Converse for US$305 million in 2003, yet managed to market it through retailers that it would not use for its own brand, to earn US$550 million in 2007 (Nager, 2008).

The merit of these tools lies in the analytical skills, management judgement and insightful strategic recommendations that can be derived from the findings (Adcock, Halborg and Ross, 2001). This requires considerable experience and careful appraisal of both context and strategy, including the often forgotten product line stretching and rationalization options.

SUMMARY

As diagnostic product development management tools, PLC and portfolio matrix analysis can assist management to quickly interpret current products, product lines, divisions and market dynamics (Kotler and Keller, 2006) and thereby predict likely characteristics of the next stage of development (Lamb, Hair and McDaniel, 2006). These analyses allow you to optimize resource allocation and so determine which strategic business units you ideally should focus your efforts on. Knowing such information helps you proactively to plan alternative strategies to individually and collectively manage a potentially challenging portfolio of SBUs.

In its most advanced form the GE multi-factor portfolio matrix can be customized to its own unique sport circumstances, and this process requires you to:

1 Determine the nature of the strategic business units.
2 Identify the factors that contribute to the dimensions of market attractiveness and business position.
3 Establish the methods of measuring market attractiveness and business position.

128

4   Score and weight each SBU driver.
5   Plot each SBU on the matrix and interpret the findings.

Limitations of any technique need to be duly recognized. For example, it could be argued that the PLC is a self-fulfilling tool and, when it is envisaged that sales have peaked, eradicating promotional strategies forces the product into the decline stage and near-certain demise. On the one hand, the extended notion of the BCG matrix offers the advantage of clarity, but it is often considered too simple, as it provides a snapshot of current activity in just two dimensions. On the other hand, the GE matrix uses a broader and more complex range of factors that require a greater level of management understanding and judgement.

In summary, if carried out robustly and insightfully, product life cycle and business portfolio analysis provide you with a useful snapshot of the current situation of single- or multi-organization strategic business units so that you can better balance your investment strategy and ensure a sustainable future.

Guides to further resources, useful web links and guideline answers to all the self-test questions featured in this chapter are available on a companion website at www.routledge.com/9780415491594.

SELF-TEST QUESTIONS

Task 1

Using Table 6.5 locate the following sports events at one or more stages of the product life cycle:

1   Commonwealth Games
2   FIFA Beach Soccer World Cup
3   FIFA World Cup
4   FINA World Swimming Championships
5   ICC Champions Trophy
6   Indian F1 Grand Prix
7   Major League Baseball World Series
8   Super Bowl
9   Tour de France
10 Twenty20 Champions League
11 US Open Grand Slam tennis
12 WrestleMania (World Wrestling Entertainment)

Table 6.5 Product life cycle sport event applications

Introduction	Growth	Maturity	Decline

What practical problems did you face with this task, and how might you be able to overcome them? Select one of these events and propose the likely characteristics of its next stage as well as possible strategies that you might use to effectively manage it.

Task 2

Using approximately 500 words in an essay format, explain how the Boston Consulting Group matrix might assist you to plan strategically, and identify the strengths and weaknesses of the model.

CHAPTER 7

CRITICAL PATH NETWORKS: COMPLETING PROJECTS ON TIME

TECHNIQUE DESCRIPTION

Critical path networks are diagrammatic representations of related tasks that collectively constitute a project. Being derived directly from project management theory, they provide managers with important resource planning information regarding the effective use of time. As well as simplifying complex projects, critical path networks can estimate the length of the total project and help you to identify the 'critical' tasks that *must* be completed on time for the project to meet its scheduled finish date.

The process of creating critical path networks involves the use of several project management techniques that have evolved and been integrated into various hybrid versions over time. Within this chapter the following project management processes and outputs will be introduced to you:

- work breakdown structure (WBS) – dividing projects into smaller, manageable, independent and measurable sub-components;
- Gantt charts – scheduling project tasks graphically, displayed via horizontal bars that represent time;
- resource allocation – assigning human and financial units to a project or individual tasks;
- activity sequencing – determining task dependencies and the nature of the logical relationships between them;
- critical path analysis (CPA) – depicting activities or tasks as a logical diagram that aids management decision making.

To better understand project management outputs and decisions, this chapter will first introduce you to manual processes, before progressing to contemporary computer applications, demonstrating their practical use through an applied sports management example.

PURPOSE

Critical path networks, particularly through computer applications such as Microsoft Project™ and ProjeX, permit managers to effectively plan and control complex projects. By pictorially displaying key information in different formats, sport managers can:

- create a clear sense of project purpose, direction and timing;
- identify task priorities and the interdependent nature of these activities;
- accurately determine the impact of starting tasks earlier or later than scheduled;
- establish clear lines of responsibility and accountability;
- estimate costs of overruns and avoid potential problems or conflicts;
- level out human resource peaks and troughs;
- improve team cooperation and communication;
- review progress and see the effect of various trade-offs between quality, resources and time.

In summary, managers who know how to use critical path network techniques can optimize their resource usage by highlighting critical tasks, foreseeing potential bottlenecks and stressful scenarios, and modelling 'What if?' solutions should the project fall behind schedule.

THEORETICAL OVERVIEW

Projects abound in every industry. Verzuh (1999) suggests that they are characterized by their goal and team orientation, finite existence (defined start and finish date) and resource intensity, and frequently become unique occurrences. A project is distinguishable from everyday operational practice, and Gray and Larson (2000: 4) suggest that it is 'a complex non-routine one-time effort limited by time, budget, resources and performance specifications designed to meet customer needs'.

The implication is that projects are temporary and require unique management activities, for individuals, organizations or new multi-organization partnerships. As a result they often involve considerable uncertainty and provide very complex and challenging management environments in which to operate. No more is this apparent than in the sports industry, where Emery (2003) has suggested that major sports events with their global participation and media interest, as well as large, pulsating, temporary and volunteer

132

dependent workforce (Hanlon and Jago, 2004), have often been considered some of the most complex projects imaginable.

Applying project management principles and techniques to these specialist project contexts involves understanding the complex macro- and micro-environment. As illustrated in Figure 7.1, whilst external macro-influences on the project are important and represented by the outer ring, it is the inner ring that identifies the interrelated micro-drivers of accountability and successful project management. This is known as the golden triangle of project management and requires the effective management of the internal drivers of quality, resources (human and financial) and time.

From the outset one or more of these drivers are likely to provide the dominant constraint(s) of any project. For example, hosting the Formula 1 Malaysian Grand Prix will be driven by quality (if the circuit is not considered safe the race will not take place) and time (once established, the event date will not be able to be changed because of the implications for other events on the circuit). In other sport scenarios, maximum budgetary spend (financial resource) may be the limiting factor, such as in the case of building a public sector swimming pool or extending the social facilities of a local voluntary cricket club. At any moment in time these three drivers vary in importance and might be traded off against each other across the different phases of the project life cycle.

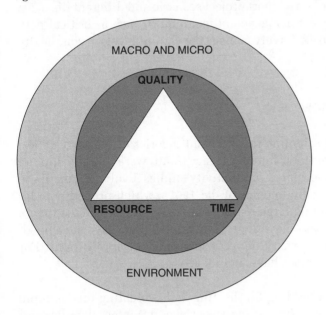

Figure 7.1 Project management environment

Source: Adapted from Briner, Geddes and Hasting (1996).

The concepts of the life cycle, as a time-bound linear progression through various clearly defined management phases of activity, have been regularly introduced into management theory and practice. For example, in the general literature there is the infamous product life cycle categorization associated with marketing (introduced in Chapter 6; see Kotler, Brown, Adam, Burton and Armstrong, 2006) and the generic project life cycle (define, plan, execute and close out phases – Verzuh, 1999). Similarly, specific sport context life cycles now exist in the literature, as illustrated by Emery's (2003) sports event management life cycle (pre-event – idea and feasibility, bidding, detailed planning and preparation; event – implementation; post-event – clearing away and feedback) and facility management stages and sub-stages (conception and development – idea and feasibility, design and construction, and detailed planning and preparation; operation – operation and perfor- mance measurement, and development or divestment; termination – transfer of ownership, and feedback).

Clearly, sport-related life cycles can span considerable time frames, as is evident by the age of venues such as Australia's Melbourne Cricket Ground, which in 2003 celebrated its 150-year history. Furthermore international sport projects can and often do contain many sub-projects, e.g. the bidding phase, torch relay or opening ceremony of the Beijing Summer Olympic Games. However, regardless of sport project scenario and different life cycle stage requirements, project management techniques, such as critical path networks, can be used to effectively manage the various levels of complexity encountered.

PRACTICAL APPLICATION

Developed through the scientific management theories of the early 1900s, Gantt charts, named after their founder Henry Gantt, were initially applied to engineering and time-oriented productivity studies. Evolving from these were the critical path methodologies of the 1950s, which proved popular and successful in managing large national defence projects. Since then a variety of other project-based techniques and applications have developed, extending their use to a variety of sport management applications. For example, different time frames have included:

- Ten-year projects of bidding for, hosting and evaluating the Olympic Games. Hosts first used them at the 1988 Calgary Winter Olympics and then the 1992 Barcelona Summer Olympics. The International Olympic Committee used them to track the organizational progress of the 2000

134

Sydney Olympic Games, whilst the British Olympic Committee made use of them to prepare their team athletes for this event.

- One-year projects. Nike International has used Gantt charts and milestones to plan its global, regional and national new product launches.
- Daily focus. For example, the 1998 FIFA World Cup first used them to plan the operational practice of each match, with management scheduling planned to the minute.
- Unit measurement of less than ten seconds. Formula 1 teams have regularly applied project management techniques to analyse both individual and collective behaviour to reduce refuelling and full tyre change times during pit stops under high-level competitive race conditions.

In the contemporary climate of the sports world, where greater accountability and professionalism are the norm, project management techniques are seen to exist in projects ranging across planning and building a golf driving range, managing a national 'get fit' promotional campaign, or even carefully managing the release of tickets at a sporting world championship.

ASSUMPTIONS AND LIMITATIONS

To use critical path networks effectively there is the assumption that project boundaries and deliverables are known and that appropriate and competent resources are fully committed to the project as well as to its scheduled time frame. Whilst the essence of a project is that there are many unknowns, the usefulness of these techniques is clearly constrained by the accuracy of the data being input. In this sense plans should be live, flexible and constantly updated so that incremental planning ensues and more accurate detail can be provided as the project progresses across its life cycle.

As presented here, critical path network techniques and computer printouts are merely considered at an introductory and junior or middle management level. They therefore possess a number of practical limitations. These include the notions that risk is not assigned to any task, staff are often working on more than one project, and on completion of the network it may be identified that there is insufficient time available to complete the project by a designated date. However, all of these limitations can be overcome through more advanced coverage of the subject matter. This could for example include greater mastery of the software, as well as the learning of additional techniques such as 'resource levelling' and the process of 'crashing a network'.

PROCESS

There are five sequential steps required in the construction and analysis of critical path networks:

1 List the project tasks.
2 Estimate the duration and resource requirements of each task.
3 Determine the relationship between the tasks and draw the network diagram.
4 Calculate the critical path.
5 Update actual performance against the baseline plan.

APPLIED EXAMPLE

To demonstrate how to carry out these steps, let us act as the working management committee of a non-profit ice hockey club in Canada. The nine members of this committee are charged with the brief of their 200 members 'to project-manage a memorable one-off international hockey tournament to celebrate 50 years of the club's existence'. In bringing this idea to fruition, let us systematically elaborate upon each of these steps to illustrate how they can be applied in practice.

1 List the project tasks

Assuming that the scope and objectives of the project have already been agreed (see Chapter 3) the first stage of planning this non-routine project is to individually or collectively brainstorm the actions required to host the event. What are the tasks that need to be achieved to meet the project objectives? The easiest way to do this is to use a Post-it pad and write down each task on a separate Post-it. This approach begins with 'bottom-up' planning (starting with operational deliverables to complete a holistic plan) and is particularly useful in project scenarios given the inherent uncertainties and uniqueness of projects. Equally the same would apply to planning a very large and complex event such as a once-in-a-lifetime opportunity to manage Olympic, Commonwealth or Asian Games. Where do you start? Because of the immensity of the project and complexity of the unknowns, it is usually impossible to initially plan projects along top-down principles, even though the project owner is likely to establish certain milestones and key performance indicators or standards to protect the integrity and quality of the final delivery.

136

In the hockey example, first thoughts could include identifying tasks such as:

- Prepare proposal.
- Construct event budget.
- Obtain sponsorship.
- Arrange accommodation and transport.
- Invite teams.
- Appoint and train staff.
- Implement event.
- Clear up.

Note that at this level of analysis it is preferable to use tasks and include a verb in the component description (e.g. 'Approve proposal') rather than merely write down one-word activities such as 'Marketing'. The advantage is that the former focuses upon practical outcomes and deliverables, whereas the latter often proves too vague in application, particularly to final users.

Once the list is complete (to the level associated with the risk of the project outcome) the tasks need to be placed in some sense of order (see the more developed 'Tasks' column in Table 7.1, which will be classified as the primary tasks). This relates to the grouping of activities at one level of management that appears to be similar in nature as well as largely sequential.

The practical purpose of using Post-its to create order is because each task (Post-it) can be placed on a flat surface and moved around as many times as required to logically group tasks together. Grouping of tasks could take many forms, the more common being arranged by activity specialism (e.g. marketing or human resource management staff), by life cycle phase or sub-stage activities (as used in Table 7.1), by previously established cost sources or reporting mechanisms, or even, in smaller events where budgetary constraints drive the project, by arranging tasks according to essential or desirable tasks.

Questions frequently encountered relate to the quantity and level of task detail. Although this is very subjective, as a rule of thumb it is suggested to initially work with no than 20 primary tasks – any more will lead to complex manual drawings or printouts, particularly if project management is new to you. Furthermore, Verzuh (1999) refers to the 8/80 rule, which suggests that tasks normally should entail between 8 and 80 hours of work.

Greater depth of detail can always be attained from the technique of work breakdown structure (WBS). This decomposition technique involves

Table 7.1 Ice hockey event: basic management data

Tasks	Duration (in days)	Preceding task(s)	Staff
Pre-event phase			
1 Prepare proposal	14		Paul
2 Approve proposal	14	1	John and Mary
3 Staff event	1	2	Paul, Sam and Jo
4 Construct budget	3	3	Paul and Richard
5 Book facilities	7	2	Ellie
6 Obtain sponsorship	84	2	Paul and Richard
7 Arrange accommodation	7	4	Ellie
8 Establish regulations	7	2	Paul and Sam
9 Obtain sport approvals	28	8	John and Mary
10 Invite teams	70	9	Ellie
11 Implement promotional plan	28	6, 10	Sam, Jo and John
12 Determine equipment needs	7	5	Su and Paul
13 Develop social programme	7	7	John and Mary
14 Arrange transport	14	9	Paul and Aileen
15 Write up systems and manuals	14	9, 13	Paul and Aileen
16 Train staff	2	15	Paul and Mary
17 Prepare facility	7	16	Paul and Sam
Event phase			
18 Implement event	7	11, 12, 14, 17	All
Post-event phase			
19 Clear away	2	18	All
20 Debrief and evaluate	14	19	All

breaking tasks down into further manageable chunks of hierarchically structured activity by drilling down to subordinate levels of detail. In exactly the same way as a report uses headings and sub-headings to create more specific meaning, different levels are logically aligned, as demonstrated in Figure 7.2 with the example of the primary task of 'Obtain sponsorship'.

This technique is used particularly where there is a high degree of task uncertainty and where tasks are considered high-risk to the successful completion of the project. This is illustrated in the ice hockey example, where the key task of 'obtaining sponsorship' will probably determine whether or not the event will actually go ahead.

138

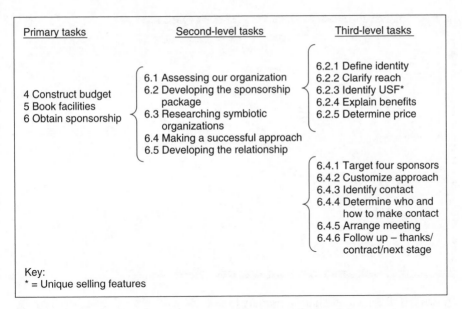

Primary tasks	Second-level tasks	Third-level tasks

4 Construct budget
5 Book facilities
6 Obtain sponsorship

6.1 Assessing our organization
6.2 Developing the sponsorship package
6.3 Researching symbiotic organizations
6.4 Making a successful approach
6.5 Developing the relationship

6.2.1 Define identity
6.2.2 Clarify reach
6.2.3 Identify USF*
6.2.4 Explain benefits
6.2.5 Determine price

6.4.1 Target four sponsors
6.4.2 Customize approach
6.4.3 Identify contact
6.4.4 Determine who and how to make contact
6.4.5 Arrange meeting
6.4.6 Follow up – thanks/ contract/next stage

Key:
* = Unique selling features

Figure 7.2 Example of work breakdown structure (WBS) levels

2 Estimate the duration and resource requirements of each task

This chronological to-do list forms the basis of the second and third steps of the critical path network process of planning. For example, and as illustrated in Table 7.1, against each of the tasks the estimated durations and persons involved with the completion of the task can be allocated (see 'Duration' and 'Staff' columns in Table 7.1). In this case staff can be assigned either personally or as a position. Such data can then be used to construct a Gantt chart, as illustrated in Figure 7.3.

Gantt charts in this basic format are a useful visual aid, as they identify all the required tasks against time. Chronologically they are read from left to right (time flow), with individual tasks being listed on the left-hand side and being read from top to bottom. The length of each horizontal bar is proportional to time. For example, Tasks 1 and 2 are the same length (14 days' duration), whereas the bars of Tasks 3, 4 and 5 are much shorter. This provides management with standard sequential information and with the added inclusion of resources (known as resource allocation) defines exactly who should be doing what and when.

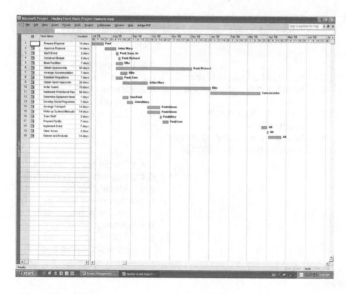

Figure 7.3 Basic Gantt chart of primary tasks

3 Determine the relationship between the tasks and draw the network diagram

Whilst Gantt charts in the 1900s provided basic scheduling information, project managers today demand greater depth of information, and this is where the scientific technique of activity sequencing developed. This involves determining task dependencies and the specific nature of the logical relationships between them. Put simply, tasks can either be carried out in a series (one after each other) or in parallel (simultaneously) and when presented as a whole collectively form a network – a diagram that shows the tasks of a project, their sequence, and the relationships between them.

However, to draw and interpret such a network a consistent and coherent form of symbols is required. To this end the most common form and the one used by most contemporary computer software packages will be described below, namely that of the precedent method. In this system each task or activity is represented by a box (classified as a node, which normally contains further information about the task) and is related to other tasks via one or more arrows. For the purpose of manually working through the applied example, each cell of the box will represent the information contained within Figure 7.4.

If we apply this example to primary Task 11, 'Implement promotional plan', for the hockey event scenario, the later, second-level tasks could include

140

Earliest start	Duration	Earliest finish
Task number and activity description		
Latest start	Float	Latest finish

Figure 7.4 Details contained within each task box

'Design poster', 'Approve poster', 'Print poster – colour 1', 'Print poster – colour 2' and 'Distribute poster'. In this case the tasks 'Design poster' and 'Approve poster' could be represented as illustrated in Figure 7.5.

At this stage do not worry about what the numbers mean, as they will be explained later. Suffice to say that the relationship between the two tasks in Figure 7.5 is suggested to use a finish to start (FS) logic. This means that before the poster can be approved (Task 11.7) the task of designing it (Task 11.6) must first be completed (Task 11.6 being classified as the predecessor and Task 11.7 the successor task). This logic is the most common encountered and is commonly the default of most software packages. But as illustrated in Figure 7.6 other possibilities exist, and these include the use of logic delays, start to start (SS) or finish to finish (FF) logic relationships.

To elaborate upon each in turn, a logic delay may relate to a task that cannot be worked on for a period of time. For example, the task of printing the second colour of the poster (Task 11.9) cannot be undertaken until the task of printing the first colour (Task 11.8) has been completed. In addition there is the time required for the print to dry, which in this case is 1 day and represented by the number (a logic delay) written on top of the arrow.

Regarding the SS relationship, once the second colour of the poster has been printed a one-day logic delay again exists for drying purposes. Equally, half of the allocation of posters can be started to be distributed before Task 11.9 is complete.

FF relationships are quite rare but can be illustrated with lower- and higher-order tasks. With 'Implement promotional plan' (Task 11) as the higher-order

80	5	85
11.6 DESIGN POSTER		
90	10	95

→

85	2	87
11.7 APPROVE POSTER		
95	10	97

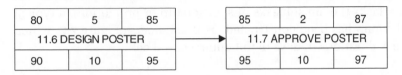

Figure 7.5 Node examples

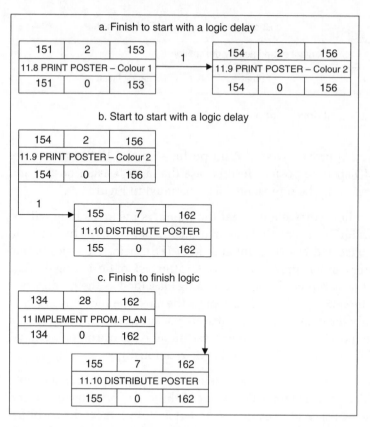

Figure 7.6 Alternative logic relationships to start to finish logic

task, as soon as the 'Distribute poster' task (Task 11.10) has been completed then the higher-order task (Task 11) is by definition also complete, and hence the description of a finish to finish relationship.

To understand as well as construct such diagrams with the accompanying logic, always note exactly where the arrow leaves and joins the respective boxes as well as note whether any logic delays exist via any number that is written on the arrow.

Using the applied example, and manually constructing the network of just the primary tasks (i.e. no subtasks of sponsorship or promotion), a typical network diagram has been constructed, as illustrated in Figure 7.7, which includes task durations in days in the upper central cell.

142

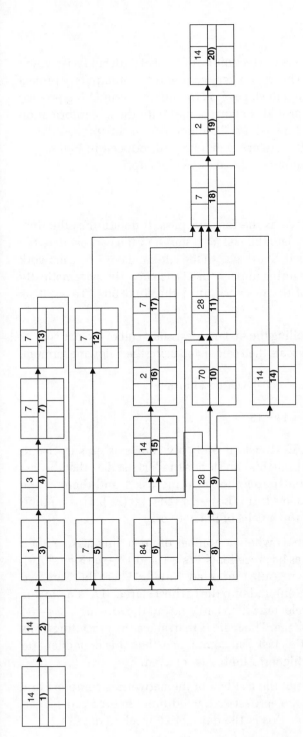

Figure 7.7 Constructing the network diagram

4 Calculate the critical path

This stage of the process covers the technique of critical path analysis, which is often considered to be the heart and very essence of contemporary project management. Involving four sub-stages it is the number-crunching process of the planning phase and provides management with the key information in which to make informed decisions. To demonstrate this process let us again refer to the case study network previously introduced in Figure 7.7. (N.B. Task names have been removed to ease readership.)

Calculate the earliest time

The first calculation is known as the forward pass. It determines the time schedule where the earliest date the task can start and the earliest date the project can finish are identified. Starting with the left-hand box of the network (Task 1) it calculates the remaining upper cells of each node by systematically moving along each path of the network until the final box (Task 20) is complete (see Figure 7.8).

The process begins with labelling the first 'earliest start' cell of the network as day 1. All upper cells of the box are then calculated using the following formula:

Earliest start (ES) + Duration (D) = Earliest finish (EF)

E.g. Task 1 equates to 1 + 14 = 15

Following the arrow to the next task, it probably comes as no surprise to understand that the earliest time this can start is the earliest date that the last task finished, i.e. Task 2 transposes the 15 from Task 1 and then, as the forward pass continues, equates to 15 (ES) + 14 (D) = 29 (EF). This method progresses across all of the upper cells of the network.

The first problem that occurs is where a number of preceding tasks enter a box (e.g. Task 15, which has as its precedents Tasks 9 and 13 – see Figure 7.8). Where this occurs the following rule is applied. Rule 1: Where there are two or more numbers that can be entered into the earliest start cell of a node it is the highest number that is selected when carrying out the forward pass – 64 as opposed to 47 in this instance. The logic is that, since the preceding tasks have to be complete before this task can commence, then it is dependent on the last task, and hence the highest number is selected.

Once the earliest finish time of the last box of the network is complete this provides the manager with the earliest estimated time that the project can finish. In the applied example this is 185 days, or 26 weeks 3 days.

144

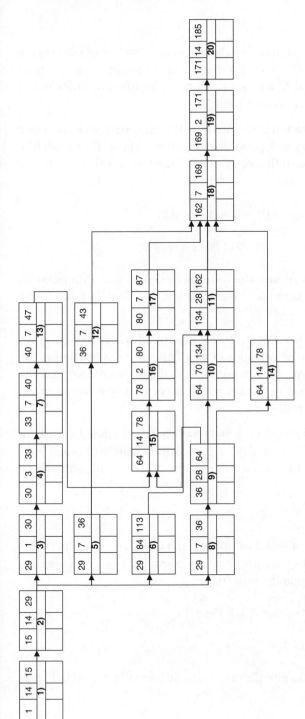

Figure 7.8 Calculating the forward pass

Calculate the latest time

Once the earliest project finish date is determined, the backward pass can be undertaken (see Figure 7.9). This provides the manager with the time schedule where the latest date a task can start is identified in order not to delay the earliest project completion date.

The first stage of this calculation is to transpose the number from the earliest finish cell of the last network task (Task 20) to that of the latest finish cell (the lower cell of Task 20). As with the forward pass, the lower cells of each task are completed using the formula:

Latest finish (LF) – Duration (D) = Latest start (LS)

E.g. Task 20 equates to 185 – 14 = 171 (see Figure 7.9)

Follow each arrow backwards and again insert the latest start number with that of the latest finish number of the preceding box, e.g. Task 19 latest finish cell is 171.

Similar in nature to the forward pass, Rule 2 is applied where there are two or more numbers that could be transposed (see Tasks 9 and 2 in Figure 7.9). Rule 2: Where there are two or more numbers that can be entered into the latest finish cell of a node it is the lowest number that is selected when carrying out the backward pass.

Complete this process until all network tasks have been calculated. Check for accuracy by making sure that in Task 1 the earliest start and latest start numbers are the same, i.e. day 1 of the project. If they are not, identify where a mistake has occurred.

Calculate the float

Completing the lower cells of each box now entails calculating the float. This is the difference between the time necessary to complete a task and the time available and is calculated via the formula:

Earliest start (ES) – Latest start (LS) = Float (F)

E.g. Task 2 equates to 1 – 1 = 0

Calculate the float for all tasks and the result should be as illustrated in Figure 7.10.

146

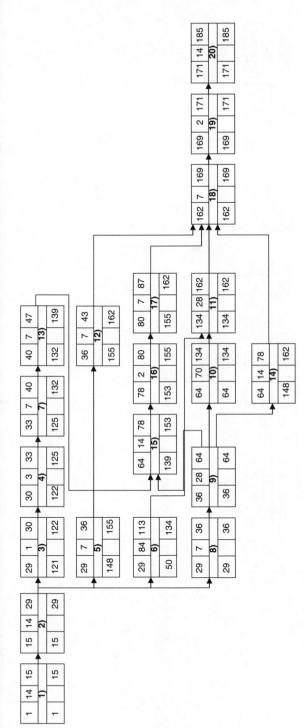

Figure 7.9 Calculating the backward pass

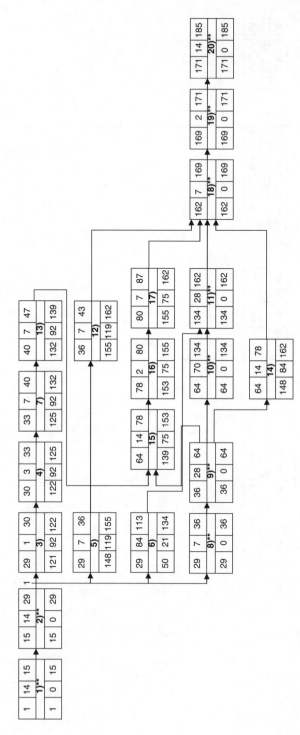

Figure 7.10 Calculating the float and determining the critical path

Determine the critical path

Now that the manual calculation of the network is complete, the critical path or in some cases paths of the project can then be determined. This relates to the longest possible time the network will take to complete without altering the earliest finish date. The critical path is identified by all the consecutive tasks that have a float of zero – in the example provided the single critical path (marked with a ** in Figure 7.10) consists of Tasks 1, 2, 8, 9, 10, 11, 18, 19 and 20.

Once the activities that lie on the critical path have been identified, what does it all mean? How can such techniques and diagrammatic representation assist you to successfully complete projects on budget and schedule and to exceed the required quality expectations? Using the case study information provided in Figure 7.10, the following important management information can be drawn from this manual representation:

■ Based upon the composite tasks and their relationship, the earliest that the event can take place is 162 days from the start date (as indicated by the earliest start cell of Task 18). Similarly the earliest the total project can be undertaken is 185 days (Task 20, earliest finish cell).
■ To meet this schedule all the tasks of the critical path must be implemented immediately the last predecessor is finished. These are the priority tasks of the network and, if they fall behind schedule, urgent action is required to determine whether the quality standard is reduced, the project can be delayed, or additional resource is required to bring the project back on schedule.
■ Other tasks, such as Tasks 3, 5 and 16, have considerable amounts of float and hence could take slippage. In Task 3's case, whilst the earliest time it can be started is 29 days, it actually could start as late as day 121 of the project without causing a delay in the 185-day project completion.

Fortunately the computer can calculate and construct similar calculations and diagrams as well as make numerous changes at the touch of a button. For example, all the information in Table 7.1, including the 'Preceding task(s)' column, can be entered into user-friendly project management software and be assigned specific calendar dates rather than merely refer just to numbers. Once input, normally in matrix format and either scheduled forward from today's date or backwards from a predetermined finish date, a wide breadth of display and printout is possible. Examples of these printouts are illustrated in the annotated Figures 7.11 to 7.15.

149

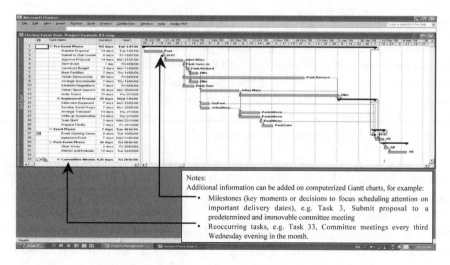

Figure 7.11 Case study Gantt chart

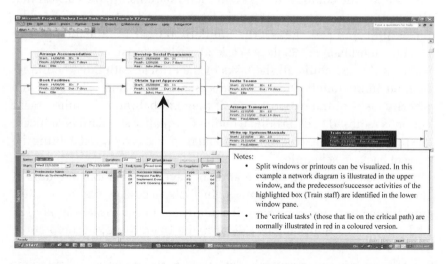

Figure 7.12 Case study network diagram and predecessor/successor tasks

5 Update actual performance against the baseline plan

A further advantage of using computers over the historical manual system is that information can be used to change and update task progress very quickly, without the need to manually redraw the network each time. For example, Figure 7.15 illustrates a tracking Gantt chart that identifies which tasks are

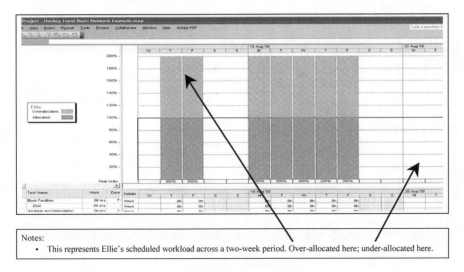

Figure 7.13 Case study resource histogram and usage

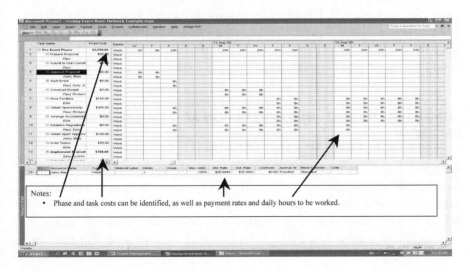

Figure 7.14 Case study cost information

complete and which tasks are behind schedule. Whilst the reality is that some tasks can be completed ahead of schedule (e.g. Task 3, where it was identified that approval could be given outside of the committee cycle), others will naturally fall behind (e.g. Task 7, where the person responsible for this was unable to get an answer before he or she went on holiday). For effective management to take place it is important to identify both

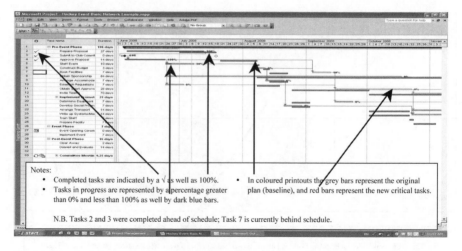

Figure 7.15 Case study tracking Gantt chart

occurrences early on. However, in the latter case, with Task 7 it is now particularly important, because the computer has rescheduled the activity, defining it as a critical task. It is this continuous comparison of actual practice against the original plan (baseline) that permits management to take remedial and appropriate action to get the project back on schedule.

COMPUTER PRINTOUT INTERPRETATION AND MANAGEMENT DECISION

With the information that can be derived from manual networks already determined, what additional information can you access from these computer printouts? Just a few examples as applied to the case study will suffice to highlight how the visual information can assist you with your decision making. From analysis of Figures 7.11 to 7.15 it is evident that the information identifies:

- Who carries out which task? For example, Figure 7.11 reveals that Paul and Richard are responsible for obtaining sponsorship, clearly defining personal levels of accountability. This provides improved communication and potentially better cooperation.
- Task priorities, their interdependence and key deadlines. Figures 7.11 and 7.12 for example highlight predecessor and successor tasks, milestones such as the 50th anniversary and event date (10 January 2009), and the critical tasks that make this date possible. If Gantt charts or

152

network diagrams are perceived to be difficult to understand the timing of tasks can be presented in a calendar format at the touch of a button.

■ Over-/under-allocation of tasks. From Figure 7.13 it can be identified that Ellie cannot give 200 per cent of her time – clearly this a case of over-allocation. Is there someone else who is under-allocated at this time (in the same way as she is not allocated any work the week after) to assist her? Alternatively, and with the costs identified in Figure 7.14, knowing this information in advance can help in determining whether the position should be offered on a casual, part-time or full-time basis. Such information can also help in avoiding potential overruns and stressful situations by rescheduling people or extending the duration of tasks to level out human resource peaks and troughs.

■ Whether the project is behind schedule, ahead of schedule or on track to meet its scheduled finish date. Figure 7.15 for example draws management attention to the fact that booking the facilities (Task 7) has not been undertaken. The task is vital, since without facilities the event will not take place. The good news though is that, although the task is behind schedule, if carried out immediately, since it is now deemed a critical activity, the event can still meet its quality and time-oriented specifications.

COMMON MISTAKES

So what are the common mistakes that inexperienced people make when using critical path networks? On the one hand mistakes can relate to the input of information. As previously mentioned, the accuracy of task knowledge and time estimates is vital for project success, since these often drive important deadlines as well as profit margins. However, the very essence of sport projects, typically involving a high dependency on volunteers, means that achieving the project's quality objectives is usually reliant on untrained staff. Whilst everyone wants to be positive and perceived as professional and reliable, they generally talk up early completion task durations and percentage progress rates. The reality is that in the complex environment of managing sport projects few people accurately meet their targeted schedules. This error can be reduced by at least communicating or ideally involving experienced personnel to determine realistic task requirements as well as durations. Additionally durations could automatically build a 10 per cent estimating error into them, the very principle behind the specialist application of the programme evaluation and review technique (PERT) methodology (a formula of applying three different estimates, a most optimistic, most pessimistic and realistic estimate of each task duration).

Another common mistake, particularly for the novice project manager, is that networks are constructed with several starting or ending nodes or conversely unconnected tasks. Remember that if tasks do not have relationships attached to them then they are by definition irrelevant to the project.

SUMMARY

In conclusion, there are many benefits of using critical path network techniques and project management software. These include:

- Complexity and uncertainty can be broken down into manageable chunks or tasks of activity from which more realistic time and resource estimates can be planned.
- A clear visual representation can highlight how external and internal tasks are linked, and how individual roles fit into the broader picture of managing the project or event.
- Over- and under-resource utilization can be identified and remedied early on in the planning process.
- Critical activities (priorities) can be established, problem areas can be determined, and 'What if?' scenarios can be planned.
- Progress can be tracked against the plan, and variance can be appropriately identified and then managed accordingly.

To effectively construct critical path networks, five sequential steps need to be followed:

1 List the project tasks.
2 Estimate the duration and resource requirements of each task.
3 Determine the relationship between the tasks and draw the network diagram.
4 Calculate the critical path.
5 Update actual performance against the baseline plan.

On the other hand, limitations of any technique need to be recognized. For example:

- Large projects involve many thousands of tasks, and it may prove impossible to identify task dependencies and vertical linkages.
- The subject matter of project management is jargonized, and for many the software is complicated; hence in combination usage might appear somewhat daunting.

154

Furthermore in using any unfamiliar software there is always a trade-off between time spent entering data into a computer and implementing practical management actions. The software will obviously involve a start-up cost, in terms of both finance and time, e.g. the software cost and the learning curve respectively. However, the advantages can far outweigh the disadvantages, particularly when the techniques are used as a means to an end and not an end in themselves.

You probably need to derive your own criteria as to the circumstances when these techniques could assist you. Determining factors are likely to be the project complexity, the resource involvement, the risk level encountered, the staff experience, and the decision-making time available. For example, it is perhaps unlikely that you would use project management software to plan an event involving just ten tasks or a local five-a-side football tournament that you have organized for the last four years. Alternatively, you would perhaps use it to plan the opening ceremony of a brand new sport centre or a national sports event that is being shown live on television. Unfortunately though, and it has to be said, completing any project on time, to budget and to exceed quality specifications appears to be a rarity these days. Using critical path networks can make the difference between project success and failure.

Guides to further resources, useful web links and guideline answers to all the self-test questions featured in this chapter are available on a companion website at www.routledge.com/9780415491594.

SELF-TEST QUESTION

Calculate the forward pass and the backward pass, and determine the earliest time the project can be finished. Which activities make up the critical path of the network illustrated in Figure 7.16?

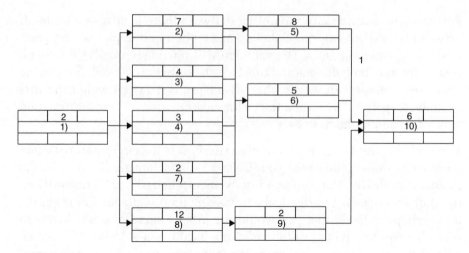

Figure 7.16 Manual calculation

CHAPTER 8

PLANNING FOR PROFIT: IDENTIFYING WHERE WE MAKE MONEY

TECHNIQUE DESCRIPTION

Most people are in business to make a profit. Whilst many sports organizations turn over large revenues, they often run at a loss. Sport managers need to know which of their products and services are profitable and which are not. In the latter case, important questions need to be asked, such as at what sales volume could you make a profit and, conversely, what might be the effect of changing the selling price to achieve designated financial objectives?

As an accounting tool, break-even analysis (BEA) calculates the break-even point (BEP) at which your total revenue covers your operating costs. In other words it identifies the point at which your production volume makes neither a profit nor a loss and from then onwards any increase in sales commences profit generation.

Determined graphically or by using a mathematical formula, BEA requires a fundamental understanding of the concepts of fixed costs (the total cost used to produce the first product or service), variable or marginal costs (the cost of producing every additional product or service) and the unit selling price (the amount charged to the customer to purchase the product or service).

Since the nature of this mathematical modelling involves predicting future sales and costs, some degree of uncertainty is inevitable. To control the changes and errors that may occur with the input data, the techniques of sensitivity analysis (the process of systematically changing the key quantitative assumptions and computations on the final outcome) and establishing the margin of safety (the amount by which the selected level of activity differs from the break-even point) commonly accompany the BEA process. These enhance the robustness and reliability of the output findings and hence improve the financial viability of the ensuing business decisions.

To further explore the relationship between income and expenditure or more specifically sales volume, costs and profits, this chapter will introduce you to cost and revenue calculations and the principle of contribution and through an applied example illustrate the process of preparing and interpreting break-even and profit/volume graphs.

PURPOSE

Since the break-even point determines the lowest limit when determining profit margins it assists managers to better understand and potentially minimize costs and maximize profits (Osgood, 2010). More specifically, given that management has virtually no control over the market or fixed costs, your profitability level is largely dependent on you effectively managing your variable costs as well as influencing your sales volume.

As a valuable pre-budgeting tool, BEA identifies the potential cash flow of each product or service and attempts to predict when your investment will make a positive return (Gutierrez and Dalsted, 2010). This allows sport managers:

- to establish and communicate through visual displays (break-even or profit/volume graphs) or through algebraic calculations, practical financial targets derived from the break-even point and the organization's accepted level of margin of safety;
- to accurately formulate pricing policies to achieve desired profit levels;
- to demonstrate the effect of various changes (sales volume, variable and fixed costs, and selling price) and 'What if?' scenarios on the profitability of a product or service;
- to compare profit potential returns on competing short- and long-term investments.

By appraising a product's cost, pricing and hence profit structure, BEA is relevant to nearly all financial plans and decisions (Stewart, 2007). In summary, managers who know how to apply such techniques can better understand, plan and control budgeted profits as well as manage 'What if?' scenarios should they occur.

158

THEORETICAL OVERVIEW

Break-even analysis, or cost–volume–profit (CVP) analysis as it is sometimes known, is the traditional approach to business financial forecasting or profitability analysis (Potter, Morse, Davis and Hartgraves, 2004). Focusing upon unit-level cost drivers, the technique examines the relationship between total costs, total revenues, sales volumes and profits over a set time period, usually an accounting quarter or year. Based upon marginal cost theory (the cost incurred to produce one additional unit), it assumes linear cost functions (remains constant regardless of output) and makes a distinction between fixed and variable costs (Steven, 2005).

Fixed costs (FC) are those that do not vary with sales volume or production output, but rather relate to a lump sum confined to a period of time. They are charged regardless of any memberships, tickets or sales being made. For example, it could cost £1,000 per night to hire a room for an annual sports presentation function regardless of whether 500 people attend or no one purchases a ticket. Commonly referred to as overheads, business expenses, outgoings or operating expenses (Small Business Development Corporation, 2010a), fixed costs typically include items such as rent, mortgages, licences, computers, permanent staff salaries, utilities and insurance, which are often required even before your first sale. Let us assume for the purpose of this example that these total £2,500 for the sports presentation function.

Variable costs (VC), on the other hand, vary with sales and production output. For example, to feed every person who attends the presentation you will incur an additional cost, such as £30 per head. These costs, sometimes referred to as your cost of sales or direct, operating, prime or on-costs, are likely to be recurring costs such as the cost of consumables, catering, giveaways, and casual staff that are absorbed within every unit of sale (Richards, 2010).

When the fixed and variable costs are added together at a particular sales volume, they indicate the total costs and can be written in formula format as:

1) Total cost (TC) = Fixed cost (FC) + Variable cost (VC)

For example, at maximum room capacity (500 people) the total costs are:

TC = £2,500 (FC) + £30 × 500 (VC) = £17,500

In comparison, at 100 and 10 ticket sales respectively the total costs are:

TC = £2,500 (FC) + £30 × 100 (VC) = £5,500

TC = £2,500 (FC) + £30 × 10 (VC) = £2,800

159

Having considered the expenditure side of the BEA equation, we now need to address the income-producing element to determine the profit or loss of the venture:

2) Profit or loss = Sales value (SV) – Total costs (TC)

This initially requires establishing a unit selling price (USP), since the sales value or revenue constitutes the quantity of sales multiplied by the USP. For example, let us assume that, for the sports presentation function, tickets will be sold at £60 per person (USP). From such data we can calculate likely sales values at different volumes, e.g. 10 sales × £60 (USP) = £600 (SV); 50 sales = £3,000 (SV); 100 sales = £6,000 (SV); 500 sales = £30,000 (SV).

This would therefore provide the following cash flows:

@ 500 ticket sales £30,000 (SV) – £17,500 (TC) = £12,500 profit

@ 100 ticket sales £6,000 (SV) – £5,500 (TC) = £500 profit

@ 10 ticket sales £600 (SV) – £2,800 (TC) = £2,200 loss

Whilst random sales volumes can be selected to determine absolute calculations of profit or loss, the calculation of the break-even point is of more use to the discerning sport manager, since it provides the fulcrum of profit generation.

Fundamental to the understanding of appraising the break-even point is the important principle of contribution (Jagels, 2007). Defined as the excess of sales over variable cost (Kotas, 1999), it is based upon the principle that every sale provides a contribution towards covering fixed costs and profit. Contribution therefore can be mathematically written as:

3) Contribution (C) = Sales value (SV) – Variable costs (VC)

4) Contribution (C) = Profit (P) + Fixed costs (FC)

$$5) \text{ Contribution/sales ratio} = \frac{\text{Contribution (C)}}{\text{Sales (S)}}$$

(sometimes referred to as the profit/volume ratio)

N.B. These formulae can be transposed, since knowing any two parameters means that the third can be calculated.

160

Calculating the contribution per unit permits identification of the break-even point (BEP) mathematically, which can be stated in terms of either units or monetary value using the formulae:

$$6) \text{ BEP (units)} = \frac{\text{Fixed cost (FC)}}{\text{Contribution per unit (C)}}$$

Alternatively:

$$\text{BEP (units)} = \frac{\text{Fixed cost (FC)}}{\text{Unit selling price (USP)} - \text{Unit variable cost (VC)}}$$

$$7) \text{ BEP (monetary value)} = \text{Fixed cost (FC)} \times \frac{\text{Sales (S)}}{\text{Contribution (C)}}$$

Equally such data can be plotted graphically with both measures being read off the x and y axes respectively as illustrated in Figure 8.1.

For example, at a given average sales price of £60 per person and a cost structure of £2,500 total fixed costs and £30 unit variable cost, the predicted BEP is 83.34 units or £5,000 in monetary value. This means that you have to sell at least 84 tickets (receive £5,040 in ticket revenue) to at least cover all

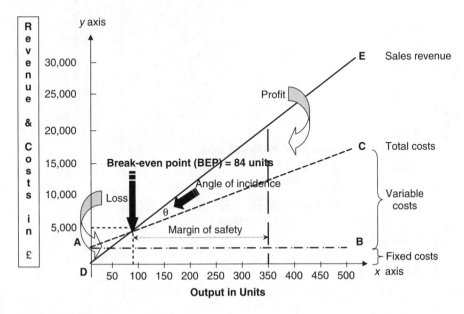

Figure 8.1 Break-even graph

of your costs. Every additional ticket sold after this contributes to you establishing a profit.

A simpler diagrammatic representation of BEA can be displayed by using profit/volume ratios and presenting the data graphically as illustrated in Figure 8.2.

Profit/volume graphs do not separate fixed and variable costs; rather they just identify the total costs and revenue at two activity levels (usually at zero sales (F) and one other random point (G)). Connecting these points with a straight line reveals the break-even point, i.e. the point where this line intersects with the x axis.

In both break-even and profit/volume graphs, production levels less than the BEP mean that a financial loss will be incurred, whereas anything greater indicates profit generation.

Further information to be extrapolated from these graphs is the margin of safety (MoS) and the angle of incidence (AoI). As illustrated in Figures 8.1 and 8.2, the MoS relates to the safety net, the quantity of units or value for

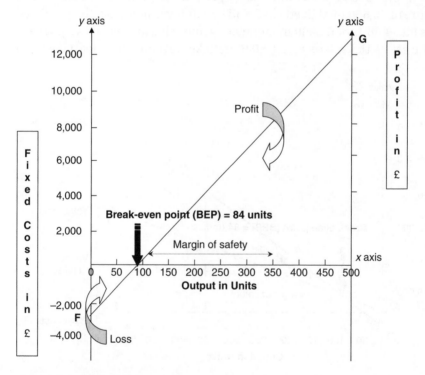

Figure 8.2 Profit/volume graph

162

which the realistically estimated sales or production level differs from the BEP. For example, let us assume that the last three years have enjoyed a minimum attendance of 350 persons, which implies that this year will be the same and hence there is a heavy confidence level of exceeding the BEP and making a profit. If the MoS is small, management needs to be aware that a little reduction in sales or production could have a disastrous effect on profit. Mathematically this can be calculated using the formulae:

$$8) \text{ Margin of safety (units)} = \frac{\text{Profit}}{\text{Contribution}} \times \text{Sales units}$$

$$9) \text{ Margin of safety (monetary value)} = \text{Profit} \times \frac{\text{Sales}}{\text{Contribution}}$$

Similarly the AoI, defined as the angle between the revenue line and the total cost line (DE and AC respectively in Figure 8.1), indicates the speed or efficiency level at which profit is made. A narrow angle (e.g. less than 30 per cent) reflects low profit margins, highlighting the fact that profits accrue slowly and many more sales may be required to break even. Collectively the MoS and AoI are efficiency indicators that help to determine the financial strength and robust nature of the decision to go ahead, particularly when you compare realistic market sales estimates with the calculated BEP.

A further method of establishing the accuracy and hence risk attached to the calculated data is by applying sensitivity analysis techniques. This involves recalculating the data by using for example up to 15 per cent positive and negative changes in the equations. For example, what would be the impact on the BEP if the price of a sale was reduced by 15 per cent or fixed costs increased by 15 per cent? This provides more complete and realistic data through which management can employ a broad array of market-driven competitive strategies, tactics and practices to suit the short- and long-term financial goals.

PRACTICAL APPLICATION

In the contemporary business climate, where greater levels of professionalism and accountability have become the norm, breaking even is often considered the financial bottom line to so many management decisions. It is used in both the profit and the non-profit sport sectors. Potter, Morse, Davis and Hartgraves (2004) suggest that break-even analysis can assist management to address practical questions such as:

- What sales volume will allow me to break even?
- How many x's do I need to sell to make a profit of £y?
- What will happen if current costs increase by 20 per cent and I increase the sales price by 10 per cent?
- How many free or concessionary sales can I offer with an annual budget of £y?
- Given the current cost structure, how much additional money do I need to raise so as not to incur a financial loss?

Break-even analysis applications are numerous. For example, Stewart (2007) suggests break-even analysis is particularly useful for establishing the feasibility of event management and sport service delivery programmes – what attendance is required and at what ticket price for what level of commercial success? Osgood (2010) similarly holds that BEA is a critical and invaluable planning, decision-making and expense control tool that can be used to determine whether to buy or lease equipment, change a pricing structure, close unprofitable strategic business units (see Chapter 6) or even appraise long-term capital investment decisions (see Chapter 9).

Furthermore, financial reports used by general and production managers, accountants, lenders and investors are based upon break-even income and expenditure data being applied to each and every product or service of the business. Without such information, decisions relating to pricing and sales volumes, the sales mix, cost structures and the all-encompassing operational budget are likely to be fundamentally flawed (Carter, Macdonald and Cheng, 1997).

ASSUMPTIONS AND LIMITATIONS

Whilst the strength of the break-even analysis technique is that it indicates the lowest amount of business activity necessary to prevent losses (Gutierrez and Dalsted, 2010), the accuracy of the findings are based upon three key assumptions (Berry, 2010):

1   The average per-unit sales price (per-unit revenue). This refers to the price, including discounts, received per unit of sales, and is derived from the sales forecast. This is not necessarily easy to calculate, particularly when most businesses sell more than one product and at many different prices, e.g. the range of ticket prices at a professional tennis tournament.
2   The average variable cost (per-unit cost). This is the incremental cost of each sales unit and is usually calculated over time by analysing a large number of sales to ensure estimate accuracy.

164

3   The fixed costs. The operating expenses or costs incurred regardless of output. These are often based upon profit and loss calculations and sometimes become more complicated owing to stepped costs. For example, hiring a 53-seater coach will be the same cost whether there is one or 53 passengers to transport. However, just one additional passenger requires another coach. Some costs therefore include both fixed and variable costs within their calculation.

Given the inherent assumptions contained within break-even analysis, the findings must only be considered accurate to the limits and estimates provided. Extrapolations sometimes prove problematic, particularly when an increase in sales volume is often accompanied by a reduction in the selling price. Furthermore the long-term return on investment (covered in Chapter 9) is not recognized in these calculations. This leads Ndaliman and Bala (2007) to propose that the technique possesses a variety of limitations, which include:

■   Whilst the technique has been used for multiple-product situations it is ideally suited to the analysis of one product at one moment in time, since multi-product sales tactics (e.g. loss leaders) cannot be easily included in the calculations.
■   The revenue and costs are not necessarily constants; therefore true linear relationships may not exist in practice, particularly where quantity discounts are commonly encountered in the industry.
■   It may be difficult to classify a cost as being entirely variable or all fixed.
■   Input data are usually based upon past experience, which may not necessarily predict the future, particularly where new sport events involve considerable uncertainty and/or may be directly influenced by inclement weather.
■   BEA assumes that opening and closing inventories are not significant. However, particularly over accounting periods, they could be, with unsold stock directly affecting profit calculations.
■   The technique predominantly focuses on the supply side and just one cost driver. What about other demand-side revenue drivers, such as price elasticity, number of customer visits or sales, and the nature of competitor activity, or other cost drivers, such as the number of units or batches produced?

Such limitations can be overcome or at least reduced by using more advanced techniques such as calculating variable costs through regression analysis techniques, including demand-side revenue drivers, and graphically plotting true revenue and cost data as a curve rather than with the currently assumed linear relationship. In practice, break-even analysis is a very common and well-established concept used in all aspects of the sport industry.

PROCESS THROUGH AN APPLIED EXAMPLE

Using the following fictitious case study, let us demonstrate two graphical and one mathematical method of calculating the break-even point of a newly planned sport video analysis business in Japan.

Let us imagine that you are looking at the feasibility of starting a part-time business, initially to complement your full-time job. It will be built upon your 20-year extensive sport coaching experience and your hobby of high-quality video/DVD production. If it is successful in the first year of operation, you may wish it to become your full-time job. Operating up to 50 weekends across the year, you decide to offer a highly customized sport analysis and improvement service to the thousands of individuals who passionately wish to improve their weekly sport performances. This entails you filming one hour of them participating in their chosen sport, followed by a two-hour editing process, and then a further hour to produce an in-depth critical analysis of their performance and possible improvements via a professionally written report. Given the time involved and limited availability owing to your full-time job, the maximum clients that you accommodate each weekend is four. You have visited a few retail stores and estimate that starting the business will cost you £2,000 for DVD/video equipment, insurance, promotion and so on, and producing each DVD will cost you approximately £25, but you will allow an additional £5 for unseen variable costs. This you hope will reduce with time as a result of learning experience and economies of scale. Currently you are working on an introductory market entrance selling price of just £60, but you believe that this can be increased once word of mouth and customer satisfaction are established.

Break-even graph/chart

The generic process of graphically displaying the break-even point using a break-even graph involves four tasks:

1   labelling and scaling the axes;
2   determining and plotting the costs;

166

3   estimating the revenue from different sales levels;

4   identifying the break-even point and margin of safety.

1 Labelling and scaling the axes

The first step entails constructing the graph parameters, namely the two axes. As illustrated in Figure 8.3, the x or horizontal axis represents the output (recorded either in actual quantities or as a percentage of maximum capacity) and the y or vertical axis represents the financial revenue and costs (as measured in local currency).

These axes need to be appropriately scaled to ensure that the break-even point can be accurately extrapolated and that realistic outputs can be achieved. This requires that the limiting factor of the output should be established, in terms of either input or demand capacity. In the sport video scenario there is an input limiting factor of four clients per weekend or 200 per year (50 weekends × 4). In other situations there may be a maximum stadium or room capacity for ticket sales, as determined by fire regulations, or limited availability owing to sporting or demand considerations. Illustrating the latter point with a more appropriate example, we might assess the weekend usage and break-even point of a synthetic pitch across a sport season. The local senior league football games will typically constitute a

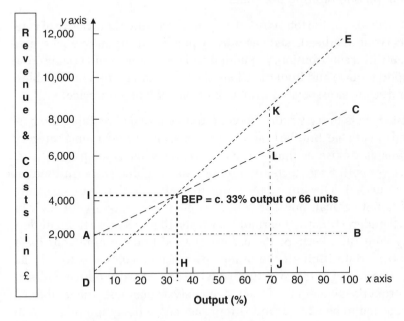

Figure 8.3 Constructing a break-even graph

maximum duration of 2 hours (i.e. 90 minutes' playing time + 30 minutes' warm-up, interlude and injury time = 120 minutes) and customers are unlikely to want to play outside the 9 a.m. to 9 p.m. time slot (demand factors), so the estimated maximum output we could achieve per weekend would be 12 bookings or sales (6 each day). Across a season (say 20 weeks) this creates a maximum usage of 240 football bookings.

Determining such limiting factors provides the outer parameter of the x axis scale and consequently explains why many break-even charts label this axis in terms of percentage output (see Figure 8.3). Knowing or estimating the 100 per cent output parameter allows you to calculate the likely maximum y axis value, particularly in terms of revenue. For example, in the video analysis scenario the best-case income is 200 videos × £60 selling price = £12,000. Alternatively, in the synthetic pitch example, assuming an average market value price for hiring a synthetic pitch (excluding floodlighting) is £150 per hour then the maximum potential income derived from this asset alone is £72,000 per season (i.e. 240 @ 2-hour bookings). Whilst optimum capacity is rarely achieved in practice, this enables you at least to start with a graphical scale from which further cost and revenue detail as well as management decisions can be made.

2 Determining and plotting the costs

Accurately calculating the total costs of any project requires knowledge of your fixed costs (your overheads such as video camera, editing suite, insurance, mortgage, utilities contribution, promotion and so on) and your variable costs (the transport costs to and from the client, the video and report consumables, postage and so on, as associated with making one unit of the service).

So the first stage is to try to allocate your known costs, classifying them as either fixed or variable. Similarly and as previously mentioned some category duplications may exist, as they are semi-variable, such as telephone costs, which possess both fixed costs (line rental) and variable costs (individual call or line usage). The important point to realize is that how costs are classified is not critical, but it will have some impact upon your BEP. In particular, underestimating variable costs is likely to result in under-estimating your BEP. Perhaps the easiest method to determine your fixed costs – and by definition all the others are variable costs – is to ask the question: what is the total cost that we will incur if we produce and sell nothing? From the given data of the video analysis business, the total fixed cost is suggested to be £2,000, and is represented on the graph (Figure 8.3) by a horizontal line (AB) drawn parallel to the x axis at point £2,000 (y axis).

168

To service the average client (a person living within a 30-kilometre radius of your home) you have calculated that the worst-case scenario for variable costs is £30 per unit. Since we already know that variable costs do not exist at zero output, we now need to find a second point to be able to draw a straight total cost line. This random point is normally calculated at maximum capacity (100 per cent or 200 units output), i.e. 200 units @ £30 per unit = £6,000. Since total costs = variable costs + fixed costs, we draw a line from point A (Figure 8.3), the fixed cost point of intersection of the y axis, to maximum capacity point C = £8,000, i.e. £6,000 (VC) + £2,000 (FC). Total costs are thus represented on the graph as anything below line AC and can be extrapolated so that we can understand practical cash flow needs at any particular output level, e.g. the 50 per cent output level will incur total costs and hence the available finance required for this production level is £5,000.

3 Estimating the revenue from different sales levels

Understanding revenue streams and the factors that affect them is the cornerstone of financial management decisions. Since sales value or revenue = unit selling price × sales volume, any calculation starts with knowledge of the sales price. In the sport video example, there is only one product under consideration and one unit selling price, namely £60. With a maximum capacity of 200 units per year we have already established that the best-case revenue scenario is £12,000 (£60 @ 200). Using such data, the sales revenue line (DE) can be plotted (Figure 8.3). This straight line is drawn from the intersection of the x and y axis (point D) (at an output level of zero there is clearly no revenue) to the 100 per cent maximum capacity revenue plot of £12,000 (point E).

Where there are variable ticket prices such as different seats in a stadium, as well as concessionary, quantity, loyalty or off-peak discounts, the average mix and price need to be determined. This can be calculated from previous sales data (e.g. last-event ticket sales: full (60 per cent) versus concessionary (40 per cent) price at each seating category, divided by the total number of tickets sold), or the ratio of the product mix has to be estimated if this is the first time the event will be held. The important point to realize is that a revenue line needs to be estimated and drawn to indicate different levels of outputs.

4 Identifying the break-even point and margin of safety

Where the total cost line (AC) and the sales revenue line (DE) intersect is the break-even point. This can be measured either in terms of production output (percentage or units), by drawing a vertical line down to the x axis (H), or in monetary value, by drawing a horizontal line to the y axis (I). Reading these values crudely from the graph displayed in Figure 8.3 provides us with an approximate BEP of 33 per cent of unit output (i.e. 66 units) or £4,200. Clearly the accuracy of these figures can be improved with detailed graphs. From a management perspective, any output less than this percentage or lower than this revenue value will indicate that you will make a financial loss, whereas anything more will indicate a profit.

Sometimes the margin of safety (the range of output over which a profit can be sustained) is additionally considered. This is to determine the relative impact on reduced sales should unforeseen circumstances be encountered. For example, in the video example, if you think that you can realistically achieve a sales output of 70 per cent (140 videos) then draw a line (JK) up from the x axis at 70 per cent (J) to cut the sales revenue line (DE) and total cost line at point L. Reading from the graph this provides a positive 33 per cent margin of safety or £2,200 profit margin (KL) as compared to the BEP. Since this is a relatively large and positive difference then a small reduction in sales activity will not be particularly disastrous, as some profit will still be achieved.

Profit/volume graph

For all practical purposes, some small businesses do not necessarily separate the fixed costs from the variable costs. If this is the case a profit/volume graph (see Figure 8.4) is constructed in a similar manner to the break-even graph (i.e. the horizontal x axis represents output in units or percentage terms), and there are two y axes – the one on the left refers to 'Costs', whereas the one on the right refers to 'Profit', both in the local currency of use.

Constructing this type of graph involves a similar process to that for the break-even graph, namely:

1   Mark a point (F), the loss, where the sales volume is zero – this equates to the fixed costs, i.e. £2,000. Mark this point on the left y axis.
2   Select a random sales volume (e.g. 100 per cent), calculate the profit (£12,000 sales value – £8,000 costs = £4,000) and plot this point (G) where it cuts the right y axis.
3   Draw a straight line to connect these two points (FG).
4   Where this line intersects with the x axis is the break-even point (BEP).
5   Draw the margin of safety line (JK) at a realistic output level; in this case it is apparent that a 70 per cent output level realizes a £2,200 profit variable relative to the BEP.

170

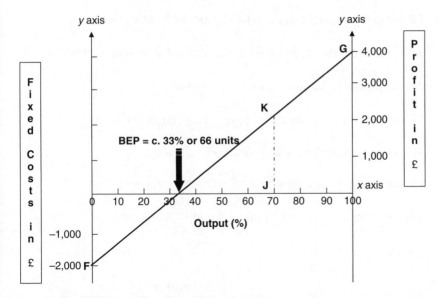

Figure 8.4 Constructing a profit/volume graph

Mathematical formulae

The third method of determining the BEP and the most accurate of all is through using the mathematical equations introduced to you in the 'Theoretical overview' section of this chapter. Before turning to a demonstration of some of their applications, let us initially restate the key elements of the video sport analysis and improvement service case study mentioned earlier:

Total fixed costs = £2,000

Unit selling price = £60

Unit variable costs = £30

Maximum capacity = 200 per year

Substituting these data into some of the previously introduced formulae, we can for example mathematically calculate:

■ Total costs at various outputs

1) Total cost (TC) = Fixed cost (FC) + Variable cost (VC)

10 per cent output (20 units) = £2,000 + £30 @ 20 = £2,600

171

70 per cent output (140 units) = £2,000 + £30 @ 140 = £6,200

100 per cent output (200 units) = £2,000 + £30 @ 200 = £8,000

- Different profits or losses at various outputs

    2) Profit or loss = Sales value (SV) – Total costs (TC)

    10 per cent output = £1,200 – £2,600 = £1,400 loss

    70 per cent output = £8,400 – £6,200 = £2,200 profit

    100 per cent output = £12,000 – £8,000 = £4,000 profit

- Break-even point

    $$3) \text{ BEP (units)} = \frac{\text{Fixed cost (FC)}}{\text{Unit selling price (USP)} - \text{Unit variable cost (VC)}}$$

    BEP = £2,000/£60 – £30 = 66.67 (to two decimal places), rounded up to 67 units*

    $$4) \text{ BEP (monetary value)} = \text{Fixed cost (FC)} \times \frac{\text{Break-even sales}}{\text{Contribution (C)}}$$

    BEP = 2,000 × 67/30 = £4,466.67 (to two decimal places)*

(* N.B. More accurate calculations are derived from the mathematical calculations as compared with graphical viewing.)

- Contribution

    5) Contribution (C) = Sales value (SV) – Variable costs (VC)

    C = £60 – £30 = £30 per unit

    6) Contribution (C) = Profit (P) + Fixed costs (FC)

    Profit @ 100 units = C × 100 units – FC

    Profit = £30 × 100 – £2,000 = £1,000

172

7) Contribution/sales ratio = $\dfrac{\text{Contribution (C)}}{\text{Sales value}}$

(sometimes referred to as the profit/volume ratio)

P/V = 30/60 = 0.5

■ Margin of safety at various output levels

8) Margin of safety (units) = $\dfrac{\text{Profit}}{\text{Contribution}} \times \text{Sales units}$

MoS @ 150 units = £30/£30 × 150 = 150 units

Break-even point (BEP) = 67 units

MoS − BEP = 150 − 67 = 83 units

9) Margin of safety (monetary value) = Profit × $\dfrac{\text{Sales}}{\text{Contribution}}$

MoS @ 70 per cent output = £8,400 − £6,200 = £2,200 profit

MoS @ 100 per cent output = £12,000 − £8,000 = £4,000 profit

To further consider the mathematical sensitivity of data accuracy, sensitivity analyses can be performed by recalculating the data using ±10 per cent variations in the equations. For example, if sales price were reduced by 10 per cent the BEP would be:

BEP (units) = $\dfrac{\text{Fixed cost (FC)}}{\text{Unit selling price (USP)} - \text{Unit variable cost (VC)}}$

BEP = £2,000/£60 × 0.9 − £30 = 83.34 (to two decimal places), rounded up to 84 units (previously it was 67 units)

Additionally if fixed costs were increased by 10 per cent the new BEP in monetary terms would be:

$$\text{BEP (monetary value)} = \text{Fixed cost (FC)} \times \frac{\text{Break-even sales}}{\text{Contribution (C)}}$$

BEP = 2,200 × 84/30 = £6,160 (to two decimal places)

Clearly the impact of such changes directly affects motivation as well as profit levels.

INTERPRETATION AND MANAGEMENT DECISION

Break-even analysis provides a theoretical framework for appraising financial estimates of revenue and costs to predict profits or losses. Break-even charts are not predictors of demand or supply, yet their data are based upon future predictions of such parameters. Given that these are estimates, the greater the accuracy of the data to real-life circumstances and appreciation of the technique's assumptions and limitations, the more likely that appropriate management decisions will occur.

Whilst you now may be able mathematically to calculate or graphically to extrapolate the break-even point, what does it actually mean? Theoretically you know the quantity of sales under these given conditions in which you can begin to make a financial profit. This is important information in itself, but in practice there are further elements to consider before you can go ahead with the decision to proceed with the venture or not. For example, does this project need to at least break even? It might be used tactically as a loss leader to provide additional revenue streams or launch other profitable activities. Similarly some private sector organizations do not merely wish to break even; they expect a minimum-percentage return on investment to justify the human and other non-financial resources involved in the project. If this is purely a return on investment decision, might there be competing and more profitable opportunities to be pursued with your limited resources? Furthermore, given multi-project commitments, is it feasible to achieve such predicted sales in the timescales suggested? The important point to realize is that break-even analysis can assist managers to understand the key financial relationships and factors involved in decisions, but there are likely to be other organizational objectives and non-financial criteria that warrant management attention.

174

However, in merely focusing on the financial aspects of interpretation, break-even analysis can help the manager determine the level of production required to create specific profits for different sales levels. Furthermore the manager can calculate the effect of reducing costs, increasing or decreasing the selling price, and achieving different sales volumes, so as to focus attention on operational tactics that can increase profit levels and/or extend the product life cycle. For example, if supply is considered to be the limiting factor in the sport video analysis business, tactics used to influence outputs could include:

- Extend business hours outside of the weekend.
- Reduce the idle time or down time (e.g. purchase an additional video camera or editing suite or change supplier to decrease the repair and maintenance time).
- Purchase cost-effective hardware and software that can reduce the production time.
- Employ additional full- or part-time staff.
- Provide a range of different products and service speeds, the more sophisticated incurring higher mark-ups (profit margins).

In essence, break-even analysis techniques can be used to appraise numerous financial 'What if?' scenarios as well as to provide focus on practical management actions, such as increasing output, reducing costs or improving sales. Combined with organizational objectives and non-financial criteria, this information provides the basis of essential budgetary management decisions upon which an organization's success is built.

COMMON MISTAKES

We have already mentioned that in practice the accuracy of the break-even data estimates needs to be questioned. Consistent methods need to be applied, such as the historical first-in, first-out (FIFO) costing technique (Granof and Khumawala, forthcoming), since costs or even sales for that matter can change quickly over time. For example, in the sport video analysis scenario more developed technologies are inevitable, which means that the costs of the editing hardware and software are likely to change. This in turn may directly affect the speed of production, as well as the quality and sophistication of the final product. Similarly, as the business becomes established there is likely to be an increase in the number of competing services, which will influence demand and the selling price. Clearly all components of the financial equation can and do change, hence the importance of considering the margin of safety and sensitivity analysis techniques alongside break-even analysis.

Interpretation errors must be avoided. It must be understood that break-even analysis is only accurate within the limits upon which it is prepared, and therefore it should not be used for extrapolation purposes. Graphical presentation of data can also be visually attractive, but take note of the scaling of the axes, as this can greatly influence the message implied or communicated. To provide more detailed and accurate information, it is recommended that mathematical formulae and calculations always accompany break-even graphs.

SUMMARY

Break-even analysis is an efficient and easy-to-understand management technique used to inform profit potential, particularly on the viability of a new product or service. Applying marginal cost principles and comparing income and expenditure data at various levels of output, it is critical in informing short- and long-term financial planning decisions. Break-even information can either be calculated via mathematical formulae or be graphically displayed using profit/volume or break-even graphs. In the latter case, this for example involves:

1   labelling and scaling the axes;
2   determining and plotting the costs;
3   estimating the revenue from different sales levels;
4   identifying the break-even point and margin of safety.

The many benefits of using break-even and allied techniques are that they assist management:

■   to identify the costs, separating them into fixed and variable, so as to focus attention on different methods of cost reduction and control;
■   to apply the concept of contribution to cover important fundamental fixed costs in the sport industry;
■   to better understand the often complex relationship between costs, sales value and profit or loss;
■   to formulate appropriate pricing policies and structures to achieve realistic profits.

On the other hand, the cited limitations of the techniques usually relate to the accuracy of both the costs and the sales data entered, particularly related

176

to the time factor and the functions' assumed linearity. However, many of these criticisms can be overcome by more sophisticated understanding of the concept, as well as more advanced multi-product technique applications.

Effective break-even analysis entails factoring in your margin of safety, understanding risk and considering other financial and non-financial goals. Regrettably, too many sport managers merely produce a break-even graph and, having calculated the break-even point, take no further action. In the more complete process of profit management, this should be just the start. Informed and evidence-based decision making should then take place to determine how you might influence the controllable aspects of profit and, if the proposed business is viable, produce robust targets and budgets that staff can realistically aspire to.

Guides to further resources, useful web links and guideline answers to all the self-test questions featured in this chapter are available on a companion website at www.routledge.com/9780415491594.

SELF-TEST QUESTION

The data contained in Table 8.1 have been extracted from the latest accounts of ABC Golf Driving Range. You have been asked to construct a break-even chart of this pay-and-play golf centre, and on the graph you need to mark the break-even point and margin of safety, both in monetary and in unit terms. To further substantiate your findings, please provide mathematical calculations.

Table 8.1 ABC Golf Driving Range profit and loss data

	Individual costs (£)	Cumulative (£)
Variable costs:		
Direct material	100,000	
Direct labour	50,000	
50% of production overhead	50,000	200,000
Fixed costs:		
Administration	100,000	
50% of production overhead	50,000	150,000
Profit		50,000
Sales revenue (80,000 golf users)		400,000

CHAPTER 9

APPRAISING INVESTMENT OPPORTUNITIES

TECHNIQUE DESCRIPTION

For the longevity of any business, managers need to continually replace and augment fixed assets to maintain the business's competitive position and ultimately help it to grow. Put simply, it takes money to make even more money. This requires prudent decisions to choose exactly where, when and how to invest limited sources of money on competing capital projects, and is known as capital budgeting (the planning process used to determine sizeable investments in the long-term assets of an organization – Dayananda, Irons, Harrison, Herbohn and Rowland, 2002). Robust financial techniques are required to carefully evaluate, compare and select between investments that optimize an organization's cash flow and rate of return.

To this end this chapter will introduce you to the most frequently used capital budgeting appraisal techniques:

- payback (PB) – ranks investments according to the period of time after which the investment is expected to break even;
- accounting or average rate of return (ARR) – uses present monetary values to compare respective returns on investment by dividing total cash flow by the number of years of the investment;
- net present value (NPV) – considers the whole project to determine its comparable worth to current value through discounting future cash flows and subtracting the initial investment;
- internal rate of return (IRR) or yield – another discounted cash flow (DCF) method, which considers the point at which the total present value of future cash flows equals the cost of the investment (Solution Matrix, 2010).

To appraise whether the investment's financial benefits outweigh the significant costs of a capital project (a business investment opportunity usually involving long-term tangible assets that possess a shelf life of at least three years and a cost of £1,000), these techniques assess likely project returns. The projects that are calculated to ideally provide positive financial net gains can then be compared with the organization's hurdle or baseline standard as well as with one another.

Applying these capital investment techniques ensures that each competing project is analysed according to the size of its financial cash flow or profit, its lifespan and in some cases the cost of obtaining the investment funds. Previously introduced tools such as assigning risk values (Chapter 4) and sensitivity analysis (Chapter 8) can additionally be incorporated so as to more accurately inform the economic viability of the decision-making process.

This chapter therefore introduces you to the purpose of capital budgeting appraisal techniques, and their underpinning theory, assumptions and limitations, before demonstrating the practical process and applied use of these techniques in a sport management setting.

PURPOSE

Would it be better to purchase or lease a new car or motorized treadmill, repair your multi-gym and aerobic capacity laboratory testing equipment, or even purchase land to expand your growing fitness business? It is especially important for you to know where and when to invest limited funds to grow your business, because capital purchases typically entail long-term decisions that are semi-permanent in nature. For example, incorrect decisions on the purchase of operating consumables such as footballs can be easily rectified within a season. However, an incorrect decision on the purchase and installation of a floodlit synthetic pitch (capital investment project) is likely to involve a significant amount of money and would be considered a largely irreversible decision (Morgan, Redman, Smith and Cooper, 2001). Having an impact on a club for at least a decade, such long-term decision making presupposes accurate information and some form of metrics to compare the return on different investments.

Managers clearly must get such decisions right first time, and capital budgeting appraisal techniques can assist. Stewart (2007) suggests that the benefits of capital budgeting, or for that matter any form of budgeting techniques, are that it helps sport managers:

- to anticipate the future and thereby assist the strategic planning process;
- to identify income shortfalls;
- to better manage and monitor spending;
- to present a clear picture of resource needs and project priorities to key stakeholders.

In summary, capital budgeting techniques help you to make informed decisions on the acquisition and disposal of assets, which in turn affects the long-term profitability of your organization (Williamson, 2003). This means that managers who know how to use capital budgeting appraisal techniques can better determine the economic viability of their short- and long-term investment decisions.

THEORETICAL OVERVIEW

According to Time Web (2010) capital budgeting is a multifaceted process that consists of the following key stages:

1   forecasting investment needs;
2   identifying project(s) to meet needs;
3   appraising the alternatives;
4   selecting the best alternatives;
5   making the expenditure;
6   monitoring project(s).

For the purpose of this chapter we will predominantly focus on the most crucial and complex of these stages (3 and 4), namely the economic or financial analysis involving the appraisal and selection of alternative investments (Dayananda, Irons, Harrison, Herbohn and Rowland, 2002).

Among the earliest appraisal methods used was the payback (PB) model, which merely determines the length of time required for the firm to recover its initial investment. Thus in its simplest form it can be considered to be very similar to break-even analysis (Chapter 8) and could be written as:

$$\text{Payback period (years)} = \frac{\text{Initial investment}}{\text{Cash inflows to cover investment cost}}$$

As payback is based upon standard historical cost accounting estimates, a project expected to pay back in two years (e.g. investment = £1 million;

180

average annual earnings = £500,000) would generally be preferred over one that would return the investment in five (e.g. investment = £1 million; average annual earnings = £200,000).

However, this approach focuses upon cash flow and does not consider project profitability (Jagels, 2007). In particular it ignores the income derived from the investment after payback has occurred. This weakness gave rise to return on investment or accounting rate of return (ARR) appraisal methods, which propose measurement of profits arising from the investment. This is logical in theory, but in practice many different interpretations in terms both of formula components (e.g. depreciation included or not included) and of formulae themselves were used to calculate the return on investment. For example, variations included:

$$\text{Return per £1 invested} = \frac{\text{Total earnings}}{\text{Investment cost}}$$

$$\text{Accounting percentage rate of return} = \frac{\text{Average annual income}}{\text{Investment cost}} \times 100$$

$$\text{Average percentage return on capital} = \frac{\text{Average profit per year}}{\text{Average capital employed}} \times 100$$

Unfortunately no standardized approach was adopted by industry and, given the inherent weakness that this method, as well as payback, ignored the time value of money, discounted cash flow techniques were introduced in the early 1950s (Kotas, 1999). These are the most frequently used investment appraisal techniques today and recognize the key principle that the value of money changes over time. For example, £1,000 today is worth considerably less than exactly the same amount ten years ago. This change in monetary value is largely attributed to the effects of inflation (reduced value over time) and explains why in practical terms managers prefer investments that provide large early returns to pay off the investment and the true cost of borrowing (the interest) as soon as possible.

In other words, reducing money estimates to current or present value overcame historical comparability issues relating to different investment amounts and earning time frames. This resulted in the DCF techniques of net present value (NPV) and the internal rate of return (IRR) being accepted as the most superior cost–benefit investment appraisal techniques (Jagels, 2007). They involve estimating the size and timing of all cash inflows, discounting them to present values, and then either totalling these values and subtracting the investment outlay as in the NPV method or calculating where the NPV = 0 in the IRR method.

In mathematical terms the net present value is represented by the formula:

$$\text{Net present value (NPV)} = \sum_{t=0}^{n} \frac{CF_t}{(1+R)^t} - CO$$

CF = Net cash flow at end of year t

CO = Cash outlay

t = Time period

R = Rate of discount

In this method the discounted cash flow is calculated for each year of the project at the cost of borrowing capital, totalled and then subtracted from the initial investment sum.

The internal rate of return method on the other hand calculates the investment efficiency by considering the discounted yield of each project. This can be written as:

$$\text{Internal rate of return (IRR)} = \sum_{t=0}^{n} \frac{CF_t}{(1+IRR)^t} = \$0 = NPV$$

CF = Net cash flow at end of year t

t = Time period

IRR = Internal rate of return

Do not worry if you do not understand these concepts or formulae at the moment. All will hopefully become much clearer when we apply them to a practical example later in the chapter.

The NPV and IRR methods might appear very similar, as they discount money over time, but the reality is that they are very different concepts. The NPV approach assumes knowledge of the discount rate and, if the NPV is calculated to be positive, suggests a financial return and therefore potential for further analysis. The IRR approach, on the other hand, does not need to evaluate the often subjective discount rate. Instead it attempts to establish the

182

rate of interest that reduces the NPV to zero. This establishes the level of interest rate a project will be able to withstand before it loses money, thereby indicating the relative risk of the project to make a profit.

As DCF models have evolved and been refined they now additionally try to include some level of risk by adding a premium (e.g. in volatile markets an additional X per cent may be added to the normal discount rate) or probabilities calculated to the cash flows. Furthermore, some level of sensitivity analysis is often carried out to model the effect of various changes in the factors that contribute to the formulae estimates (e.g. changing the material costs, the sale volumes and prices by X per cent).

When these moderated capital budgeting techniques were applied to a broad range of financial settings, it also became apparent that the nature of the project relationship may become an important facet in project selection. For example, Tajirian (1997) argues that, if the objective of the manager is merely to maximize value, then for independent projects all projects where NPV > 0 could be accepted. On the other hand, if the choice is between mutually exclusive projects, the one with the highest NPV should be chosen. This has led Dayananda, Irons, Harrison, Herbohn and Rowland (2002) to argue that different acceptance decisions are likely to apply to independent, mutually exclusive or contingent project applications.

PRACTICAL APPLICATION

Regardless of the nature of the project relationship to others, there are normally two primary types of capital investment decisions:

1 selecting new or expanding business facilities to exploit profitable opportunities via new products and markets, e.g. investing in an overseas plant, refunding a long-term debt, or decisions to purchase or lease new equipment;
2 repair, replacement or improvement of existing assets to improve quality, productivity and/or safety levels, e.g. repairing technology, replacing a manual system with a computerized one, removing obsolete assets, or improving security practices with the addition of a closed-circuit television system.

Within these general application parameters of expansion or maintenance, capital goods can be seen to relate to property, equipment, consultancy, research or even extensive promotional campaigns.

More specifically in terms of sporting applications, Stewart (2007) suggests that these techniques are commonly used to consider facility and sport playing surface purchases, as well as maintenance expenditure, player salary and coaching staff employment, and equipment upgrades.

Capital project decisions, whether funded from equity or from debt, are usually used to compare the financial returns on investment on competing applications. As the decisions are nearly always constrained by financial availability at a moment in time (Stewart, 2007), the ceiling of the investment and hence the optimum return on the investment are likely to be dependent upon an organization's assets, which provide access to further secured or unsecured loans.

However, contemporary sport with its common political and emotional connotations does not necessarily conform purely to the highest returns on investment or the profit maximization models of other industries. For example, the financial bottom line of many sport projects is often stated as being merely to break even (the payback approach). Carvalho (2009) cites the Abu Dhabi Motorsports Management Company, which in hosting its first ever Formula One race hopes to meet the financial target of breaking even within three years. This could be considered a very positive target when compared with the 1976 Montreal Summer Olympic Games, which took 33 years to break even (Wilson, 2010).

Other sport projects may never break even yet still be approved. For example, the development of a local sport club's social and welfare facilities may be approved on the basis of minimal levels of expectation and competing offerings, rather than profit or payback principles. In this sense the application of capital investment appraisal techniques may be considered to cover a broad cross-section of projects, at one end of the continuum being used to establish the cheapest viable project of choice and at the other end to determine the most profitable return on investment.

ASSUMPTIONS AND LIMITATIONS

Time Web (2010) believes that each technique possesses its own specific assumptions and limitations. Payback for example is intuitively very simple, with financial investments expecting a speedy return. However, the technique lacks objectivity. For example, who determines the optimal payback period? In reality this is usually obtained by comparing payback periods with those of other investments and then prioritizing the projects that return the earliest paybacks. But all competing projects at a moment in time could be

184

either very weak or very strong, making this a very subjective assessment of project viability.

In comparison, the accounting rate of return method provides a more meaningful and accurate relative comparison between projects. Being based upon fundamental accounting measures such as return on capital employed financial ratios, it makes the financial findings relatively easy to understand and apply. On the other hand, Time Web (2010) suggests that the limitation of the technique is that it does not consider the timing of the cash flows or the duration of the project return. So, whilst projects may create viable long-term returns, they may also present serious cash flow problems on a short-term basis. Furthermore, Time Web (2010) argues that the concept of profit can be interpreted differently between businesses and hence considers investment decisions made solely on this method to be very subjective.

Through the notion of discounted cash flows, the NPV and IRR methods consider such time-oriented failings. However, Investopedia (2010) elaborates that these relatively complex techniques make assumptions on the accuracy of the selected discount rate as well as the receipt of quite specific cash flows. Where there are multiple and uncertain cash flows or variable discount and hurdle rates, then the accuracy of the calculations must be questioned. More sophisticated and refined tools have been developed, such as the modified internal rate of return (MIRR) (Investopedia, 2010), which considers reinvestment of the cost of capital to overcome multiple IRRs, but this technique is beyond the scope of this text.

Whilst the validity of any financial calculation always assumes accurate inputs, Morgan, Redman, Smith and Cooper (2001) suggest that the greatest limitation of traditional present value techniques is that they rely on quantifiable cash flows. In practice, they argue, these are sometimes difficult to quantify, particularly in service industries where increased flexibility and improved customer relations cannot be easily reduced to cash flow figures. Morgan, Redman, Smith and Cooper (2001: 4) elaborate:

> As a result of the complex nature of today's projects, new methods, such as multiattribute decision models and the analytical hierarchy process have been developed to incorporate the 'softer' measures into the decision process. These approaches weigh and rate for importance, impact, and probability all factors that can be identified as relevant, from the ones that can be measured to those that are more subjective.

Despite these individual technique limitations and recent refinements, Morgan, Redman, Smith and Cooper (2001) conclude that, in corporate

America at least, capital budgeting evaluation techniques are more often used in combination than in isolation, with the most frequent combination being the IRR technique followed by the payback method.

PROCESS THROUGH AN APPLIED EXAMPLE

Once investment proposals have been generated, basic appraisal typically entails undertaking the following sequential actions:

1 Estimate each project's cash flows (amounts and timing).
2 Determine and apply the appropriate discount rate over time (usually only applied to the DCF methods of NPV and IRR).
3 Calculate each project's annual net cash flow.
4 Compute the payback, accounting rate of return, net present value or internal rate of return.
5 Compare the findings of each project investment.
6 Decide whether to accept or reject each investment opportunity.

To illustrate each technique as well as more advanced developments of this process let us apply it to fictitious data drawn from the Beijing Olympic Games and the evolving Bird's Nest stadium project. Awarded the hosting rights to the 2008 Summer Olympic and Paralympic Games in 2001, China expected to enjoy typical host nation improved trade exports of 30 per cent (Bhusnurmath, 2009). Highlighting its emergence on the world stage, the country continuously invested heavily in this national stadium, which was officially opened in June 2008 at a reported investment cost of US$423 million (Pasternack, 2008). Since the very successful games, the stadium has unfortunately experienced problems in attracting sport events, despite the fact that it draws nearly 30,000 people daily to view the facility, at an admission price of 50 yuan (Reuters, 2009). With annual venue costs being reported at US$9 million, owners and operators have begun to encourage other complementary activities to the area, with a recent announcement of a new shopping complex, entertainment outlets and a hotel to be built within five years (Demick, 2009).

For the building of one of these small entertainment outlets, you as a private sector investor have decided to look at the feasibility of offering a tourist-focused electronic games area. Themed within a new larger snow park project, you have identified five competing project proposals, but have the funds to invest in only one of them. Which do you decide to invest in and why? Data for each project are summarized, with rounded-up estimated cash flows to ease calculations, in Table 9.1.

186

Table 9.1 Comparative project cash flows of themed outlet proposals

Year	Project A cash flow (£ 000)	Project B cash flow (£ 000)	Project C cash flow (£ 000)	Project D cash flow (£ 000)	Project E cash flow (£ 000)
0	(100)	(100)	(200)	(100)	(200)
1	25	15	70	40	10
2	25	30	60	30	20
3	25	45	40	20	30
4	25	60*	20	20	40
5				20	50
6				20	50
7					60*

* = Includes a residual value of selling off the asset.

Project A represents a four-year venture with an initial outlay of £100,000. (N.B. A negative cash flow is represented by the brackets in each of the projects.) It then is estimated to provide a positive cash flow of £25,000 per annum.

Payback method

The formula is:

$$\text{Payback period (years)} = \frac{\text{Initial investment}}{\text{Cash inflows to cover investment cost}}$$

i.e. where Investment cost (I) = Cash inflow (CI)

This is applied to the example:

I = £100,000

CI = £25,000 (year 1) + £25,000 (year 2) + £25,000 (year 3) + £25,000 (year 4) = £100,000

Project A payback = 4 years

Project B payback = 3 years 2 months (N.B. 3 years = 90% of investment plus £10,000/£60,000 × 12 months = 2 months)

187

Project C payback = Investment cost (£100,000) ≠ Total cash inflow (£190,000), i.e. no recovery of cost

Project D payback = 3 years 6 months (N.B. 3 years = 90% of investment plus £10,000/£20,000 × 12 months = 6 months)

Project E payback = 6 years

With this technique ranking investments according to the earliest payback period it is apparent that, purely on financial return grounds and assuming mutually exclusive projects, the only projects that should be accepted are A, B, D and E and, given the time value of money, in the following rank order: B, D, A and E. Project C is likely to be rejected on the basis that it is not financially viable, namely that it will never pay back on the initial investment.

Accounting rate of return (ARR) method

The formula is:

Accounting percentage rate of return =

$$\frac{\text{Average annual income (AI)}}{\text{Investment cost (I)}} \times 100$$

When this is applied to the four financially viable projects the following computations occur:

Project A example:

$$AI = \frac{£25,000 + £25,000 + £25,000 + £25,000}{4} = £25,000$$

$$I = £100,000$$

$$\text{Project A} = \frac{£25,000}{£100,000} \times 100 = 25\%$$

$$\text{Project B} = \frac{£37,500}{£100,000} \times 100 = 37.5\%$$

$$\text{Project D} = \frac{£25,000}{£100,000} \times 100 = 25\%$$

$$\text{Project E} = \frac{£37,143}{£200,000} \times 100 = 18.57\%$$

Using this methodology it is apparent that all the projects are estimated to return investment rates in excess of 18 per cent, the order of preference at this stage being B, D and A equal, and then E (the general principle being that the highest ARR provides the best financial return).

Net present value (NPV) method

Given that money does change in value over time, future cash flows need to be discounted to present values. This can be calculated by using present values tables (Table 9.2) or access to a present value calculator (see Moneychimp, 2010 at http://www.moneychimp.com/calculator/present_value_calculator.htm), both of which are derived from the formula:

$$PV = \frac{A}{(1 + R)^n}$$

PV = Present value

A = Amount of initial cost

R = Rate of interest

n = Number of years ahead of initial investment

Demonstrating the method using Table 9.2, this calculation involves determining two dimensions: the appropriate discount rate (percentage) and the number of years it needs to be discounted for (i.e. the timing of the receipt of the money, normally identified in years or months). Where the percentage column and the period row intersect in Table 9.2 is the factor the cash flow needs to be multiplied by. For example, a positive cash flow of £30,000 received in three years' time with a depreciation or cost of capital (interest rate) of 7 per cent per annum is suggested to be worth £30,000 × 0.816 = £24,480 today. Applying the respective discount rate multiplier to each year

Table 9.2 Present value tables

Year	1%	2%	3%	4%	5%	6%	7%	8%	9%	10%	11%	12%	13%	14%	15%
1	0.990	0.980	0.971	0.962	0.952	0.943	0.935	0.926	0.917	0.909	0.901	0.893	0.885	0.877	0.870
2	0.980	0.961	0.943	0.925	0.907	0.890	0.873	0.857	0.842	0.826	0.812	0.797	0.783	0.769	0.756
3	0.971	0.942	0.915	0.889	0.864	0.840	0.816	0.794	0.772	0.751	0.731	0.712	0.693	0.675	0.658
4	0.961	0.924	0.888	0.855	0.823	0.792	0.763	0.735	0.708	0.683	0.659	0.636	0.613	0.592	0.572
5	0.951	0.906	0.863	0.822	0.784	0.747	0.713	0.681	0.650	0.621	0.593	0.567	0.543	0.519	0.497
6	0.942	0.888	0.837	0.790	0.746	0.705	0.666	0.630	0.596	0.564	0.535	0.507	0.480	0.456	0.432
7	0.933	0.871	0.813	0.760	0.711	0.665	0.623	0.583	0.547	0.513	0.482	0.452	0.425	0.400	0.376
8	0.923	0.853	0.789	0.731	0.677	0.627	0.582	0.540	0.502	0.467	0.434	0.404	0.376	0.351	0.327
9	0.914	0.837	0.766	0.703	0.645	0.592	0.544	0.500	0.460	0.424	0.391	0.361	0.333	0.308	0.284
10	0.905	0.820	0.744	0.676	0.614	0.558	0.508	0.463	0.422	0.386	0.352	0.322	0.295	0.270	0.247
11	0.896	0.804	0.722	0.650	0.585	0.527	0.475	0.429	0.388	0.350	0.317	0.287	0.261	0.237	0.215
12	0.887	0.788	0.701	0.625	0.557	0.497	0.444	0.397	0.356	0.319	0.286	0.257	0.231	0.208	0.187
13	0.879	0.773	0.681	0.601	0.530	0.469	0.415	0.368	0.326	0.290	0.258	0.229	0.204	0.182	0.163
14	0.870	0.758	0.661	0.577	0.505	0.442	0.388	0.340	0.299	0.263	0.232	0.205	0.181	0.160	0.141
15	0.861	0.743	0.642	0.555	0.481	0.417	0.362	0.315	0.275	0.239	0.209	0.183	0.160	0.140	0.123
16	0.853	0.728	0.623	0.534	0.458	0.394	0.339	0.292	0.252	0.218	0.188	0.163	0.141	0.123	0.107
17	0.844	0.714	0.605	0.513	0.436	0.371	0.317	0.270	0.231	0.198	0.170	0.146	0.125	0.108	0.093
18	0.836	0.700	0.587	0.494	0.416	0.350	0.296	0.250	0.212	0.180	0.153	0.130	0.111	0.095	0.081
19	0.828	0.686	0.570	0.475	0.396	0.331	0.277	0.232	0.194	0.164	0.138	0.116	0.098	0.083	0.070
20	0.820	0.673	0.554	0.456	0.377	0.312	0.258	0.215	0.178	0.149	0.124	0.104	0.087	0.073	0.061

of income allows us to calculate the net present value of each project using the formula:

$$\text{Net present value (NPV)} = \sum_{t=0}^{n} \frac{CF_t}{(1+R)^t} - CO$$

CF = Net cash flow at end of year t

CO = Cash outlay

t = Time period

R = Rate of discount

Applying this to Project A:

CF = Σ £23,400 (year 1) + £21,800 (year 2) + £20,400 (year 3) + £19,100 (year 4) = £84,700

CO = £100,000

t = 4 years

R = 7%

The NPV of Project A = £84,700 – £100,000 = –£15,300

Repeating the same process for all projects provides us with the data contained in Table 9.3, with the highlighted final row indicating the total NPV of each project.

Any NPV that is positive implies that the project is financially viable and worthy of further consideration. Given that Projects A, C and E are negative they are likely to be rejected, whereas this method suggests that only Projects D and B should initially be considered, in that order.

Internal rate of return (IRR) or yield method

Largely dependent upon trial-and-error calculation, the yield method often produces a similar evaluation to the NPV method. Its advantage though is that it is normally used to compare projects against an organization's 'hurdle' or minimum threshold rate of return, hence its name 'internal rate of return'.

Table 9.3 Project net present values @ 7% discount rate

Year	Project A PV cash flow (£ 000)	Project B PV cash flow (£ 000)	Project C PV cash flow (£ 000)	Project D PV cash flow (£ 000)	Project E PV cash flow (£ 000)
0	(100)	(100)	(200)	(100)	(200)
1	25 × 0.935 = 23.4	15 × 0.935 = 14	70 × 0.935 = 65.5	40 × 0.935 = 37.4	10 × 0.935 = 9.4
2	25 × 0.873 = 21.8	30 × 0.873 = 26.2	60 × 0.873 = 52.4	30 × 0.873 = 26.2	20 × 0.873 = 17.5
3	25 × 0.816 = 20.4	45 × 0.816 = 36.7	40 × 0.816 = 32.6	20 × 0.816 = 16.3	30 × 0.816 = 24.5
4	25 × 0.763 = 19.1	60 × 0.763 = 45.8	20 × 0.763 = 15.3	20 × 0.763 = 15.3	40 × 0.763 = 30.5
5				20 × 0.713 = 14.3	50 × 0.713 = 35.7
6				20 × 0.666 = 13.3	50 × 0.666 = 33.3
7					60 × 0.623 = 37.4
Net cash flow total	84.7	122.7	165.8	122.8	188.3
Total NPV	**−15.3**	**+22.7**	**−34.2**	**+22.8**	**−11.7**

For example, given the lessons learnt from the Bird's Nest stadium experience, an organization may suggest that financially it will only consider projects that provide a yield of more than 10 per cent of investment. This will be determined by trying various rates until you find the rate of discount at which the NPV is zero. Positive NPV values mean that the rate being tried is too low, and negative values conversely imply too high a rate has been selected.

Initially this method requires selecting a random discount rate, so having already used a 7 per cent discount rate in Table 9.3 let us use these data to illustrate the calculation process. Selecting Project B we have found, at this 7 per cent rate, that it would provide an NPV return of +£22,700. Since this is positive let us try a higher rate, such as 15 per cent, using the NPV tables found at Cengage Learning (2010). (N.B. Please open the second tab, entitled 'Present Value of Lump Sum', at http://www.swlearning.com/finance/brigham/ifm7e/pvtables.xls.)

Project B:

$$CF = \Sigma \; £15,000 \times 0.870 \; (\text{year 1}) + £30,000 \times 0.756 \; (\text{year 2}) + £45,000 \times 0.658 \; (\text{year 3}) + £60,000 \times 0.572 \; (\text{year 4})$$

$$= £13,050 + £22,680 + £29,610 + £34,320 = £99,660$$

$$NPV = £99,660 - £100,000 = -£340$$

This implies that the IRR or yield is likely to be just less than 15 per cent (because of the negative sign).

If by chance the two selected rates are not particularly close to locating the point where NPV= 0 then using the following formula can prove useful in determining a more appropriate percentage estimate:

$$\text{Internal rate of return (IRR)} = X + \frac{a}{a+b} \; (Y - X)$$

X = Lower rate of interest

Y = Higher rate of interest

a = Difference between present values of the outflow and inflow at X%

b = Absolute value (i.e. ignore any negative sign) of the difference between present values of the outflow and inflow at Y%

Project B example:

$$IRR = 7 + \frac{22{,}700}{22{,}700 + 340} \ (15 - 7)$$

$$= 7 + 0.9852 \ (8) = 14.88\% \ \text{(to two decimal places)}$$

Alternatively a rough approximation can be extrapolated graphically by plotting the discount rate as the x axis and NPV as the y axis. Plot where the two rates have been determined and then draw a straight line to join the two points. Where this line crosses the x axis is the IRR.

Applying the same calculation process to the other projects would reveal rounded-up project yields of: Project A – 10 per cent negative; Project B – 15 per cent positive; Project C – 10 per cent negative; Project D – 15 per cent positive; Project E – 8.5 per cent negative.

As for the NPV method, the financial decision to invest or not will depend upon the ranking of project profitability, since IRR is a relative measure of value creation. Hence Projects B and D are jointly the most profitable, since they provide the highest positive yields, with the remainder being unlikely to be considered unless there were other compelling reasons for their selection.

Risk premiums, probabilities and sensitivity analysis

In the current NPV example the discount base rate is assumed to be 7 per cent. To include an element of uncertainty in this prediction let us include an additional risk premium of say 3 per cent to this rate, making it 10 per cent. Calculating at this new rate provides the following NPV project findings: Project A –£20,700; Project B +£13,200; Project C –£43,100; Project D +£13,600; Project E –£34,500. Although these NPV project findings are obviously lower than for the 7 per cent calculations, this does not change the fact that Projects B and D are still considered financially viable, as they both provide positive returns above this new hurdle rate.

Another method to include uncertainty is to attach probabilities to each cash flow. For example, the probability of Project B's expected initial outlay or investment cost could be estimated as possessing a 10 per cent chance of being at £80,000, a 50 per cent chance of being at £100,000, and a 40 per cent chance of being at £130,000.

194

$$
\begin{array}{lll}
 & & \pounds \\
\pounds 80,000 \times 0.1 & = & 8,000 \\
\pounds 100,000 \times 0.5 & = & 50,000 \\
\pounds 130,000 \times 0.4 & = & \underline{52,000} \\
 & & 110,000
\end{array}
$$

Assigning such probabilities could give us a revised outlay of £110,000, which when recalculated using the NPV method reveals a +£12,700 NPV for Project B. Whilst this represents a reduced NPV of £10,000, it is still positive, but Project B could prove to be an unprofitable venture if the inflows similarly included amalgamated probabilities.

Using sensitivity analysis (Chapter 8) we can also ascertain the NPV under its base assumptions, as well as likely variations in the key parameters. For example, to test the sensitivity of the calculations we could flex material costs by 10 per cent, and sales prices and volume by 5 per cent, as shown in Table 9.4, where the changed parameters in the Year 1 cash flows of Project B are presented.

This would directly mean recalculating each year of the NPV permutation for each project. Where numerous calculations are anticipated, it might be worth considering purchasing some analytical software, such as TedCo's (2010) Discounted Cash Flow Analysis Calculator, which can evaluate 14 projects against many different discount rates.

Sensitivity analysis should be applied and used with common sense. For example, if future sales are based upon well-established trend data and only small changes are anticipated in sales prices and sales volumes (as witnessed in Table 9.4), using sensitivity metrics does not justify its application. However, if volatile market conditions exist and reliance is placed upon key costs that are highly variable, such as investments reliant on the foreign

Table 9.4 Project B changed parameters

Material costs:			
	Base case	+10%	−10%
Year 1	£45,000	£49,500	£40,500
Sales prices:			
	Base case	+5%	−5%
Year 1	£3	£3.15	£2.85
Sales volumes:			
	Base case	+5%	−5%
Year 1	20,000	21,000	19,000

exchange rate, stock markets or even the price of petrol, then the impact of even small changes should be factored in, as this could significantly influence your investment decision.

INTERPRETATION AND MANAGEMENT DECISIONS

As previously alluded to, the findings from a combination of capital investment appraisal techniques, as well as non-financial factors, are likely to be considered in the management capital decision-making process. In the Beijing example, Projects B and D appear most economically viable, but the choice between them, assuming that capital rationing exists to fund only one of them, is likely to depend upon other qualitative factors. These could relate to positive and/or negative considerations of the competitiveness of the industry, management competence, effective infrastructure, opportunity costs, project risks or even regulatory legal imperatives.

In practice, financial calculations usually drive the investment decision process. With this in mind, Dayananda, Irons, Harrison, Herbohn and Rowland (2002) suggest that management are likely to use the following sequence of events to accept or reject projects:

1   Screen each project initially to see whether it meets fundamental payback or accounting rate of return expectations. Eliminate marginal and unsound projects that do not meet this minimum standard.
2   Financially evaluate the remaining projects using discounted cash flow techniques of NPV or IRR.
3   Consider the qualitative benefits or weaknesses of each project.
4   Consider the specific funding opportunities available, such as independent, mutually exclusive or contingent project funding.
5   Rank projects or selection of projects, decide and allocate funds accordingly.

In most cases the NPV and IRR techniques produce the same financial results, where the highest positive returns, relative to the borrowing rate, convey worthwhile project investments. Despite a strong academic preference for the former, it is IRR that tends to be preferred in practice (Jagels, 2007; ACCA, 2008). However, in using the latter you need to be aware of some of its recently identified pitfalls. For example, IRR does not account for changing discount rates, and net cash flows that frequently change from positive to negative produce multiple IRRs (Investopedia, 2010). For this reason, some managers now prefer to use a more advanced and modified version of IRR,

196

referred to as MIRR (modified internal rate of return). This avoids the inter-pretation problems created by multiple IRRs, as well as takes into account that the cost of capital can be reinvested into the project before its end date.

Other factors that sometimes complicate DCF calculations and hence man-agement decisions include changes in price levels, whether or not to include income tax, unequal project lives, and how to quantify social benefits.

COMMON MISTAKES

Quantifying uncertainty, particularly over long time periods in the future, will always create problems for sport management decision makers. To reduce this level of uncertainty, managers will attempt to track trends so as to be more knowledgeable about future events. The dilemma, as suggested by a commentator on Chinn's (2007) article, is:

> A trend is a trend.
> The question is when will it bend?
> Will it climb higher and higher?
> Or eventually expire
> And come to an untimely end.

This does not mean that we should ignore trends, since the future is directly related to the past; rather, as Boehlje and Ehmke (2005: 1) recommend, 'you should make a considerable effort to evaluate investment alternatives as thoroughly as possible'. In practice this means that you should question the accuracy of the financial estimates. What are they based on, and what are their underlying assumptions? Do they take into account down times or transition periods of reduced productivity, where temporary lay-offs or redundancies are likely to be encountered?

Another error commonly encountered is that managers frequently make a decision based on the findings of just one financial tool. A mix of appraisal tools is recommended, since discounting cash flow methods identify the most profitable investments, but longer payback periods create increased uncer-tainty and can involve large discounting errors (Boehlje and Ehmke, 2005).

Should financial profit be the only consideration of investment? Sometimes the qualitative elements that are difficult to quantify in monetary terms, such as political, social or environmental factors, are unfortunately ignored. In some instances, they may actually become more important than the quanti-tative findings, particularly if they refer to mandatory occupational health

197

and safety requirements (Dayananda, Irons, Harrison, Herbohn and Rowland, 2002).

And finally, one of the most common reasons for sport organization failure is that managers try to expand their business too quickly, stretching their limited resources too far. For example, a fitness centre business may be performing so well that you decide to open another in a different location. But the mere purchase and launch of such a new venture may place your entire business portfolio in jeopardy.

Clearly an awareness of the underpinning principles and assumptions of these tools, accompanied by thoughtful and prudent decision making, will avoid many of these common mistakes.

SUMMARY

Managing capital assets involves long-term decision making, and mistakes can prove costly, resulting in long-term ramifications. Whereas purchasing a capital item usually involves immediate payment, the income or benefits that derive from the decision can accrue over a long period of time (Boehlje and Ehmke, 2005).

Specifically focusing upon the appraisal and selection phase of the capital budgeting process, this chapter has introduced you to the capital investment appraisal tools of payback, accounting rate of return, net present value and internal rate of return. Using these tools in conjunction with risk premiums, probabilities and sensitivity analysis, you should be able to carefully evaluate, compare and select between investments. The benefits accrued from appropriately applying these tools mean that you can begin to prioritize your short- and long-term resource needs, identify your shortfalls, but most importantly plot a path to a predetermined future.

The process to achieve this goal requires you to undertake the following actions:

1 Estimate each project's cash flows (amounts and timing).
2 Determine and apply the appropriate discount rate over time (usually only applied to the DCF methods of NPV and IRR).
3 Calculate each project's annual net cash flow.
4 Compute the payback, accounting rate of return, net present value or internal rate of return.

198

5 Compare the findings of each project investment.
6 Decide whether to accept or reject each investment opportunity.

Accurately quantifying future cash flows, over-reliance on one financial tool, and ignoring qualitative considerations are the primary limitations and errors of application.

In conclusion, the basis behind capital budgeting is to determine and justify which projects contribute most to the value of your organization. Whilst completing a detailed capital investment appraisal may appear difficult and complex to some, getting it wrong or misapplying the mix of tools could mean you losing your business as well as your livelihood.

Guides to further resources, useful web links and guideline answers to all the self-test questions featured in this chapter are available on a companion website at www.routledge.com/9780415491594.

SELF-TEST QUESTIONS

To gauge your understanding and decision making derived from the application of capital budgeting techniques, have a go at the following tasks.

XYZ Adventure Tours is planning to add one additional activity to its current portfolio of adrenalin sports. Project A is a jet-skiing option requiring an initial outlay of £40,000. Project B on the other hand is a micro-light project requiring an outlay of £60,000. Both have a predicted five-year life; assume no residual value. Their estimated net cash flows are summarized in Table 9.5.

1 For each project calculate:
   a. Payback
   b. Accounting rate of return
   c. Net present value assuming a cost of capital of 8 per cent
   d. Internal rate of return

Table 9.5 Comparative project cash flows

Year	Project A (£)	Project B (£)
1	20,000	4,000
2	12,000	16,000
3	16,000	40,000
4	8,000	12,000
5	4,000	8,000

199

2   Which project would you recommend on financial grounds and why? What other non-financial considerations might there be?

3   Explain why net present value may be preferable to accounting rate of return as an aid to management decision making.

4   Do you agree or disagree with the following statements. Please offer a brief explanation to justify your chosen answer.

    a.   Payback methods have no use, since they do not consider project profitability.

    b.   All projects with an NPV > 0 should be accepted.

    c.   If IRR < cost of financing it should be accepted.

    d.   If an organization is investing in a capital project then it is creating additional long-term value to its shareholders.

    e.   The IRR approach asks if the project return is greater than the borrowing rate.

CHAPTER 10

CASE STUDY: THE GREAT NORTH RUN

INTRODUCTION

The event industry and particularly the sports event industry offer some of the most challenging and exciting opportunities in management. As people continuously search for difference and memorable personal experiences, hosting and participating in sports events have become increasingly popular.

A sports event that manages to successfully combine local community and elite-level competition with highly sustainable levels of participation is that of the Great North Run (GNR). Developed by and for runners, regardless of ability or background, this road race has become one of the most prestigious and largest half-marathons in the world. Such has been the success of the event that the event organizers, Nova International Limited, have become the UK market leader in event management and sport marketing, and since the millennium have progressed on a transformative path of both local and global expansion.

Compiled through considerable desk and field research of stakeholder perspectives, this case study allows you to apply and demonstrate your understanding, analysis and application of the various sport management tools introduced within this text. Accounts of the GNR, its origins, growth and current portfolio, will be followed by a description of the key stakeholders to be managed and its current level of impact. This will provide contextual information to which the management tools from each chapter will be concisely applied albeit in a fictitious manner to improve practice.

GREAT NORTH RUN HISTORY

In 2010 the 30th Bupa Great North Run took place in the north-east of England, where once again participant demand (100,000) massively out-stripped supply (54,000). Being described as 'one of the most famous runs in the world' (Tyne Tees Television, 2000), 'a North East institution' (Nirvana Europe, 2000: 1) and more recently 'the most iconic half-marathon on the planet' (Great Run, 2010a), the Great North Run has evolved into a major sporting event by any criterion. The quantity of participants (54,000 runners and 120,000 spectators), the quality of participants (world record holders and performances), the complexity and diversity of stakeholders (more than 60 organizations annually involved), the widespread international media coverage (185 countries) and the millions of pounds raised for charities mean that the Great North Run has made a significant social, sporting and economic impact in what was once one of England's most depressed regions (Nova, 2000; Smith, 2001).

The origin of the aptly named 'Great North Run' event can be traced back to the rich heritage of athletics in the region and, more specifically, to one particular person, Olympic medallist and local runner Brendan Foster. In the preparations for his final Olympic Games, his winter training took him to Auckland in New Zealand, where he encountered the 10-kilometre Round the Bays Race. Captivated and inspired by the scene of 80,000 participants having so much fun, he set himself the goal of creating a mass-participation community event in north-east England – an event that would offer friend-ship, rivalry, challenge and above all enjoyment for everyone. With four of his athletic club runner friends, John Caine, Max Coleby, Dave Roberts and John Trainor, and over a few beers, the Great North Run concept was born (Caine, 2001).

The rest, as they say, was history, with the first Great North Run taking place on Sunday, 28 June 1981. As the event was developed as a philanthropic voluntary hobby, it was never envisaged that it would be so popular or would go on to affect so many lives. Overwhelmed by the initial response, the Race Director, John Caine (2001), recalls: 'In 1981, there was no feel for it, or real grasp of the scale of it. . . . We expected it to attract about 5,000 runners. However, applications just avalanched and we ended up with 12,000 entries.'

Since then, and as illustrated in Table 10.1, the event has grown considerably, in terms of size, service offering and quality of running experience.

The Great North Run quickly progressed to a professionally organized and managed major sports event or, more precisely, series of events. For example,

Table 10.1 Historical milestones of the Great North Run

1981	First Great North Run on 28 June (12,000 runners; 10,677 finishers).
1984	25,000 runners: Europe's biggest organized road race.
1986	Musyoki established a world record of 1 hour 43 seconds.
	Incorporated the final of the Pearl Assurance half-marathon series, the AAA national championships and the British Disabled Association championships.
1987	Introduced the first Junior Great North Run (5 miles).
1988	Festival of Sport initiated, involving a week of different activities, i.e. the Great North Walk, Great North Ride, Tyne River Races, Junior Great North Run, Great North Roadshow and Great North Run.
1990	Introduced a Great Run Series that included the Great South, the Great Caledonian, the Great Midlands, the Great London and the Great Welsh runs alongside the Great North Run.
1992	IAAF staged the first ever world half-marathon championships in the Great North Run (33 countries).
	Masya set a world half-marathon record time of 1 hour 24 seconds.
1993	Introduced mass warm-ups; bands on the run; more non-sporting celebrities.
2000	50,173 entries – the world's biggest half-marathon.
	Initiated the first Great North Open (golf event).
2001	Introduced the first Great North Women's Run in Manchester.
2003	Radcliffe broke the women's world record over the distance in a time of 1 hour 5 minutes 40 seconds.
2005	Zersenay recorded new world record time of 59 minutes 5 seconds.
2009	IAAF Gold Label road race status awarded to the event.

Information primarily sourced from Great Run (2010a).

such was the popularity of the Great North Run that by the early 1990s horizontal and vertical diversification was evident in the form of the Festival of Sport, which included a Junior Great North Run, a 10-mile family walk and a 30-mile bike ride, and a national Great Run Series; and the event had gained international governing body world half-marathon championship status. More recently the International Association of Athletics Federations (IAAF) has awarded Gold Label road race status, the ultimate world standard in road race organization, not just to the Great North Run but also to Nova's Great Manchester and Great South events.

Based upon the Great North Run formula of integrating elite, celebrity, club and fun runners into a mass-participation event, this premier event is now established as the world's most popular half-marathon, with its tried and tested methods of implementation. From the outset it has been Nova's jewel in the crown of its portfolio of annual sport events. As illustrated in Table 10.2 Nova manages running, swimming and walking events.

The UK Great Run series alone involves more than 150,000 participants each year (Great Run, 2010d). In addition, Nova has established numerous smaller junior and mini events for younger runners, as well as the Tesco Great School Run, a national school-based activity campaign that involves more than 3,000 schools and a million children (Great Run, 2010c). As evident from Table 10.2, Nova has more recently expanded both into overseas markets and into other sports. As explained by their Managing Director:

> It's about looking at new markets and those outside of running and swimming. So, we will look at doing mass participation cycling. We will also build our television arm so we can start producing more programmes. We will also look at how we can monetise the website in terms of advertising, click-throughs and so on.
>
> (Business Link, 2010)

On the basis of such developments, Nova International has quickly grown to become an international company of 52 employees with an annual turnover of more than £12 million (Business Link, 2010).

MANAGEMENT AND IMPACT

Given the significant growth of the event and its strategically aligned and evolving portfolio, it was inevitable that the amateur voluntary hobby would have to give way to more professional management. As the magnitude and complexity of these projects developed, more public, private and voluntary organizations, primarily from the diverse sectors of sport, health, education and tourism, became involved. With all the stakeholders possessing their own reasons and demands for involvement, more professional management became a necessity. From a three-month project, the Great North Run progressed to a 15-month management project, as it is today.

Figure 10.1 is a stakeholder map providing a general understanding of the stakeholders involved in delivering this annual event.

204

Table 10.2 Nova International Limited 2010 brand portfolio

Event	Inaugural year	Month held	Participant numbers	Further details
Bupa Great Run series:				
Bupa Great Winter Run	2005	Early January	3,000	http://www.greatrun.org/Events/Default.aspx
Bupa Great Edinburgh Run	2005	Early May	10,000	N.B. Junior (aged 9–16 years) and/or mini (aged
Bupa Great Manchester Run	2003	Mid-May	34,000	3–8 years) running events are additionally staged in
Bupa Great North 10k	2009	Late July	12,000	association with many of these events, as are other
Bupa Great Yorkshire Run	2007	Early September	8,000	annual events such as the Bupa Great North Run
Bupa Great North Run	1981	Mid-September	54,000	Culture (http://www.greatnorthrunculture.org) and
Bupa Great South Run	1990	Late October	22,000	the 2-kilometre Tesco Great School Run
				(http://www.greatschoolrun.org).
International running events:				
Great Ireland Run	2003	Early April	10,000	http://www.greatirelandrun.org
Great Ethiopian Run	2001	Mid-November	35,000	http://www.ethiopianrun.org
Great Australian Run	2008	Late November	4,000	http://www.greataustralianrun.com.au
Great City Games:				
Great City Games Manchester	2009	Mid-May	Elite performers	http://www.greatcitygames.org
Great Manchester 150	2009	Mid-May		
Great North City Games	2009	Mid-September		
British Gas Great Swim series:				
British Gas Great East Swim	2009	Late June	2,000	http://www.greatswim.org
British Gas Great London Swim	2009	Early July	2,000	
British Gas Great Scottish Swim	2009	End August	2,000	
British Gas Great North Swim	2008	Early September	7,000	
British Gas Great Salford Swim	2010	Late September	N/A	
Diabetes UK Great North Walk	1988	Late June	Recreation	http://www.greatwalk.org

Information sourced from Great Run (2010b) and Great Run (2010c).

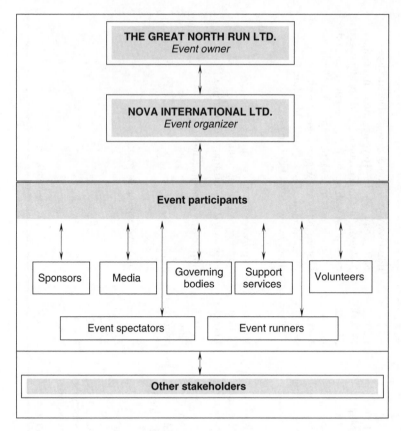

Figure 10.1 Original stakeholder map of the Great North Run event

The event was initially owned by a charitable trust (registered number 3093780), The Great North Run Limited, which commissioned Nova International Limited, a private sector sporting events and marketing agency, to organize, market and promote the event on its behalf. Since then the charity has been wound up, and Nova now owns all the rights associated with this and its other events. It earns money by selling these rights to sponsors (such as Bupa, Nike, British Gas and Powerade), television partners (such as Sky Sports, BBC and Five), location partners (such as Newcastle, Gateshead and South Tyneside city councils) and, as participant entries, the general public (Business Link, 2010). As elaborated by Nova's Managing Director, this is achieved through 'a dedicated team which coordinates the events, a marketing team and we have our own television company, so we can do complete turnkey solutions, staging the event, marketing the event, promoting it and televising it' (Business Link, 2010). From concept to implementation, the

206

original founders of the GNR are employed in either a full- or a part-time basis to make each event happen.

As highlighted in Figure 10.1, the event participants of the Great North Run come from a broad array of different organizations. In just considering sponsors this typically entails a title sponsor, official media, a location, sportswear, a sports drink, water, and a timing partner, as well as other official suppliers. Such sponsorship opportunities reflect both above- and below-the-line financial or in-kind sponsorship, with the complexity of each being dependent upon the appropriate levels of negotiation and contractual legislation of each event. In addition, individual sponsors possess their own business network and partners. For example, Bupa, an international health care leader, has been the Great North Run event title sponsor since 1993, one of the longest-running sponsorships in any sport. It has sponsored countless sports events and fitness initiatives, including a network of Bupa-approved health clubs across the UK and a teenage health and fitness website to inspire teenagers to get off the couch and live more active lifestyles. With a reported 7,000 leads from each Great North Run event (Nova, 2000), Bupa has a global reach of 10 million insurance customers from more than 190 countries (Bupa, 2009).

The media possess considerable power as a significant enabler of mass communication and sponsorship. Using extensive television (terrestrial and satellite), radio and print media, the Great North Run enjoys excellent international, national, regional and local coverage, which is enhanced by its own in-house television production company FilmNova. The events accommodate up to 100 media personnel each race day and can generate a global audience in excess of 150 million (Great Run, 2010c).

To attract the very best elite performers and officials from around the world, the event requires official sanctioning from the international and national governing bodies of the sport. These include organizations such as the International Association of Athletics Federations, UK Athletics, the English Federation of Disability Sport and the British Wheelchair Racing Association.

Furthermore, it is the support services that are vital in providing their quality services before, during and after any major event that determine its success. In the case of the Great North Run, the three public sector authorities through which the run passes – Newcastle, Gateshead and South Tyneside city councils – have always been heavily involved in the event, as have the British Red Cross, St John Ambulance, Northumbria Ambulance Service, Northumbria Police, and the Tyne and Wear Fire and Rescue Service.

As for most major sport events, it is the volunteers and community groups that form the backbone of the Great North Run. Volunteers alone amount to approximately 1,300 persons on race day, 100 at the start, 600 around the course, and 600 dispersed at the finish. This equates to 98 per cent of the workforce. As elaborated by Allan Wilson (2001), the Great North Run Finish Director, '15 voluntary organizations, from both sport and non-sport backgrounds, have provided excellent voluntary support at the finish – 95 per cent of them have always been involved and in most cases it is exactly the same people, year after year'.

Whilst volunteers make up the vast majority of the workforce, it is the event runners and event spectators who constitute 99 per cent of stakeholder involvement at the event. They are obviously the Great North Run's *raison d'être* and, as briefly illustrated in Table 10.3, it appears that everyone possesses his or her own personal motivation and inspirational story to tell.

And finally there are the many other stakeholders that are associated with the Great North Run. Their diversity varies from national, regional and local education, health, sport and tourism organization projects through to the hundreds of charities that annually benefit from runner participation. For example, in 2008 there were over 400 charities registered as Great Run charity partners, and every year Great Run series runners raise more than £28 million for charitable causes (Great Run, 2010c).

Nova International Limited and the Great North Run are a perfect example of a sport organization with growth and dynamism that has provided social and economic benefits to the individual, community and region, across both short- and long-term timescales. From a hobby and individual vision, the event has evolved into a significant focus for effective partnerships, an inspiration and personal challenge to so many. More than a million runners have already completed the event. In excess of 4 million spectators have watched it, and the event has probably touched the life of every person in the region.

Demonstrating a genuine and socially inclusive approach to sport, the Great North Run has proved that disability (wheelchair athletes were included in the inaugural 1981 event), age (17- to 88-year-olds regularly run) and running ability (novice through to elite) are not a barrier to participation. Shoulder to shoulder, all participate as one and, best of all, the local community can join the party, as viewing the event is free! But, as every runner knows, the experience, memories and anecdotes last so much longer than the day of competition. Behind every runner there exist family and friends who support and share in the training rituals, the preparations, the disappointments, the serious and joyous moments, and the final celebrations. From lifestyle guidance and choice of pre-race meal, to what should be worn on 'the day', everyone becomes an expert.

208

Table 10.3 Great North Run motives

Participant category	Personal story
First-time runner	'I underwent a quadruple heart bypass operation at Papworth Hospital. I discovered recently that it took four attempts to bring me round in intensive care. Having been fortunate enough to be provided with a second chance, I want to give back something to others who suffer from similar life-threatening illnesses. This is where I stop being an 'also ran' and become a runner with a destination! . . . One or two people who know me well will be aware that in normal circumstances I cannot run more than 100 yards. . . . I started training for the race in October last year and can now comfortably run 3,000 metres. I *will* complete the Great North Run and, in doing so, my goal is to raise £1 million for the Gift of Life Commemorative Trust' (Ellis, 2000).
Disabled runner	'Derek chose the Tommy Campaign to benefit from his fund raising efforts because he and his wife Angela lost two daughters born sleeping several years ago. . . . To run the half marathon is all the more remarkable because of Derek's disabilities. Not only is he deaf, he has suffered with arthritis in his feet for more than 10 years, so much so that he had to have a toe removed and the bones in his feet fused. . . . "I reckon that I raised £1,508 per mile of the half marathon, and I am just so chuffed that I managed to complete the run"' (*Rothwell and District Record*, 2000: 23).
Unusual running experiences	'We had one runner who couldn't make it to the event as he had to work, so he did it on the oil rig he was working at!' (Roy, 2001: 1).
Overseas runner from USA	'She stumbled on the event when she was on holiday ten years ago over here. Entered at the last minute, begged for an entry, and we let her run. And she has come back every year, makes the pilgrimage; she comes on her own. She's in her sixties and has a whale of a time' (Caine, 2001).
Proud parent/ spectator	'When I saw Jenny enter the finish straight, a lump came in my throat. I began to cry and just hugged my husband – we were so very, very proud of our daughter's achievement' (Anonymous).

Through effectively managing a complex network of individual and collective stakeholders, the Great North Run has become a catalyst to regeneration, developing active and healthy lifestyles, enhancing citizenship and improving the vibrancy and quality of life in north-east England. Through continuous innovation, reflection and commitment, as well as a very sincere concern for the quality of the runner experience, Nova International Limited has captivated, inspired, educated and entertained people both in the region and beyond.

MANAGEMENT TOOL APPLICATION

But where do the organization and event go from here? For this final section, we address this question by systematically applying each chapter management tool to some element of the case study. Please note that, even though these scenarios are based upon case study contexts, the information contained must be considered fictitious and does not represent the views of Nova International Limited. The examples introduced are merely developed for learning purposes, providing you with specific contexts in which to recognize applied and competent management practice. Furthermore, given the breadth and depth of tools covered within each chapter, only brief and concise snapshots will be selected here. More comprehensive analysis and evidence-based reporting would be expected in your work-related practice.

Applied SWOT analysis (Chapter 2)

Introduction

Planning presupposes an understanding and appraisal of the current situation. Using the organization as the unit of analysis, yet focusing predominantly on its primary product, the Great North Run, Table 10.4 provides you with a very basic SWOT analysis. From just three identified strengths, weaknesses, opportunities and threats, the use of other chapter planning tools can be demonstrated.

Management implications

Derived from this very short SWOT analysis, strategic planning options could include:

- Building and maintaining strengths, e.g. communicating and exploiting the sustainable, inspirational and socially inclusive elements of mass-participation events.
- Reducing or ideally eradicating weaknesses, e.g. formalizing Great North Run procedures, processes and plans, and employing as well as training new staff to ensure event sustainability.
- Prioritizing and optimizing the identified opportunities, e.g. developing national programmes that address health agendas and exploit technological reach. Currently started with the Nova (2009) 'Take to the streets' programme (http://www.taketothestreets.org/) that helps people train for their goal, whether this be at a local gym or at a Nova event.

210

Table 10.4 Great North Run SWOT analysis example

Strengths	Weaknesses
1 A mass-participation sports event that can appeal to all ages and abilities and has been the catalyst to regional regeneration, creating significant and sustained social and economic impact.	1 The Great North Run is at maximum capacity. Increasing the number of road runners would be too dangerous given the historical start, finish and route, without losing the fundamental values of the event.
2 The organizing team is a long-established small group of former athletes with unrivalled road race expertise and contacts in the athletic world, e.g. multi-world record holder Haile Gebrselassie, a personal friend of Brendan Foster the GNR founder, was instrumental in establishing the Great Ethiopian Run.	2 A number of deaths have occurred naturally on race day (Bird, Powell and Goodbody, 2005). Not unusual given the volume of spectators and participants, but this has created negative press on what should be an enjoyable celebration of life.
3 Key components and decisions can be controlled from within one organization, e.g. Nova historically possessed an event division, a media division (FilmNova), a clothing division (View From) and a marketing division.	3 The organizing team and many volunteers have largely been the same for three decades, which has meant excellent contemporary practical knowledge but little has been written down and no project management plan exists.

Opportunities	Threats
1 Sport and business expectations, professional management training and career opportunities have significantly developed at both local and international levels.	1 With an increased frequency of sports and events there are now cluttered schedules with unprecedented competitive offerings, e.g. London Marathon or new sports such as parkour (free running).
2 Governments are establishing fitness, health and wellness campaigns to stem rising obesity rates and reduce health costs.	2 Increased accountabilities, safety expectations and hosting costs, e.g. 2010 saw its open water British Gas Great Scottish and North Swim events cancelled owing to toxic algae (Great Run, 2010b).
3 Technological developments and reliance on computers and mobile phones have grown exponentially in the last decade. This has significant implications for participant pre- and post-communications and race day operations, e.g. IPICO timing chips used by all runners as their race timing device (Great Run, 2010e).	3 Developed societies are increasingly valuing and expecting socially responsible ethical and environmental management practices.

211

- Combating the threats, e.g. highlighting the social causes of runners and corporate socially responsible behaviours of environmentally friendly management practices.

Meeting these goals and further growing the business are likely to entail one or more of Ansoff's (1957) growth strategies, namely:

- market penetration (current product, current market), e.g. within or across years offering discounts or creating loyalty schemes for participants who engage in Nova's multi-events programme;
- product development (new product, current market), e.g. introducing a developmental programme of mass dance or cycling events to key UK cities already used so as to help reduce obesity rates;
- market development (current product, new market), e.g. using the tried and tested Great North Run formula to enter and establish a series of events in other potentially untapped economic countries such as India or China;
- product diversification (new product, new market), e.g. creating new product ranges such as healthy sport drinks, watches or even an in-house radio station.

Some of these directional strategies will be further exploited via the applied management tool examples to follow.

Applied performance criteria and measures (Chapter 3)

Introduction

Each organization involved with the Great North Run should possess its own reasons and purpose for being so. This should include establishing performance criteria and measurements that will determine the effectiveness of its actions. Table 10.5 illustrates two such organizational examples, with the establishment of hierarchical and logically aligned criteria.

Management implications

Such aims, objectives and key performance indicators provide clarity, focus and shared commitment towards goal achievement. They in turn act as planning and motivating targets from which subsequent processes, systems and actions can be determined and justified.

212

Table 10.5 Great North Run performance criteria and measures

Organization	Performance criterion	Performance measure	
Nova International	Event mission	To organize the world's best, safest and most enjoyable running event.	
	Event aims	1	To stage an enjoyable and competitive event that provides an opportunity for community involvement, as well as national and international participation
		2	To facilitate participants' raising money for charity.
	SMART objectives (examples relating just to aim 1 above)	1.1	Develop and implement recruitment strategies by 1 January 20XX that will attract: – 5 of the top 10 IAAF world-ranked male and female half-marathon runners; – 20 female celebrity runners; – at least 5 per cent more wheelchair participants than last year; – at least 30 per cent of runners from previous Great North Run events; – runners from more than 50 countries, five continents and every postcode in the UK.
		1.2	Host four pre- and two post-race events that allow members of the general public to meet, have photos with and autographs signed by the elite and celebrity runners.
		1.3	Employ 25 volunteers at least one month before the event to help local runners produce press releases and capture photos that can successfully capture their inspirational story for local media coverage.
	Key performance indicators (examples relating just to objective 1.3 above and ranked in order of importance)	■	At least 100 × 10-centimetre column stories printed in different local papers before the GNR.
		■	Five of these stories to be captured by FilmNova and then broadcast on television with the theme 'a race within a race'. To be shown one week before the event and then followed up during and after the event to inspire others to participate in next year's event.
		■	Award five prize winners of the best 'community photograph' the opportunity to participate in an all-expenses-paid Nova event as well as to see their photo and name printed in a national newspaper.

Table 10.5 Continued

Organization	Performance criterion	Performance measure	
Nike (official sportswear partner of the Bupa Great Run series)	Event aims	1	To enhance the experience of a Great North Run runner in a fun and exciting way.
		2	To inspire and empower new and existing communications with Nike+ (see Table 2.3 and Chapter 2) runners at the event.
	SMART objectives (examples relating just to aim 2 above)	2.1	Develop and implement a 16-week pre-event and post-event communication strategy with all Nike+ runners by 30 April 20XX.
		2.2	Recruit at least 200 new mobile phone users to the Nike+ hotline one month before the event.
		2.3	Sell at least 500 Nike+ running products to this year's Great North Run entrants within one month of the event date.
	Key performance indicators (example relating to just objective 2.1 above)	■	Provide at least 1,000 signed-up Nike+ runners with a pre- and post-run networking forum that will include: – pre-event training schedules, expert advice, and access to new running partners and products; – post-event graphically displayed split times and certificate immediately after the event; – post-event Nike+ VIP runners comfort zone situated in the finish area that will permit docking stations for Nike+ equipment, a family meeting point, a chill-out music area and massage.

Ideas sourced from Connelly (1996) and Great Run (2010c).

Applied risk analysis (Chapter 4)

Introduction

As identified in the SWOT analysis, one of the Great North Run's weaknesses is the participant deaths that have been encountered in the race's history. Given that the road race is at maximum capacity and uses a route that is not specifically designed for running, risk assessment, treatment and control practices must be continuously appraised and documented. An example of an output of this process is provided in the brief risk assessment extract in Table 10.6.

214

Table 10.6 Great North Run risk assessment

Risk number and type	Identified hazard	People affected	Existing precautions	Probability	Severity	Risk level	Further actions
1.1 Human factor	Start: Large numbers of people assembling at the start area	Competitors, spectators and start officials	Operational management plan in place for the start; competitors are pre-informed via information booklet and mail-out; use of information and directional signage; marshals provided to manage assembly procedure; police presence to assist with event safety; use of PA to keep crowds informed; use of big screens to relay messages.	4	1	4 = low/medium	Local authority and emergency services major incident plans would be brought into operation in the event of the need to evacuate the start area for any reason.
1.2 Human factor	Start: Construction of start gantry	Start area set-up team, competitors and officials	Use of professional contractors working to relevant industry standards.	2	1	2 = low	Visual inspection – Start Director.
1.3 Human factor	Route: Pinch point at XXX	Competitors	Police presence and deployment as identified in Northumbria Police operational support plan.	4	2	8 = medium	Signage to be introduced; padding to be added to street furniture; video footage to be taken for future analysis; event control decision to control roundabout on the day if required.

Table 10.6 Continued

Risk number and type	Identified hazard	People affected	Existing precautions	Probability	Severity	Risk level	Further actions
1.4 Human factor	Route: General participant and spectator injuries	Competitors and spectators	Duty of care and medical arrangements as set out in the event's multi-agency medical response operation plan. Under the auspices of British Red Cross Northumbria Branch, the NEAS paramedic motorcycles and VAS ambulances.	4	3	12 = high	Comprehensive review of medical arrangements each year through the race doctor.

Source: Adapted from Nova International (2000).

Management implications

Having proactively identified, evaluated, categorized and prioritized the event risks, you can establish thresholds to trigger either management actions to control the risks or acceptance of the consequences. In the case of managing the Great North Run, normal and emergency operation procedures are annually reviewed and approved by multi-agency specialist emergency services. Nova's safety plan alone documents more than 300 pages of detail that includes pre- and post-road closures, traffic management arrangements, runner route maps, start and finish area plans, command flow charts, management of emergency situations and even fatality procedures (Nova International, 2000).

Applied job description (Chapter 5)

Introduction

With international development being one of Nova's immediate growth strategies, a new position has been created in the company, namely a Logistics and Transport Manager for the Great Run event series. A fictitious job description for this position (with some common areas omitted) is presented in Table 10.7.

Management implications

Having identified the context-specific nature and requirements of the position, as well as the essential and desirable characteristics of the ideal person, you can plan your recruitment, selection and induction processes. Remember that to improve your operational performance and future productivity in any service industry people are your most valuable assets.

Applied product life cycle and Boston Consulting Group matrix (Chapter 6)

Introduction

In 2005 Nova reviewed its event portfolio. Based upon running numbers (sales) and the year of inaugural event (sales volume), it located each event on the product life cycle, as illustrated in Figure 10.2.

In addition, Nova considered broader data sources that related to the control it had over its market (measured as market share) as well as the attractiveness

Table 10.7 Great Run series Logistics and Transport Manager job description

Title of position: Logistics and Transport Manager	*Reports to: Event Director*

Purpose of the role	To ensure that Nova events run on time, to budget and to defined quality standards, a Logistics and Transport Manager is required to take responsibility to scope and implement the freight, logistic and regional transport services of the Great Run Event series. This position will involve working closely with Event Services to develop policies and procedures for the transport of equipment between sport and non-sport venues.
Responsibilities	1 Freight
	■ Develop and implement policies and procedures for the transport of equipment between event bases.
	■ Provide an effective operational link between any appointed freight service provider and Nova events.
	■ Meet monthly with the Event Director to plan and review freight operations and provide regular work plans.
	2 Logistics
	■ Scope the equipment requirements at venues, such as, but not limited to, the start and finish areas, the main operations centre, and the media and VIP centres.
	■ Coordinate the fit-out, bump-in and decommissioning of the sport and non-sport venues.
	■ Manage one of the on-site storage facilities.
	3 Staff management and training
	■ Manage and motivate a team of logistics and transport volunteers.
	■ Provide training and development initiatives to improve performance, efficiency and safety.
	■ Oversee and support the projects undertaken by the Logistics Operations Assistants.
	4 Regional transport coordination
	■ Scope, plan and coordinate the transport requirements through the event's Transport Network and Communication Plan.
	■ Develop timely route plans for the arrival and departure of elite athletes from the airport or train station to hotel and official sport and non-sport venues.
	■ Ensure transport suppliers are appropriately booked and confirmed, and scheduled information is communicated to all relevant stakeholders.
	5 Risk management
	■ Assist in the development of the logistic and transport policy, procedures and risk register.

6 General
- ■ Ensure positive working relationship with all stakeholders through efficient communication.
- ■ Undertake other duties as determined by the Event Director to meet organization objectives.

Key relationships
External – venues; sponsors; suppliers; border control agencies.
Internal – accreditation; corporate hospitality and VIP services; ICT Manager; Event Services; volunteers.

Key competencies required
Essential criteria:
- – Project management experience of hosting international events.
- – Advanced knowledge of Microsoft Project, Word, Excel, PowerPoint.
- – Excellent organizational skills, able to juggle conflicting priorities professionally and cope effectively under pressure.
- – Willingness to take ownership and be held accountable.
- – Ability to communicate effectively with senior levels of management.

Desirable criteria:
- – Qualifications in logistical management or a related discipline.
- – Proven experience in providing leadership and direction to staff.

Additional information
As well as offering staff the opportunities to work on some of the biggest and best sporting events in the world, we provide them with training opportunities, competitive salaries and a supportive environment in which to develop their careers. All staff receive 25 days' holiday per year, a generous pension scheme, annual bonuses, staff discounts and a range of other flexible benefits.

Source: Adapted from Great Run (2010f) and International Rugby Board (2010) recruitment positions.

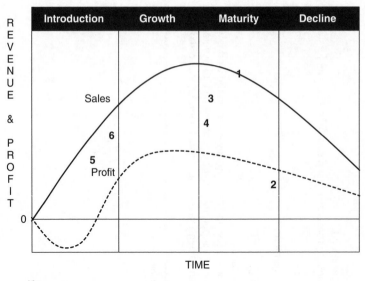

Key:
1 = Great North Run; **2** = Great North Walk; **3** = Great South Run; **4** = Great
Ethiopian Run; **5** = Great Manchester Run; **6** = Great Ireland Run

Figure 10.2 Nova's product life cycle of events

and potential future sales of this market (market growth). Nova had previously reviewed its strategic business units of events (E), marketing (M),
television (T) and clothing (C) divisions, and plotted the BCG matrix findings
as shown in Figure 10.3.

Management implications

From the findings it was apparent that the majority of events could be found
in the maturity stage of the PLC as well as primarily just in one market,
running. This left Nova particularly vulnerable in terms of its long-term
future and limited product range. From Figure 10.3 it was additionally
evident that the events division was its most profitable strategic business
unit and that its clothing division was its poorest. Management decisions
derived from these data led to the following growth strategy actions:

- new running events in the UK and overseas, e.g. the introduction of the
  Great Winter and Edinburgh Runs in 2005, the Great Yorkshire Run in
  2007, the Great Australian Run in 2008 and the Great North 10k race in
  2009;
- new types of running events in the UK, e.g. Great City Games in 2009;

220

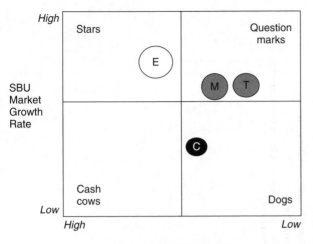

Figure 10.3 Boston Consulting Group matrix applied to Nova's strategic business units

- new sports events in the UK, e.g. the Great North Swim in 2008; the Great East, London and Scottish Swims in 2009 and the Great Salford Swim in 2010;
- to maintain a balanced portfolio, the sale of its clothing line (View From), with the money used to invest in the marketing and television divisions.

Applied project management analysis (Chapter 7)

Introduction

Another of the weaknesses identified in the SWOT analysis was that the very experienced event team possessed considerable practical knowledge but very little had been formalized on paper, not least the vital planning schedule. Furthermore, aligned with professional and technological developments, planning and tracking software became readily available to grow the business and share the expertise within the company. This led to the software printouts presented in Figures 10.4 to 10.7.

Management implications

Management interpretation of the project management information contained within Figures 10.4 to 10.7 include:

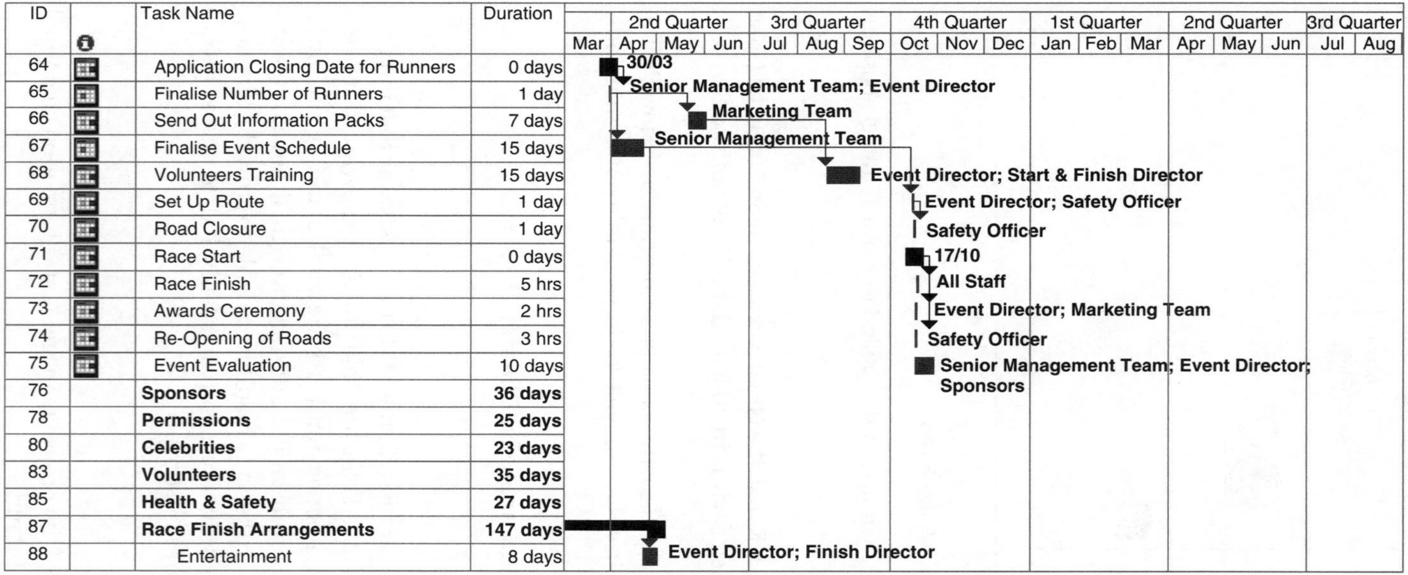

ID
Task Name
Duration
2nd Quarter
3rd Quarter
4th Quarter
1st Quarter
2nd Quarter
3rd Quarter
Mar
Apr
May
Jun
Jul
Aug
Sep
Oct
Nov
Dec
Jan
Feb
Mar
Apr
May
Jun
Jul
Aug
64 Application Closing Date for Runners 0 days
65 Finalise Number of Runners 1 day
66 Send Out Information Packs 7 days
67 Finalise Event Schedule 15 days
68 Volunteers Training 15 days
69 Set Up Route 1 day
70 Road Closure 1 day
71 Race Start 0 days
72 Race Finish 5 hrs
73 Awards Ceremony 2 hrs
74 Re-Opening of Roads 3 hrs
75 Event Evaluation 10 days
76 Sponsors 36 days
78 Permissions 25 days
80 Celebrities 23 days
83 Volunteers 35 days
85 Health & Safety 27 days
87 Race Finish Arrangements 147 days
88 Entertainment 8 days
30/03
Senior Management Team; Event Director
Marketing Team
Senior Management Team
Event Director; Start & Finish Director
Event Director; Safety Officer
Safety Officer
17/10
All Staff
Event Director; Marketing Team
Safety Officer
Senior Management Team; Event Director; Sponsors
Event Director; Finish Director

Figure 10.4 Gantt chart of the Great North Run

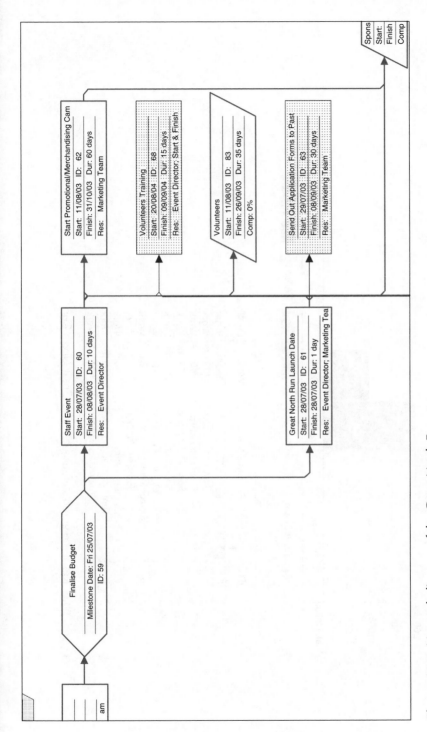

Figure 10.5 Network diagram of the Great North Run

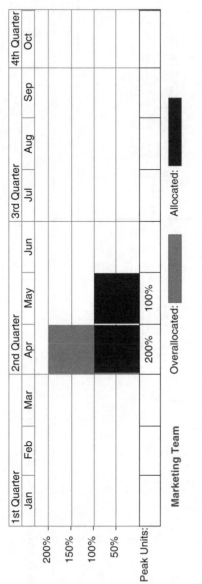

Figure 10.6 Resource graph staff usage of the Great North Run

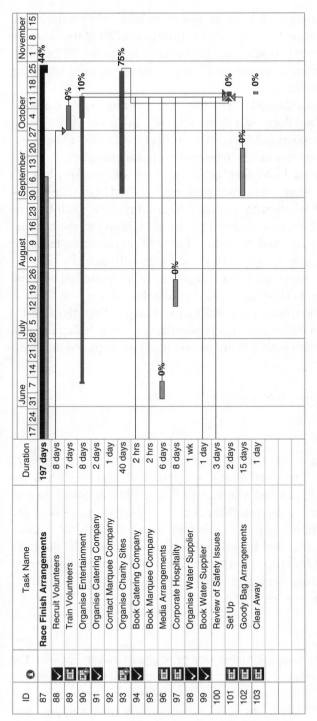

Figure 10.7 Tracking Gantt chart of the Great North Run

- From Figure 10.4 it should be apparent that there are two key milestones, namely the 'Application Closing Date for Runners' of 30 March and the 'Race Start' date, which was scheduled to be held on Sunday, 17 October. These are target dates, which have a direct impact on the successful completion of the event.
- Figure 10.5 shows that the tasks of 'Volunteers Training' and 'Send Out Application Forms' are the only non-critical tasks of the network shown. All other tasks must be completed on time; otherwise a trade-off between quality, resource and time needs to be carefully managed.
- Figure 10.6 reveals that the Marketing Team is over-allocated on specific tasks and dates. On other dates, such personnel are not being used. This has implications for whether they should be employed on a full-time or part-time basis, and for management decisions relating to them being given additional support and/or reallocated to other roles and tasks for this event or other projects, where they are under-utilized.
- Figure 10.7 suggests that all the tasks with a tick are complete and on time, but for whatever reason there has been considerable slippage on the task of 'Organise the Entertainment' at the finish and on the 'Organise Charity Sites' task. Urgent management action is now required, which should focus on addressing these two issues, if the project is to be completed on time.

Applied profit/volume graph (Chapter 8)

Introduction

As already mentioned, one very successful growth strategy adopted by Nova has been to expand the Great North Run concept to new markets both in the UK and overseas. Having enjoyed a decade of the Great Ethiopian Run and more recently the Great Australian Run, you have decided to look at the feasibility of entering a new and potentially very large international market, namely India. Having consulted heavily with your world athletic contacts and the local experts in India, you have calculated race costs and prices for a 10-kilometre introductory event and presented the information as a profit/volume graph, as shown in Figure 10.8.

Management implications

Assuming the accuracy of your estimates, this provides management with the following important information. For the inaugural Great Indian Run the worst-case scenario is a cost of £20,000 and at best, if 10,000 runners participate, you could make a profit of £20,000. The break-even point is 5,000 runners, and

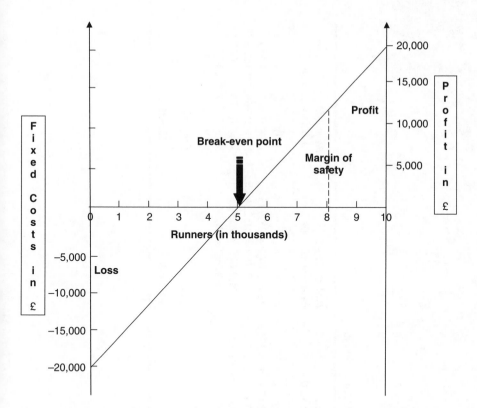

Figure 10.8 Profit/volume graph of the Great Indian Run

local estimates suggest that 8,000 runners for this type of event (the margin of safety) are likely to be a realistic participation figure for this inaugural event.

Whilst the costs and profit are not particularly high, this could be the start of a Great Indian Run series with similar long-term effects accruing as witnessed in the UK model.

Applied capital investment analysis (Chapter 9)

Introduction

Whilst UK business growth has meant new offices in Manchester and London, with headquarters remaining in Newcastle (Business Link, 2010), Nova now requires a similar capital investment decision to be made for an office base in India. Currently you have viewed four offices in different Indian cities and calculated investment costs and returns based on various lease or buy options, as indicated in Table 10.8.

Table 10.8 New Indian office projects: net present values @ 14% discount rate

Year	Project A PV cash flow (£000)	Project B PV cash flow (£ 000)	Project C PV cash flow (£ 000)	Project D PV cash flow (£ 000)
0	(45)	(55)	(70)	(110)
1	18 × 0.877 = 15.786	40 × 0.877 = 35.08	25 × 0.877 = 21.925	15 × 0.877 = 13.155
2	18 × 0.769 = 13.842	30 × 0.769 = 23.07	25 × 0.769 = 19.225	25 × 0.769 = 19.225
3	18 × 0.675 = 12.15	60* × 0.675 = 40.5	35 × 0.675 = 23.625	35 × 0.675 = 23.625
4			35 × 0.592 = 20.72	35 × 0.592 = 20.72
				100* × 0.519 = 51.9
Net cash flow total	41.778	98.65	85.495	128.625
Total NPV	**−3.222**	**+43.65**	**+15.495**	**+18.625**

* Includes a residual value of selling off the asset.

Management implications

Using the current national inflation rate, it is apparent that all positive NPV office investments, namely B, C and D are at least financially viable and worthy of further consideration. Given that project A is negative it is likely to be rejected, unless there are other significant factors to be considered. This investment appraisal tool suggests that projects B, D and C should warrant further analysis in that order. However, financial decisions alone should not decide the outcome. Other very practical considerations in this case could include distance from the international airport, location from elite and running clubs, city population and catchment area, public transport infrastructure, access to a running-specific sporting venue, or even negative influences such as city-specific terror alerts or the dengue fever outbreak warnings that have recently been issued for the city of New Delhi (Fakkert, 2010).

REFERENCES

7 News (2008) Nike contractor used forced labour. Online. Available http://cosmos. bcst.yahoo.com/up/player/popup/?rn=248153&cl=8922679&ch=&src=y7news (accessed 2 September 2009).

ACCA (2008) *A better measure?* ACCA. Online. Available http://www.accaglobal. com/pubs/students/publications/student_accountant/archive/sa_apr08_ryan2.pdf (accessed 15 September 2010).

Adcock, D., Halborg, A. and Ross, C. (2001) *Marketing principles and practice*, 4th edn. Harlow: Pearson Education.

AIRMIC, ALARM and IRM (2002) *A risk management standard*. Online. Available http://www.theirm.org/publications/documents/Risk_Management_Standard_03 0820.pdf (accessed 22 February 2010).

Ambler, G. (2006) *10 steps to setting SMART objectives*. Online. Available http://www.thepracticeofleadership.net/2006/10/15/10-steps-to-setting-smart-objectives/ (accessed 17 July 2009).

American Express (2010) *Know who you want to hire: an interactive hiring tool*. Online. Available http://www133.americanexpress.com/osbn/tool/hiring/intro. asp (accessed 26 May 2010).

Ansoff, I. (1957) Strategies for diversification. *Harvard Business Review*, 35 (5): 113–124.

Anthony, W.P., Kacmar, K.M. and Perrewé, P.L. (2006) *Human resource management: a strategic approach*, 5th edn. Mason, OH: Thomson Custom Solutions.

Asia Pacific Marketing Federation (2010) *Business portfolio analysis*. Marketing Institute of Singapore. Online. Available http://www.apmf.org.sg/Lt2—BusiPortfo Analysis.ppt (accessed 22 July 2010).

Audit Commission (2000) *On target: the practice of performance indicators*. Online. Available http://www.audit-commission.gov.uk/SiteCollectionDocuments/Audit CommissionReports/NationalStudies/archive_mptarget.pdf (accessed 5 October 2009).

Australian Communications and Media Authority (2005) *Appendix 4 – Risk management plan*. Online. Available http://www.acma.gov.au/webwr/_assets/ main/lib299/appen%204%20-%20risk%20management%20plan.pdf (accessed 22 February 2010).

Australian Public Service Commission (2002) *Performance management*. Canberra: Commonwealth of Australia.

230

Bacal and Associates (2009) *What is the critical incident method of performance appraisal?* Online. Available http://performance-appraisals.org/faq/criticalincident. htm (accessed 26 May 2010).

Balanced Scorecard Designer (2009) *Leadership balanced scorecard metrics template.* Online. Available http://www.strategy2act.com/solutions/leadership_excel.htm?s 14lea1google&gclid=CJf9raLlyp4CFYctpAodF17jqw (accessed 10 December 2009).

Barksdale, H.C. and Harris, C.E. (1982) Portfolio analysis and the product life cycle. *Long Range Planning*, 15 (6): 74–83.

Beech, J. and Chadwick, S. (Eds) (2004) *The business of sport management.* Harlow: Pearson Education.

Berry, S. and Thomas, R. (2009) *Use SMART objectives to focus goals, plans and performance.* Online. Available http://www.projectsmart.co.uk/use-smart-objectives-to-focus-goals-plans-and-performance.html (accessed 9 October 2009).

Berry, T. (2010) *Break-even analysis*. Online. Available http://articles.bplans.com/ writing-a-business-plan/break-even-analysis/131 (accessed 22 August 2010).

Bhusnurmath, M. (2009) The special thing about the Olympics. *Economic Times*, 6 October.

Bird, S., Powell, D. and Goodbody, J. (2005) Four die as runners feel heat of Great North Run. *The Times*. Online. Available http://www.timesonline.co.uk/tol/ news/uk/article568295.ece (accessed 13 September 2010).

Black, F. and Scholes, M. (1973) The pricing of options and corporate liabilities. *Journal of Political Economy*, 81 (3): 637–654.

Blanchard, K., Zigarmi, P. and Zigarmi, D. (1986) *Leadership and the one minute manager.* London: Collins.

Blythe, J. (2001) *Essentials of marketing*, 2nd edn. Harlow: Pearson Education.

Boehlje, M. and Ehmke, C. (2005) *Capital investment analysis and project assessment.* West Lafayette, IN: Purdue University.

Boston Consulting Group (2010) *The Boston Consulting Group.* Online. Available http://www.bcg.com/ (accessed 22 July 2010).

Brand Finance (2009) *Kolkata Knight Riders is richest in IPL.* Online. Available http://www.brandfinance.com/Uploads/pdfs/JBIPL070509.pdf (accessed 22 July 2010).

Brassington, F. and Pettitt, S. (2003) *Principles of marketing*, 3rd edn. Harlow: Pearson Education.

Bratton, J. and Gold, J. (2003) *Human resource management*, 2nd edn. London: Lawrence Erlbaum Associates.

Briner, W., Geddes, M. and Hasting, C. (1996) *Project leadership*, 2nd edn. Aldershot: Gower.

Bupa (2009) *Annual reports and accounts 2009: Helping people live longer, healthier, happier lives.* Online. Available http://www.bupa.com/jahia/webdav/site/bupa com/shared/Documents/PDFs/financial-information/annual-report-and-accounts-2009.pdf (accessed 13 September 2010).

Businessballs.com (2009) *Project management.* Online. Available http://www. businessballs.com/project.htm (accessed 16 September 2009).

Businessballs.com (2010) *Job descriptions.* Online. Available http://www.business balls.com/jobdescription.htm (accessed 26 May 2010).

Business Link (2010) *Case study: Nova International.* Online. Available http://www. businesslink.gov.uk/bdotg/action/detail?site=101&itemId=5001497643&type=ON EOFFPAGE (accessed 13 September 2010).

Business Week (2008) The 100 top brands. Online. Available http://images.business week.com/ss/08/09/0918_best_brands/30.htm (accessed 2 September 2009).

Buzzell, R.D. (2004) The PIMS program of strategy research: a retrospective appraisal. *Journal of Business Research*, 57 (5): 478–483.

Caine, J. (2001) Informal interview on 13 July 2001 at Nova International Limited.

Carter, S., Macdonald, N.J. and Cheng, D.C.B. (1997) *Basic finance for marketers*. Rome: Food and Agriculture Organization of the United Nations.

Carvalho, S. (2009) Abu Dhabi's F1 firm reveals break even target. *Arabian Business*. Online. Available http://www.arabianbusiness.com/550788-abu-dhabis-f1-firm-reveals-break-even-target (accessed 15 September 2010).

Cengage Learning (2010) *Present value tables*. Online. Available http://www.sw learning.com/finance/brigham/ifm7e/pvtables.xls (accessed 15 September 2010).

CFA (2010) *CFA exam prep: level 2 capital budgeting process*. Online. Available http://www.youtube.com/watch?v=YewEQ_AL0X0 (accessed 15 September 2010).

CFAR (Centre for Applied Research) (n.d.) *Mini case study – Nike's 'Just do it' advertising campaign*. Online. Available http://www.cfar.com/Documents/nike cmp.pdf (accessed 2 September 2009).

Change Factory (2009) *Customer needs analysis*. Online. Available http://www.changefactory.com.au/articles/article_224.shtml (accessed 16 December 2009).

Chartered Institute of Personnel and Development (2010) *Recruitment: an overview*. Online. Available http://www.cipd.co.uk/subjects/recruitmen/general/recruitmt. htm (accessed 26 May 2010).

Chelladurai, P. (2006) *Human resource management in sport and recreation*, 2nd edn. Champaign, IL: Human Kinetics.

Chinn, M. (2007) Do we know a trend is a trend? *Econbrowser*. Online. Available http://www.econbrowser.com/archives/2007/12/do_we_know_a_tr.html (accessed 15 September 2010).

Commonwealth of Australia (2009) *Notes for using the job analysis template*. Online. Available http://www.cpsisc.com.au/Resources/A_Construction%20HR/GC%20 Notes%20for%20using%20the%20Job%20Analysis%20Template.doc (accessed 26 May 2010).

Connelly, H. (1996) An investigation to determine the demographic, geographic and motivational influences of the 1995 Great North Run participants and the evaluation of two 1996 promotional mediums from a student perspective to determine marketing implications. Unpublished BA (Hons) Sport Studies dissertation, University of Northumbria.

Cox, T. and Beale, R.L. (1997) *Developing competency to manage diversity*. San Francisco: Berrett-Koehler.

Dayananda, D., Irons, R., Harrison, S., Herbohn, J. and Rowland, P. (2002) *Capital budgeting: financial appraisal of investment projects*. Cambridge: Cambridge University Press.

Demick, B. (2009) Beijing's Olympic building boom becomes a bust. *Los Angeles Times*. Online. Available http://articles.latimes.com/2009/feb/22/world/fg-beijing-bust22 (accessed 15 September 2010).

Department for Business, Innovation and Skills (2009) *Defining the job*. Online. Available http://webarchive.nationalarchives.gov.uk/20090902222257/http://www. dius.gov.uk/higher_education/widening_participation/professional_recruitment_gu ide/recruitment_step_by_step/defining_the_job.aspx (accessed 26 May 2010).

232

Det Norske Veritas (DNV) (2010) *Risk – a word from ancient Greece.* Online. Available http://www.dnv.com/focus/risk_management/more_information/risk_origin/inde x.asp (accessed 22 February 2010).

Drucker, P.F. (1954) *The practice of management.* New York: Harper & Row.

Economic Times (2010) IPL franchisees failed to file annual reports. Online. Available http://economictimes.indiatimes.com/articleshow/5863434.cms (accessed 22 July 2010).

Ehmke, C., Fulton, J., Akridge, J., Erickson, K. and Linton, S. (n.d.) *Industry analysis: the five forces.* West Lafayette, IN: Purdue University.

Eisenhauer, S. (2005) *Sports events and risk management in New Zealand: how safe is safe enough?* Research Master's thesis, University of Otago. Online. Available http://eprints.otago.ac.nz/675/1/EsienhauerS.pdf (accessed 22 February 2010).

EIU (Economic Intelligence Unit) (2007) *Just doing it.* Online. Available http:// sponsor.sap.manufacturingcentre.eiu.com/articles/12 (accessed 11 September 2009).

Elliott, D. (2004) Risk management in sport. In J. Beech and S. Chadwick (Eds), *The business of sport management.* Harlow: Pearson Education.

Elliott, G., Rundle-Thiele, S., Waller, D. and Paladino, A. (2008) *Marketing: core concepts and applications,* 2nd Asia-Pacific edn. Milton, Queensland: John Wiley & Sons Australia.

Ellis, P. (2000) BUPA Great North Run 2001. The Gift of Life promotional material. The Gift of Life Commemorative Trust.

Emery, P.R. (2003) Sports event management. In L. Trenberth (Ed.), *The business and management of contemporary sport.* Palmerston North: Dunmore Press.

EPM Review (2009) Online. Available http://www.epmreview.com/KPI-library.html (accessed 17 July 2009).

Evans, M. (2010) *Course 3: capital budgeting analysis.* Online. Available http://www. exinfm.com/training/pdfiles/course03.pdf (accessed 15 September 2010).

Fakkert, J. (2010) Militant attack warnings put New Delhi on alert. *Epoch Times.* Online. Available http://www.theepochtimes.com/n2/content/view/34589/ (accessed 13 September 2010).

Fleisher, C. and Bensoussan, B. (2007) *Business and competitive analysis: effective application of new and classic methods.* Upper Saddle River, NJ: FT Press.

Fortune (2009) Fortune 500. Online. Available http://money.cnn.com/magazines/ fortune/fortune500/2009/full_list/101_200.html (accessed 2 September 2009).

Government of Western Australia (2007) *Can you risk it? An introduction to risk management for community organizations,* 3rd edn. Online. Available http:// www.vicsport.asn.au/Assets/Files/WADSR%20%20Introduction%20to%20 Risk%20Management%20for%20Community%20Organizations.pdf (accessed 22 February 2010).

Granof, M.H. and Khumawala, S.B. (forthcoming) *Government and not-for-profit accounting: concepts and practices,* 5th edn. Hoboken, NJ: John Wiley & Sons.

Gray, C. and Larson, E. (2000) *Project management: the managerial process.* Boston, MA: McGraw-Hill International.

Great Run (2010a) *Bupa 30th Great North Run.* Online. Available http://www.great run.org/events/Event.aspx?id=1 (accessed 13 September 2010).

Great Run (2010b) *All events.* Online. Available http://www.greatrun.org/All Events.aspx (accessed 13 September 2010).

Great Run (2010c) Corporate information. Online. Available http://www.greatrun. org/Corporate/Default.aspx (accessed 13 September 2010).

Great Run (2010d) *Charity advertising and fundraising packages 2010*. Newcastle upon Tyne: Nova International.

Great Run (2010e) *Bupa Great North Run 2010 competitor's information booklet*. Online. Available http://www.greatrun.org/App_Files/Gr_Files/Bupa-30th-Great-North-Run-2010-Magazine.pdf (accessed 13 September 2010).

Great Run (2010f) *Recruitment*. Online. Available http://www.greatrun.org/ Recruitment/Recruitment.aspx (accessed 13 September 2010).

Gutierrez, P.H. and Dalsted, N.L. (2010) *Break-even method of investment analysis*. Online. Available http://www.ext.colostate.edu/pubs/farmmgt/03759.html (accessed 22 August 2010).

Halpern, S. (2009) *Step up to Nike (NKE): a 'great company'*. Online. Available http://www.bloggingstocks.com/2009/07/02/step-up-to-nike-nke-a-great-company/ (accessed 19 August 2009).

Hanlon, C. and Jago, L. (2004) The challenge of retaining personnel in major sport event organizations. *Event Management*, 9: 39–49.

Hartley, H.J. (2001) *Exploring sport and leisure disasters: a sociolegal perspective*. London: Cavendish Publishing.

Haughey, D. (2009) *SMART goals*. Online. Available http://www.projectsmart. co.uk/smart-goals.html (accessed 12 December 2009).

Health and Safety Executive (2006a) *Example risk assessment for an office-based business*. Online. Available http://www.hse.gov.uk/risk/casestudies/pdf/office. pdf (accessed 22 February 2010).

Health and Safety Executive (2006b) *Example risk assessment for a village hall*. Online. Available http://www.hse.gov.uk/risk/casestudies/pdf/villagehall.pdf (accessed 22 February 2010).

Health and Safety Executive (2009) *Risk management: five steps to risk assessment*. Online. Available http://www.hse.gov.uk/risk/fivesteps.htm (accessed 22 February 2010).

Health and Safety Executive (2010) *Guidance on using the risk assessment and policy template*. Online. Available http://www.hse.gov.uk/risk/guidance.htm (accessed 22 February 2010).

Helbig Consulting (2010) *Project risk assessment questionnaire*. Online. Available http://www.helbig.com.au/pmo/templates/Risk_Assessment_Questionnaire_Tem plate.doc (accessed 22 February 2010).

House of Commons (2007) *Preparations for the London 2012 Olympic and Paralympic Games – risk assessment and management: thirty-ninth report of session 2006–2007*. London: The Stationery Office. Online. Available http://www. publications.parliament.uk/pa/cm200607/cmselect/cmpubacc/377/377.pdf (accessed 22 February 2010).

Hoye, R., Smith, A., Nicholson, M., Stewart, B. and Westerbeek, H. (2009) *Sport management: principles and applications*, 2nd edn. Oxford: Elsevier Butterworth-Heinemann.

hr.guide.com (2001) *Job analysis: overview*. Online. Available http://www.hr-guide.com/data/G000.htm (accessed 26 May 2010).

HR Management (2009a) *Purpose of job analysis*. Online. Available http://www. humanresources.hrvinet.com/purpose-of-job-analysis/ (accessed 26 May 2010).

234

HR Management (2009b) *Job analysis methods*. Online. Available http://www.humanresources.hrvinet.com/18-methods-of-job-analysis/ (accessed 26 May 2010).

HR Management (2009c) *Process of job analysis*. Online. Available http://www.humanresources.hrvinet.com/process-of-job-analysis/ (accessed 26 May 2010).

HR Management (2009d) *Practical problems with job analysis*. Online. Available http://www.humanresources.hrvinet.com/practical-problems-with-job-analysis/ (accessed 26 May 2010).

HR Management (2010) *Job analysis methods*. Online. Available http://www.humanresources.hrvinet.com/18-methods-of-job-analysis/ (accessed 26 May 2010).

ICMR (International Centre for Management Research) (2001) *Nike – the 'goddess of marketing'*. Online. Available http://www.icmrindia.org/casestudies/catalogue/Marketing/MKTG088.htm (accessed 2 September 2009).

IMF (International Monetary Fund) (2009) *The implications of the global financial crisis for low income countries*. Online. Available http://www.imf.org/external/pubs/ft/books/2009/globalfin/globalfin.pdf (accessed 24 September 2009).

Institute of Risk Management (2010) *What is risk management?* Online. Available http://www.theirm.org/aboutheirm/ABwhatisrm.htm (accessed 22 February 2010).

International Rugby Board (2010) *Recruitment*. Available http://www.rugbyworldcup.com/destinationnewzealand/recruitment.html (accessed 13 September 2010).

Investopedia (2010) *Which is a better measure for capital budgeting, IRR or NPV?* Online. Available http://www.investopedia.com/ask/answers/05/irrvsnpvcapitalbudgeting.asp (accessed 15 September 2010).

IPL (2010) *Record ratings for IPL in the UK*. Online. Available http://www.iplt20.com/news_detail.php?id=958 (accessed 22 July 2010).

Jagels, M.G. (2007) *Hospitality management accounting*, 9th edn. Hoboken, NJ: John Wiley & Sons.

Jobsinsports.com (2010) Online. Available http://www.jobsinsports.com/ (accessed 26 May 2010).

Johnson, G. and Scholes, K. (2002) *Exploring corporate strategy: text and cases*, 6th edn. Harlow: Pearson Education.

Johnson, P. (2009) *Product life cycle theory*. Online. Available http://www.buzzle.com/articles/product-life-cycle-theory.html (accessed 22 July 2010).

Kennemer, B. (2004) *Show me! Microsoft Office Project 2003*. Indianapolis, IN: Que.

Kenyon, P. (2000) *Gap and Nike: no sweat?* London: BBC.

Kerzner, H. (1995) *Project management: a systems approach to planning, scheduling, and controlling*, 5th edn. New York: Van Nostrand Reinhold.

Key Note (2010) *Sports market market review*. London: Key Note. Online. Available http://www.keynote.co.uk/market-intelligence/view/product/2361/sports-market?utm_source=kn.reports.browse (accessed 22 July 2010).

Klein, N. (2000) *No logo: taking aim at the brand bullies*. Toronto: Random House of Canada.

Klinke, A. and Renn, O. (2001) Precautionary principles and discursive strategies: classifying and managing risks. *Journal of Risk Research*, 4 (2): 159–173.

Koontz, H. and Weihrich, H. (2006) *Essentials of management*, 7th edn. New York: McGraw-Hill.

Kotas, R. (1999) *Management accounting for hospitality and tourism*, 3rd edn. London: International Thomson Business Press.

Kotler, P. (1994) *Marketing management: analysis, planning, implementation and control*, 8th edn. Englewood Cliffs: Prentice Hall International.

Kotler, P. (2000) *Marketing management*, millennium edn. Englewood Cliffs, NJ: Prentice Hall.

Kotler, P. and Keller, K.L. (2006) Marketing management, 12th edn. Upper Saddle River, NJ: Pearson Education.

Kotler, P., Brown, L., Adam, S., Burton, S. and Armstrong, G. (2006) *Marketing*, 7th edn. Frenchs Forest, NSW: Pearson Prentice Hall.

KPI Portal (2009) Online. Available http://www.kpi-portal.com (accessed 17 July 2009).

Lamb, C.W., Hair, J.F.H. and McDaniel, C. (2006) *Marketing*, 8th edn. Mason, OH: Thomson South-Western.

Lashley, C. and Lee-Ross, D. (2003) *Organization behaviour for leisure services*. Oxford: Butterworth-Heinemann.

Leisure Media Company (2010) Online. Available http://www.leisureopportunities. co.uk (accessed 26 May 2010).

Leopkey, B. and Parent, M.M. (2009) Risk management issues in large-scale sporting events: a stakeholder perspective. *European Sport Management Quarterly*, 9 (2): 187–208.

Levitt, T. (1965) Exploit the product life cycle. *Harvard Business Review*, 43: 81–94.

Life Cycle Initiative (2010) *Benefits of life cycle approaches*. Online. Available http://jp1.estis.net/builder/includes/page.asp?site=lcinit&page_id=E9606E46-72E7-43A9-A6BE-E27854134FB9 (accessed 22 July 2010).

Locke, E. (1968) Toward a theory of task motivation and incentives. *Organizational Behavior and Human Performance*, 3 (2): 157–189.

London 2012 (2009) *London 2012 appoints the Boston Consulting Group as Tier Three Provider*. Online. Available http://www.london2012.com/press/media-releases/2009/01/london-2012-appoints-the-boston-consulting-group-as-tier-three-provider.php (accessed 22 July 2010).

London Organising Committee of the Olympic and Paralympic Games (2007) *Changing places programme – how to improve your local area*. Online. Available http://www.london2012.com/documents/locog-publications/changing-places-toolkit.pdf (accessed 22 February 2010).

Lussier, R.N. and Kimball, D. (2004) *Sport management: principles, applications, skill development*. Mason, OH: Thomson South-Western.

Mallinger, M. (2009) *Management skills for the 21st century*. Pepperdine University. Online. Available http://gbr.pepperdine.edu/982/skills.html (accessed 14 September 2010).

Marketing Teacher (2000) *SWOT analysis – POWER SWOT*. Online. Available http://www.marketingteacher.com/Lessons/lesson_power_swot.htm (accessed 21 May 2009).

Markowitz, H.M. (1987) *Mean-variance analysis in portfolio choice and capital markets*. Oxford: Blackwell.

Martin, C. (2010) *Perfect phrases for writing job descriptions*. New York: McGraw-Hill.

236

Maxi-Pedia (2010) *SPACE matrix strategic management method.* Online. Available http://www.maxi-pedia.com/SPACE+matrix+model+strategic+management+ method (accessed 22 July 2010).

Mercer, D. (2001) *Marketing,* 2nd edn. Oxford: Blackwell Publishers.

MICA (Ministerial Conference on Ageing) (2002) *The world population is ageing.* Online. Available http://www.bagso.de/mica/demographic%20changes.htm (accessed 11 September 2009).

Michman, R.D. and Mazze, E.M. (2006) *The affluent consumer: marketing and selling the luxury lifestyle.* Westport, CT: Praeger Publishers.

MindTools (2010) *The Boston matrix.* Online. Available http://www.mindtools.com/ pages/article/newTED_97.htm (accessed 22 July 2010).

Minten, S. and Foster, W. (2009) Human resource management. In K. Bill (Ed.), *Sport management.* Exeter: Learning Matters.

ModelRisk (2010) Online. Available http://www.vosesoftware.com/ (accessed 22 February 2010).

Moneychimp (2010) *Present value calculator.* Online. Available http://www.money chimp.com/calculator/present_value_calculator.htm (accessed 15 September 2010).

Moore, M. (1998) *The big one.* London: BBC.

Morgan, M.J. and Summers, J. (2005) *Sports marketing.* Melbourne: Thomson Learning.

Morgan, R., Redman, A., Smith, M. and Cooper, W. (2001) Capital budgeting models: theory vs. practice. *Business Forum.* Online. Available http://www.allbusiness. com/ (accessed 15 September 2010).

Morrison, M. (2008a) *Prime practice health and safety audit and review.* Online. Available http://www.rapidbi.com/created/primepractice.html (accessed 22 February 2010).

Morrison, M. (2008b) *Developing the innovative capacity of individuals, teams, leaders and organizations.* Online. Available http://rapidbi.com/creatrix/ (accessed 22 February 2010).

Nager, F.J. (2008) *Cows and dogs in a bear market: applying the BCG matrix to marketing.* Online. Available http://coolrulespronto.wordpress.com/2008/07/06/ bcgmatrix/ (accessed 22 July 2010).

National Audit Office (2007) *Preparations for the London 2012 Olympic and Paralympic Games: risk assessment and management.* London: The Stationery Office. Online. Available http://www.nao.org.uk/publications/0607/preparations_ for_the_olympics.aspx (accessed 22 February 2010).

Ndaliman, M.B. and Bala, K.C. (2007) Practical limitations of break-even theory. *AU Journal of Technology,* 11 (1): 58–61.

NDTV (2009) *All about the Indian Premier League (IPL).* Online. Available http://www.ndtv.com/convergence/ndtvcricket/showstory.aspx?id=SPOEN20090 082651 (accessed 22 July 2010).

Netball Western Australia (2009) *Netball Western Australia Development Manager position description.* Online. Available http://www.netballwa.com.au (accessed 26 May 2010).

Nike (2009a) Nikebiz. Online. Available http://www.nikebiz.com (accessed 19 August 2009).

Nike (2009b) *Nike Inc. 2009 annual report*. Online. Available http://media.corporate-ir.net/media_files/irol/10/100529/AnnualReport/nike-sh09-rev2/docs/Nike_2009_10-K.pdf (accessed 2 September 2009).

Nike (2010) Online. Available http://www.nikebiz.com (accessed 22 July 2010).

Nirvana Europe (2000) *Great North Run economic impact assessment*. Newcastle upon Tyne: Nirvana Europe.

Nova (2000) *Bupa Great North Run 2000 media pack*. Newcastle upon Tyne: Nova International.

Nova (2009) *Take to the streets*. Online. Available http://www.taketothestreets.org/ (accessed 13 September 2010).

Nova International (2000) BUPA Great North event safety plan. Unpublished document.

Office of Sport and Recreation Tasmania (1999) *A sporting chance*. Online. Available http://www.development.tas.gov.au/__data/assets/pdf_file/0014/4514/riskman1.pdf (accessed 22 February 2010).

Olympic Delivery Authority (2007) *Olympic, Paralympic and legacy transformation planning applications*, Volume 14A: *Flood risk assessment*. Online. Available http://planning.london2012.com/upload/publicaccessodalive/07-02-06%20vol14a%20flood%20risk%20assessment%20(387).pdf (accessed 22 February 2010).

Osgood, W.R. (2010) *Breakeven analysis*. Online. Available http://www.buzgate.org/8.0/wi/ft_beven.html (accessed 22 August 2010).

O'Toole, W. and Mikolaitis, P. (2002) Corporate event project management. New York: John Wiley & Sons.

Ozanian, M.K. and Schwartz, P.J. (2007) *Forbes sports values: the world's top sports brands*. Online. Available http://www.forbes.com/2007/09/26/sports-brands-teams-biz-sports_cz_mo_0927sportsbrands.html (accessed 2 September 2009).

Pannell, D.J. (1997) *Sensitivity analysis: strategies, methods, concepts, examples*. Online. Available http://cyllene.uwa.edu.au/~dpannell/dpap971f.htm (accessed 22 August 2010).

Pasternack, A. (2008) National stadium. *Architectural Record*. Online. Available http://archrecord.construction.com/projects/portfolio/archives/0807nationalstadium-1.asp (accessed 15 September 2010).

Patel, P. and Younger, M. (1978) A frame of reference for strategy development. *Long Range Planning*, 11: 6–12.

Pearson, B. and Thomas, N. (1991) *The shorter MBA: a practical approach to business skills*. London: Thorsons.

Piekarz, M. (2009) Risk management and the sport manager. In K. Bill (Ed.), *Sport management*. Exeter: Learning Matters.

Porter, M.E. (1979) How competitive forces shape strategy. *Harvard Business Review*, 57 (2): 137–145.

Porter, M.E. (1985) *Competitive advantage: creating and sustaining superior performance*. New York: Free Press.

Porter, M.E. (2004) *Competitive advantage: creating and sustaining superior performance*. New York: Free Press.

Potter, G., Morse, W.J., Davis, J.R. and Hartgraves, A.L. (2004) *Managerial accounting*, 4th edn. Cambridge: Cambridge Business Publishers.

Project Management Institute (2009) Online. Available http://www.pmi.org/Pages/default.aspx (accessed 16 September 2009).

Project Smart (2009) *PMBOK and PMP books*. Online. Available http://www.project smart.co.uk/pmbok-books.html (accessed 16 September 2009).

Q-BPM (n.d.) *SWOT*. Online. Available http://en.q-bpm.org/mediawiki/index.php/ SWOT (accessed 16 December 2009).

Ransdell, E. (2007) The Nike story? Just tell it! *Fast Company*. Online. Available http://www.fastcompany.com/magazine/31/nike.html (accessed 2 September 2009).

RapidBi (2009) *How to write SMART objectives and SMARTer objectives*. Online. Available http://rapidbi.com/created/WriteSMARTobjectives.html (accessed 10 December 2009).

Ravindran, S. and Gollapudi, N. (2010) *Pune and Kochi unveiled as new IPL franchises*. Online. Available http://www.cricinfo.com/ipl2010/content/story/ 452856.html (accessed 22 July 2010).

Read, R. (2008) *Nike's focus on keeping costs low causes poor working conditions, critics say*. Online. Available http://www.oregonlive.com/business/oregonian index.ssf?/base/news/121790850350380.xml&coll=7 (accessed 2 September 2009).

Reuters (2009) In pictures: Beijing's Bird's Nest winter wonderland. *BBC News*. Online. Available http://news.bbc.co.uk/2/hi/asia-pacific/8442051.stm (accessed 15 September 2010).

Richards, D. (2010) *How to do a breakeven analysis*. Online. Available http:// entrepreneurs.about.com/od/businessplan/a/breakeven.htm (accessed 22 August 2010).

Riskbase (2010) Online. Available http://www.icwa.wa.gov.au/cif/cif_riskbase.shtml (accessed 22 February 2010).

RiskSense (2010) Online. Available http://www.reliancerisk.com.au (accessed 22 February 2010).

Robinson, S.J.Q., Hichens, R.E. and Wade, D.P. (1978) The directional policy matrix – tool for strategic planning. *Long Range Planning*, 2 (3): 8–15.

Roitha, D. (2007) *Impact analysis*. Online. Available http://e-articles.info/e/a/ title/Impact-Analysis/ (accessed 16 December 2009).

Rothman, J. (2004) *Hiring the best knowledge workers, techies and nerds: the secrets and science of hiring technical people*. New York: Dorset House Publishing.

Rothwell and District Record (2000) Disabled man raises almost £20k for charity. 10 November: 23.

Roy, S. (2001) Email entitled 'SPARKS GNR Statistic' sent on 27 July.

Rugby World Cup 2011 (2009) *Accreditation Manager position overview*. Online. Available http://www.rugbynz2011.com (accessed 18 August 2010).

Sarbanes–Oxley Act (2002) Online. Available http://www.soxlaw.com/ (accessed 22 February 2010).

Service Canada (2010) *Job analysis template*. Online. Available http://www. gestionrh.gc.ca/gol/hrmanagement/site.nsf/vDownload/hiring_job_analysis_e.pdf /$file/hiring_job_analysis_e.pdf (accessed 20 February 2010).

Shank, M.D. (2009) *Sports marketing: a strategic perspective*, 4th edn. Upper Saddle River, NJ: Pearson Education.

Shilbury, D., Westerbeek, H., Quick, S. and Funk, D. (2009) *Strategic sport marketing*, 3rd edn. Sydney: Allen & Unwin.

Shin, Eui-Hang (2009) *State, society, economic development in sports life cycle: the case of boxing in Korea*. Online. Available http://www.allacademic.com/meta/

p_mla_apa_research_citation/1/7/6/8/7/p176873_index.html (accessed 22 July 2010).

Small Business Development Corporation (2010a) *Break-even analysis*. Online. Available http://www.smallbusiness.wa.gov.au/break-even-analysis (accessed 22 August 2010).

Small Business Development Corporation (2010b) *Biztools*. Online. Available http://www.smallbusiness.wa.gov.au/assets/BIZTools/biztool-breakeven-analysis.xls (accessed 22 August 2010).

SmartBiz (2010) *Sample job analysis questionnaires to define the duties of a new job.* Online. Available http://www.smartbiz.com/article/articleprint/1001/-1/29 (accessed 26 May 2010).

Smith, A. (2001) The dangerous north. *News Post Leader*, 9 August: 25.

Smith, A. and Stewart, B. (1999) *Sports management: a guide to professional practice.* Crows Nest, NSW: Allen & Unwin.

Smith, C.W. (1998) Corporate risk management: theory and practice. *Journal of Derivatives*, 2 (4). Online. Available http://ssrn.com/abstract=6414 (accessed 22 February 2010).

Society for Human Resource Management (2010) Online. Available http://www.shrm.org/ (accessed 26 May 2010).

Solution Matrix (2010) *Internal rate of return*. Online. Available http://www.solutionmatrix.com/internal-rate-of-return.html (accessed 15 September 2010).

Sonfield, M. and Lussier, R.N. (1997) The entrepreneurial strategy matrix: a model for new and ongoing venture. *Business Horizons*, 40, May/June: 73–77.

Soucie, D. and Doherty, A. (1994) *An overview of past, present and future sport management research in North America*. Proceedings of second European Association of Sport Management conference. Florence: EASM.

Sportretort (2009) *Nike and the jester: a tale of arrogance*. Online. Available http://sportretort.wordpress.com/2009/07/22/nike-and-the-jester-a-tale-of-arrogance/ (accessed 2 September 2009).

Sports Management Worldwide (2010) Online. Available http://www.sports managementworldwide.com/ (accessed 26 May 2010).

Sportspeople (2010) Online. Available http://www.sportspeople.com.au/ (accessed 26 May 2010).

Sport Taranaki (2009) *Program Manager job description*. Online. Available http://www.sporttaranaki.org.nz (accessed 18 May 2010).

Steven, G. (2005) Management accounting fundamentals. *Financial Management*, September: 51.

Stewart, B. (2007) *Sport funding and finance*. Oxford: Elsevier.

Stewart, B. and Smith, A. (1999) The special features of sport. *Annals of Leisure Research*, 2: 87–99.

Strategic Planning Institute (2010) *About PIMS database*. Online. Available http://pimsonline.com/about_pims_db.htm (accessed 22 July 2010).

Sullivan, M. (2004) Sport marketing. In J. Beech and S. Chadwick (Eds), *The business of sport management*. Harlow: Pearson Education.

Summers, J., Gardiner, M., Lamb, C., Hair, J. and McDaniel, C. (2003) *Essentials of marketing*. Melbourne: Thomson Learning.

Tajirian, A. (1997) Chapter 9: *Capital budgeting process*. Online. Available http://www.morevalue.com/i-reader/ftp/Ch9.PDF (accessed 15 September 2010).

Taylor, P. and Godfrey, A. (2003) Performance measurement in English local authority sport facilities. *Public Performance and Management Review*, 26 (3): 251–262. M.E. Sharpe. Online. Available http://www.jstor.org/stable/3381286 (accessed 15 December 2009).

TedCo (2010) *Discounted cash flow analysis calculator*. Online. Available http://www.discountedcashflowanalysis.com/ (accessed 15 September 2010).

Tennis Auckland (2009) *Tennis Auckland job description*. Online. Available http://www.sportspeople.co.nz (accessed 26 May 2010).

Tennis Australia (2009a) Online. Available http://www.tennis.com.au/pages/default.aspx?id=4&pageId=127 (accessed 14 December 2009).

Tennis Australia (2009b) *2008/9 annual report*. Online. Available http://www.tennis.com.au/Pages/default.aspx?id=4&pageId=14675 (accessed 14 December 2009).

Tennis Victoria (2006) *2006–10 strategic plan*. Online. Available http://www.tennis.com.au/pages/image.aspx?assetid=RDM38896.3769053472 (accessed 14 December 2009).

Tennis Victoria (2009a) Online. Available http://www.tennis.com.au/pages/default.aspx?id=3&pageId=554 (accessed 14 December 2009).

Tennis Victoria (2009b) *2008/9 annual report*. Online. Available http://www.tennis.com.au/pages/default.aspx?id=3&pageId=1523 (accessed 14 December 2009).

Textiles Intelligence (2008) *Green textiles and apparel: environmental impact and strategies for improvement*. Online. Available http://www.emergingtextiles.com/?q=stu&s=TI-green-textiles&c=stu080423-&peu=eu395&pus=us632 (accessed 24 September 2009).

Thirdway (2006) *Converse finds more than one way to kill a cat*. Online. Available http://www.thirdwayblog.com/category/converse/ (accessed 11 September 2009).

Thompson, K.N. (2002) *Product life cycles: theoretical and practical issues*. Online. Available http://courses.unt.edu/kt3650_9/sld004.htm (accessed 22 July 2010).

TimeAnalyzer (2006) *The action priority matrix*. BossEye. Online. Available http://www.timeanalyzer.com/lib/priority.htm (accessed 22 July 2010).

Times of India (2010) Indian Premier League brand value $4.13bn. Online. Available http://timesofindia.indiatimes.com/iplarticleshow/5713042.cms (accessed 22 July 2010).

Time Web (2010) *Investment appraisal*. Online. Available http://www.bized.co.uk/timeweb/reference/using_experiments.htm (accessed 15 September 2010).

Toohey, K. and Taylor, T. (2008) Mega events, fear, and risk: terrorism at the Olympic Games. *Journal of Sport Management*, 22: 451–467.

Torrington, D., Hall, L. and Taylor, S. (2005) *Human resource management*, 6th edn. Harlow: FT/Prentice Hall.

Trading Economics (2010) India inflation rate. Online. Available http://www.tradingeconomics.com/Economics/Inflation-CPI.aspx?Symbol=INR (accessed 22 July 2010).

Turnbull Report (1999) Online. Available http://portal.surrey.ac.uk/portal/page?_pageid=823,181361&_dad=portal&_schema=PORTAL/ (accessed 22 February 2010).

Tyne Tees Television (2000) Cited in Nova (2000) *Bupa Great North Run 2000 media pack*. Newcastle upon Tyne: Nova International.

Uchitelle, L. (1997) The world; global good times, meet the global glut. *New York Times*. Online. Available http://www.nytimes.com/1997/11/16/weekinreview/the-world-global-good-times-meet-the-global-glut.html (accessed 24 September 2009).

Vanguard Software Corporation (2010) *Portfolio management software*. Online. Available http://www.vanguardsw.com/solutions/application/portfolio-analysis/ (accessed 22 July 2010).

Varma, A., Budhwar, P.S. and DeNisi, A. (2008) *Performance management systems: a global perspective*. London: Routledge.

Verzuh, E. (1999) *The fast forward MBA in project management*. New York: J. Wiley.

Vicsport Triathlon Sport (2003) *Case study – an event risk management plan – triathlon race*. Online. Available http://fulltext.ausport.gov.au/fulltext/2003/vic/Help_Sheet7.pdf (accessed 22 February 2010).

Volunteering Australia (2007) *Designing volunteer roles and position descriptions: toolkit*. Online. Available http://www.volunteeringaustralia.org/html/s02_article/article_view.asp?id=2759 (accessed 26 May 2010).

Watt, D.C. (2003) *Sports management and administration*, 2nd edn. New York: Routledge.

Westerbeek, H. and Smith, A. (2003) *Sport business in the global marketplace*. London: Palgrave Macmillan.

Williamson, D. (2003) *Capital budgeting: the key numerical techniques*. Online. Available http://www.duncanwil.co.uk/invapp.html (accessed 15 September 2010).

Wilson, A. (2001) Informal interview on 13 July 2001 at Nova International Limited.

Wilson, B. (2010) Will Vancouver count cost of Olympics? *BBC News*. Online. Available http://news.bbc.co.uk/2/hi/business/8510177.stm (accessed 15 September 2010).

Wilson, R.M.S. and Gilligan, C. (1997) *Strategic marketing management: planning, implementation and control*, 2nd edn. Oxford: Elsevier Butterworth-Heinemann.

YiHou Huang, A. (2009) A value-at-risk approach with kernel estimator. *Applied Financial Economics*, 19 (5): 379–395.

YouTube (2010) *Breakeven analysis*. Online. Available http://www.youtube.com/watch?v=TLOo2mY6FIw (accessed 22 August 2010).

INDEX

243

248

249

250

252

253

254